PASTIMES

The Context of Contemporary Leisure

6th Edition

Ruth V. Russell

SAGAMORE
PUBLISHING

Publishers: Joseph J. Bannon and Peter L. Bannon
Sales and Marketing Managers: Misti Gilles
Director of Development and Production: Susan M. Davis
Technology Manager: Mark Atkinson
Production Coordinator: Amy S. Dagit
Graphic Designer: Marissa Willison

ISBN print edition: 978-1-57167-820-1
ISBN ebook: 978-1-57167-821-8
Library of Congress Control Number: 2016955124
All photos provided by Shutterstock.com unless otherwise indicated.

Printed in the United States.

SAGAMORE
PUBLISHING

1807 N. Federal Dr.
Urbana, IL 61801
www.sagamorepublishing.com

For Aunt Ruth

Whose example gave me the original inspiration to get into the recreation field.

Contents

Preface

The purpose of this sixth edition of *Pastimes* is to extend the discussion about contemporary leisure to new concepts supported by the latest research findings and commentary. Throughout, I have pursued the most interesting, relevant, exciting, and up-to-date information possible. This wasn't at all difficult; leisure is simply a very intriguing subject.

First, as an introduction to the phenomenon of leisure, the book must be current. Momentous changes, actual and alleged, have always been the root of leisure expressions and experiences. To match, *Pastimes* again reflects a wide range of material from the disciplines of leisure studies, sociology, psychology, economics, political science, history, anthropology, geography, the humanities, and media and cultural studies.

Second, as a learning tool, this sixth edition teaches more. It contains new illustrations of concepts through field-based cases, biographical features, exploratory activities, statistics, and research studies. While the basic organization remains similar, in addition to updated material throughout, some concepts have been extended and broadened. For example, in Chapter 1, a new section on Ancient Egypt is added, and in Chapter 6, more discussion of virtual geography is presented. Also, Chapter 7, on leisure and technology, has been completely rewritten to reflect a new organization, and ever-changing content.

More than a textbook, *Pastimes* is very much a point of view. Leisure is presented as a human phenomenon that is individual and collective, vital and frivolous, historical and contemporary, factual and subjective, good and bad.

This edition is the result of what I have learned from years of engagement with leisure theory, research, and personal and professional practice. Signs of my worldwide wanderings are also evident. Learning is the greatest of joys, and I am lucky to be able to devote my life to it.

Ruth V. Russell

Acknowledgments

Throughout all six editions, I have felt grateful to many people: family, friends, students—at bachelor and doctoral levels, university and practitioner colleagues, and fellow recreation participants. In particular, I have learned a great deal from my IU collaborators: Rasul Mowatt, Trish Ardovino, Boyd Hegarty, Jeff Nix, Debbie Smith, and Agnes Kovacs.

Most especially I wish to thank Pat Setser not only for moral support, but for life-saving assistance with the photo program for this edition. As well, based on a 30-year career in technology in industry, public schools, at the university level, and as a consultant, she is coauthor of Chapter 7 on leisure and technology.

About the Author

Dr. Ruth V. Russell is professor emeritus in the Department of Recreation, Park, and Tourism Studies at Indiana University. She is a former trustee of the National Recreation and Park Association and has served as president of the Society of Park and Recreation Educators. Professional experience includes the San Diego Recreation and Parks Department, San Diego–Imperial Counties Girl Scout Council, and Chateau La Jolla Retirement Center. Dr. Russell has authored numerous textbooks (and a cookbook), published research in refereed journals, and lectured internationally. Presently her pursuits include RVing, walking, swimming, reading, watercolor painting, and culinary projects, as well as class enrollments in Spanish.

PART 1

Leisure as a Condition of Being Human: Personal Context

We are human in large part because of our leisure

We begin our exploration of leisure by considering its significance for us personally. Leisure helps shape us as human beings–our growth, health, motives, feelings, and actions.

Chapter 1

Demonstrates leisure's meanings for us through the humanities, in ancient and contemporary histories, and according to today's connotations.

Chapter 2

Discusses benefits of leisure to us, including our happiness, freedom, pleasure, and spirituality.

Chapter 3

Offers some explanations about our leisure choices and behaviors.

Chapter 4

Traces the ways leisure helps us grow and stay healthy.

CHAPTER 1

The Meanings of Leisure

What is leisure?

Leisure is an intricate and dynamic concept with different meanings, depending on context.

What are the contexts of leisure's meaning?

Leisure's meanings can be found in the humanities, history, and today's connotations.

Where do we find meanings of leisure in the humanities?

Perhaps leisure can be best understood through the ideas portrayed in a story, a song, or a picture.

What are the clues to meanings of leisure in history?

From the beginning of human culture, leisure has been part of everyday life—legacies that endure today.

What do we understand leisure to mean today?

Leisure is individually and culturally defined, but most common are the themes of free time, recreational activity, and a special spirit.

To have leisure is one of the oldest dreams of human beings: to be free to pursue what we want, to spend our time meaningfully in pleasurable ways, to live in a state of grace (Godbey, 2008, p. 1). In this chapter, we set the stage for understanding the essential humanness of leisure by exploring its foundational meanings.

Because leisure is a complex concept with different meanings depending on the people, the place, and the time, defining it requires journeys to different peoples, places, and times. First, we define leisure through its reflections in the humanities: literature, art, and music. Next, we examine some of the original meanings of leisure in history, and finally, we summarize leisure's contemporary connotations. Throughout the discussion, you'll notice that leisure has multiple, and even contradictory, meanings.

Meanings in the Humanities

First, the complexity of leisure's meanings can be reflected through the **humanities**. The subjects of the humanities include the arts, such as music, paintings, and stories, which convey what it is like to be human. The word *art* itself comes from the same root as the word *artificial*, meaning something made by humans.

Humanities: Human creations that describe human experience

In creating a song or a poem, songwriters and poets portray their own experiences. So, when we listen to a musical performance or read a poem, we understand something about the experience of its creator. In these expressions are ideas, images, and words that serve as a kind of self-reflection, telling us who and what we may be and informing us of our humanness. As well, the humanities introduce us to people we have never met, places we have never visited, and ideas that may have never crossed our minds.

Literature

Literature, in the broadest sense, is widely apparent in everyday life. It is the written art form found in magazine articles, greeting card verses, Internet blogs, as well as in poetry and novels. Reading literature in itself is a popular leisure expression, and to prove it, Americans spent about $29.2 billion in 2014 on books (both paper and e-book formats) (Association of American Publishers, 2015). Another example of the vitality of literature today is the role-playing literary camps sprouting up across the United States (Otterman, 2010). Structured around children's books such as *Harry Potter, Percy Jackson and the Olympians, Twilight*, and *Clash of the Titans*, both residential and day camp programs feature kids acting out book scenes and situations.

Like looking into a mirror, literature offers a view of human life, including leisure. For example, American fiction writer F. Scott Fitzgerald wrote many short stories that tell us about the good-time culture of the 1920s. Labeled his "flapper stories," short stories such as "The Camel's Back" glamorized the social life of the young:

> Now during the Christmas holidays of 1919 there took place in Toledo, forty-one dinner parties, sixteen dances, six luncheons, male and female, twelve teas, four stag dinners, two weddings, and thirteen bridge parties. It was the cumulative effect of all this that moved Perry Parkhurst on the twenty-ninth day of December to a decision. This Medill girl would marry him and she wouldn't marry him. She was having such a good time that she hated to take such a definite step. (Fitzgerald, 1920, p. 35).

In contrast, Maya Angelou's (1971) poem, "Harlem Hopscotch," uses the rhythm of a children's street game to express a serious problem in society:

One foot down, then hop! It's hot.
Good things for the ones that's got.
Another jump, now to the left.
Everybody for hisself.

In the air, now both feet down.
Since you black, don't stick around.
All the people out of work,
Hold for three, then twist and jerk.
Cross the line, they count you out.
That's what hopping's all about.
Both feet flat, the game is done.
They think I lost, I think I won. (p. 100)

In the poem, Angelou uses the game of hopscotch to vent frustration and a sense of betrayal. Although the poem is about the injustices of race and social class, it makes light of it by putting it into the rhythm of a classic children's pastime. Or does it? What do you think is meant by the game's outcome in the last line: "They think I lost, I think I won"?

Art

People have always had an interest in the beauty of pattern. We enjoy designs of contrast and balance for their own sake. We create our own aesthetic experience every day; we doodle during class, wear jewelry and tattoos, and make figures with the mower in our yard. The use of pattern also has a commemorative function. The most important events in our social, political, and religious lives, for example, are reflected in images and icons. We post photos of our experiences on Facebook, and we hang out flags to celebrate national holidays. In other words, art mirrors what we consider to be both beautiful and important.

Perhaps one of the most readily recognized reflections of leisure in art comes from the paintings of the impressionist period. Impressionism is a style of art that presents an immediate "impression" of an object or event. Impressionist artists try to show what the eye sees at a glance, so the image seems spontaneous. Although painters have created impressionistic works in several periods of history, the term is most commonly applied to the work of a group of painters exhibiting in Paris from about 1870 to 1910. What is the impression of leisure in this art?

Figure 1.1. Claude Monet. Garden at Sainte-Adresse, 1867.
Source: The Metropolitan Museum of Art. Used with permission.

One answer is in the painting "Garden at Sainte-Adresse" (Figure 1.1) by Claude Monet. Painted in 1867, Monet's painting depicts vacationers. Out in the water are pleasure boats moored on the left and steamers on the right. In the middle-distance is a fishing boat (just above the parasol). This perhaps represents the transitions from sail to steam, and away from the local and traditional life, with the arrival of tourism. This mirrors what was happening at that time in most of coastal France. Fishing villages were changing into resorts, with broad avenues, sidewalks, formal gardens, and large buildings, just as many waters-edge locations have in the years since. The creation of artificial spaces for the visiting tourists changed forever the lives of the fishermen and shopkeepers who once lived there (Herbert, 1988).

Figure 1.2. Mary Cassatt. Woman in Black at the Opera. 1879. The Hayden Collection. Courtesy of the Museum of Fine Arts, Boston.

Another impressionist painter of the time, Mary Cassatt, painted "Woman in Black at the Opera" (Figure 1.2). Cassatt presents a woman using her upward-tilted opera glasses to scan the audience. With a bit of humor, Cassatt also placed a man in the distance leaning out of his box to point his glasses in the woman's direction, emphasizing the fun of spying on others (Herbert, 1988). We can also learn from this painting that leisure defined the upper social class of this era.

Even this brief glance at the western art of the late 1800s reveals clear meanings of leisure. Indeed, idle hours and entertainment greatly expanded during this period, particularly for the upper class. As thousands of paintings by impressionist artists portray, by the end of that century, daily life was dominated by theaters, operas, cafes, restaurants, dances, racetracks, gardens, and parks. Tourism expanded as well, with a focus on the beauty of the seaside.

Box 1.1
Web Explore

Romanticism

Another artistic tradition that provides an interpretation of leisure's meaning is Romanticism. While Impressionism suggests leisure is a daily life dominated by theaters, operas, cafes, gardens, and racetracks, Romanticism suggests something different. What is that? Explore the web for both images and interpretations of the landscape paintings of Casper Friedrich, Thomas Cole, J.M.W. Turner, and others. Search "Romanticism and nature and emotion" for clues. For example, you might begin with http://www.newworldencyclopedia.org/entry/Romanticism.

Music

Music is perhaps the most universal activity of humankind. Beginning as the natural sound of the human voice, music over the centuries has taken many forms and reflected many ways of life. For example, people today express themselves through jazz, rock, rhythm and blues, country, rap, gospel, classical, bluegrass, K-pop, Latin, and many other musical styles. In fact, through the purchase of CDs, ringtones, digital downloads, music videos, and other musical recordings, the music industry worldwide saw revenues of $15 billion in 2015, 45% of which were in digital format (International Federation of Phonographic Industry, 2016).

How might music portray leisure? All forms of music reflect leisure's meanings, but as an initial illustration, we'll consider rock and roll, and Elvis Presley in particular, who remains rock's most indelible image. In Elvis, millions of American young people found more than a new entertainer; they found themselves, or at least an idealized version of themselves, which stood in stark, liberating contrast to the repressed atmosphere of the 1950s.

What was this new identity? In Elvis's "Hound Dog" and the flip side's "Don't Be Cruel," the highest selling single record of that decade, we find a summary of how Elvis's rock and roll represented young people and their leisure of that time. While the straight rock of screaming guitars and drums in "Hound Dog" emphasizes a wild and raucous sound, a light beat and gentler accompaniment in "Don't Be Cruel" highlight a sweet melody and lyrics. This makes for a big difference between the sexually aggressive and the playfully innocent. Thus, just like the two sides of this single record, youth of the 1950s were bumping, although timidly, against the outer edges of a sort of rebellion.

Comparing this image of leisure for young people from the 1950s with a popular music genre today provides some different contrasts. Rap is a genre of popular music of U.S. black origin in which words are recited rapidly and rhythmically over a prerecorded, typically electronic instrumental backing. According to a study of young people by Scott (2008), when rap music uses the word "chillin," the interpretation of leisure is of relaxation and "doing nothing."

While there are multiple types of rap music (i.e., gangsta, East Coast, etc.), a specific example in the lyrics of the metal-rap group Gang of Four (Metrolyrics, 2016) gives us a glimpse of leisure as consumerism:

The problem of leisure
What to do for pleasure
Ideal love a new purchase
A market of the senses
Dream of the perfect life
Economic circumstances
The body is good business
Sell out, maintain the interest

Box 1.2
The Study Says

Music Lyrics

Can the lyrics of popular songs reveal something about those who listen to them? Based on a computer analysis of lyrics from three decades (1980-2007) of hit songs, a statistically significant trend toward narcissism and hostility in popular music was found by researchers at the University of Kentucky. The study was controlled for genre to prevent the results from being skewed by the growing popularity of hip-hop and rap. In general, it was found that hit songs in the 1980s were more likely to emphasize happy togetherness (Diana Ross and Lionel Richie sang of "two hearts that beat as one"), while today's songs are more likely to be about one very special person: the singer (e.g., Justin Timberlake proclaiming "I'm bringing sexy back" and Beyoncé exulting "It's blazin', you watch me in amazement").

Source: Tierney, 2011

Meanings from Human History

It is not known exactly where and when human civilization originated. While glaciers are still retreating today, the most recent glacial period during the Pleistocene Age (when great sheets of ice up to two miles thick covered most of Greenland, Canada, and the northern United States, as well as northern Europe and Russia) began to retreat about 10,000 years ago (Dictionary.com, 2016). At some point afterward, successive periods of cultural evolution began. As people gathered together into communities, more formalized rules of conduct emerged, including governments, religions, work occupations, and of course, leisure.

Our contemporary meanings of leisure have been shaped by the histories of these past societies. Let's explore some of them.

Stone Age: Art

The Stone Age was a broad prehistoric period during which sharpened stone was the major tool. The period lasted roughly until about 2000 BC with the beginning of metalworking. Our understanding of life for these earliest humans is very much conjecture, but recent discoveries made of 50 samples of symbol-based art from 11 caves in northwestern Spain (Wilford, 2012) suggest our earliest ancestors may have given us our notion of leisure as artistic expression.

From these discoveries, an international team of scientists determined that the art in a cave known as El Castillo was part of the earliest known art. The red handprints found in the cave, for example, were probably made from blowing pigment on a hand placed against the cave wall. Thus, the scientists said, this motif "implies that depictions of the human hand were among the oldest art known" (Wilford, 2012, p. 1). Until these discoveries, archaeologists usually saw prehistoric people as incapable of creating artistic works much beyond simple abstract markings and personal ornamentation.

Figure 1.3. Perhaps in the spirit of prehistoric cave art, contemporary sidewalk chalk art, or pavement art, is a similar leisure expression? Numerous festivals held around the world today celebrate chalk artists, some who create 3-D images. Denver, Colorado-June 4, 2011: Chalk Art Festival on Larimer Square.

Ancient Egypt: The Family That Plays Together Stays Together

Ancient Egypt includes several civilizations of northeastern Africa, concentrated along the lower Nile River, that joined together around 3150 BC. Its rich and diversified culture thrived until 30 BC, when under Cleopatra, it fell to the Roman Empire and became a Roman province.

From the study of burial tomb artifacts, it appears that family leisure was vital to the ancient Egyptians. The nuclear family was the core of society and even many of the gods were arranged into such groupings (Brewer & Teeter, 2007). There was tremendous pride in one's family, and respect for one's parents was a cornerstone of morality. Indeed, the most important duty of the eldest son (or occasionally daughter) was to ensure that parents received a proper burial.

The ancient Egyptians expected that life after death would follow the general pattern of life on earth, so they kept in their burial tombs food to eat, clothing to wear, and sport and game equipment (Hamed, 2015). Indeed, excavating ancient Egyptian tomb sites provides clues to common family leisure expressions. For example, all family members played a variety of musical instruments. Popular were flutes made of reed or wood, as well as large floor harps and various percussion instruments, including bone or ivory clappers. Many types of toys have been found at tomb sites, too: balls, horses on wheels, and baby rattles. The board game of Senet is perhaps the most well known, but also dice and other board games have been identified. As well, ancient hieroglyphs depict ancient Egyptians as excellent swimmers and aquatic athletes.

Ancient Greece: The Leisure Ideal

Although much has been debated about Greek concepts of leisure (see Sylvester, 1999), one constant theme from this ancient culture seems to be its focus on leisure as a means to the good life. The philosopher Plato, for example, believed there were spiritual as well as physical rewards from participating in gymnastics. Further, throughout his writings, Aristotle considered the power to think to be the most unique of human qualities and thus was convinced that a life of contemplation was the proper use of leisure. Yet, to him, life should be devoted not only to thinking noble thoughts, but also to doing civic and productive deeds (Hemingway, 1988).

Leisure scholars have labeled Aristotle's and Plato's philosophical ideas the "leisure ideal." That is, leisure is a force that can ignoble us. This interpretation comes from the Greek concept σχολή, which was translated as **schole.** This word is also related to the Latin (*licentia* and *licere*) and French (*loisir*) and English (leisure and school) words. Extending these associations, then, the ideal pastime was in pursuit of scholarship: reading, thinking, debating, discussing, and studying.

Schole: An ancient Greek term for scholarship that is translated today to the word leisure

How this society interpreted this advice from the philosophers into daily life provides a legacy for leisure's meaning today. For ancient Greeks, such intellectual pursuits as mathematics, poetry, and music, as well as dance, drama, and sport were exalted as part of an ideal of religious expression. For example, excavation of the ancient Olympic site in western Greece shows that the first formalized Olympic Games took place in 776 BC as worship to the god Zeus.

Figure 1.4. An artist's rendering of Olympia in ancient Greece. Source: Pierers Universal-Lexikon, 1891. Source: Public domain

While originally the games owed their purity and importance to religion, later the games incorporated a mixture of not only religious festival, but also athletic and artistic competitions and politics. Held every four years (or Olympiad), the Ancient Olympic Games continued for nearly 12 centuries. They were a series of mostly athletic contests among representatives of the city-states, intended to encourage good relations, but ultimately became a political tool used by them to assert dominance. Politicians would announce political alliances at the games, and in times of war, priests would offer sacrifices to the gods for victory. Sculptors and poets would also congregate at each Olympiad to display their works of art to potential patrons.

At the first Olympiad, a footrace of 180 meters was the only event. Later, longer running races, as well as horse races, chariot racing, jumping, discus throwing, weight lifting, and running with armor were added. One particularly savage sport, called pankration (which translates as "all of might"), was introduced in 648 BC and combined boxing and wrestling. Scholars tell us that in pankration, all types of empty-handed physical attack were encouraged, with eye gouging and biting the only hits not allowed.

The athletes in the games were the aristocratic young men who had the privilege of leisure. Indeed, social distinctions were prominent in all of ancient Greek life. What Plato and Aristotle taught about the leisure ideal was available only to native-born males who were citizens. Their control of a system of slaves and the limitations on women empowered their lives of leisure.

Yet, within this contradiction to the leisure ideal, there is another contradiction. There is some evidence that women had their own games in Olympia (Pausanias, 1918). These were the Heraean Games, also held every 4 years to honor the goddess Hera, the consort of Zeus. Here, unmarried women competed in foot races, with the winners receiving the traditional olive branch garland.

Putting all this rich complexity of leisure meaning together, we can conclude that for the ancient Greeks, leisure meant developing the mind and the body through participation, learning, and noble actions. The good life of leisure for the Greeks was a privileged "ideal" of maintaining knowledge and physicality toward virtuous choices and conduct, which in turn lead to true pleasure.

Ancient Rome: Mass Leisure

Films often portray the ancient Romans as military conquerors as well as ardent pleasure seekers. While there is some accuracy in these images, this civilization also shaped many other cultures with important advancements. These included legacies of language, astronomy, religion, politics, and architecture.

The ancient Roman Empire centered in the city of Rome, in what is now Italy. It was the most extensive western civilization of ancient times, beginning around 753 BC and lasting for over 1,000 years. During that time, the Empire grew to rule much of Europe, Western Asia, and Northern Africa. It owed its prosperity to a policy of expansion backed by both military and political methods. Although the ancient Romans borrowed a good deal of Greek philosophy and copied Greek art and architecture, they had a unique notion about leisure.

For example, as Rome conquered its neighbors, the problem of overseeing an immense empire began to require control of the social order. Discipline and careful regulation of a growing middle class of people were required. They accomplished this by what today we would refer to as **mass leisure**. There were heated public baths, parade grounds for various ball games, buildings for gymnastics, wrestling rooms, and grand athletic stadiums.

Mass leisure: Leisure expressions adopted by the collective of many people in a culture; mass entertainment is an example today

Often the middle-class masses of people were spectators to professional gladiators fighting each other—often to the death, and to political prisoners, criminals, and slaves being thrown to wild animals. Based on the policy of "bread and circuses," leisure as mass entertainment was used as a form of social control and appeasement, and as a means whereby rulers and officials could win popular favor. For example, beginning about 31 BC, ***ludi,*** or public games, became annual events in the Roman calendar (Ibrahim, 1991). By the end of the Roman Empire, each year included 175 official holidays, with 101 of them for theatrical entertainments, 64 devoted to chariot races, and 10 for gladiatorial combats (Roberts, 1962).

Ludi: A Latin word for public games and festivities

Specialized facilities were provided for these events. The oldest of these, the Circus Maximus, was built for horse races, trick riding, mock cavalry battles, and chariot races. Amphitheaters hosted gladiatorial combats, with the largest, the Colosseum, holding thousands of spectators. The Colosseum also sponsored the ***naumachia,*** a ship battle requiring the flooding of the Colosseum floor. However, the greatest of all *naumachiae* is believed to be that staged by Claudius outside Rome in Lake Fucine. A total of 19,000 men boarded a fleet of 50 ships and battled each other beginning at 10 a.m., and by 3 p.m., 3,000 of them were dead (Butler, 1971).

As the mass entertainments became more popular, and more widely used by emperors to gain support from the people, they also became more lavish and depraved as each tried to outdo his predecessor. Enormous amounts of money and human resources were spent on the *ludi*, which many historians conclude ultimately degraded the Roman culture. Restrictions began to be imposed on these practices. For example, gladiator fights ended in the east of the empire at the end of the fourth century, and in the west at the end of the fifth century.

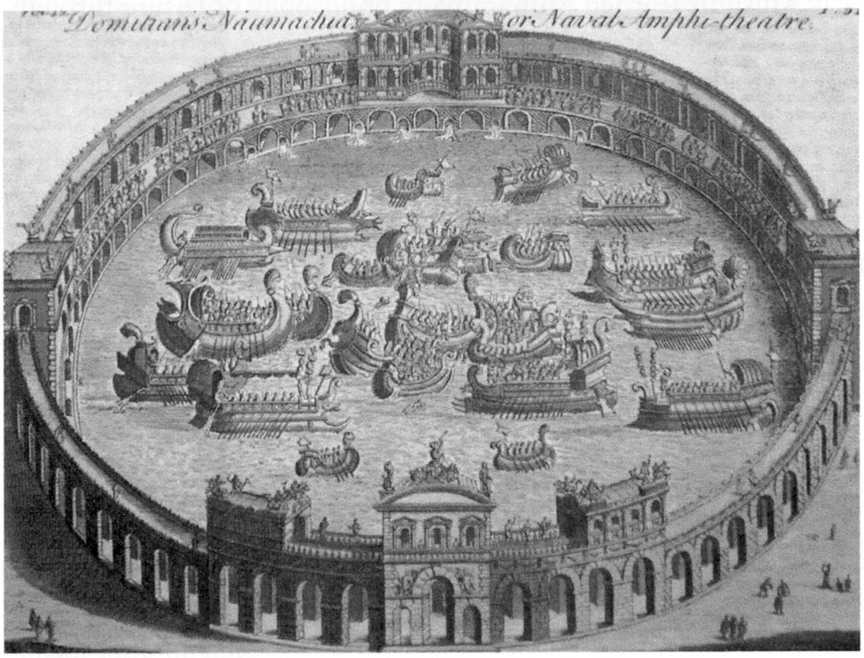

Figure 1.5. Artist's rendering of Naumachiae, the staging of naval battles as mass entertainment. Source: Public domain www.albion-prints.com

Early Polynesians: Tourism

Today, Hawaii is one of the world's most popular tourist destinations. Ironically, its early settlement can perhaps be viewed as the effect of tourism itself. Polynesian seafarers were skilled ocean navigators and astronomers who traveled long distances at a time when boats rarely went out of sight of land. While scholars still debate the founding history of Hawaii, some believe the first Polynesians arrived there around 200 AD from the Marquesas (Kamakau, 1992).

These Polynesian voyagers (sometimes an entire village) loaded up their double-hulled canoes with animals, plants, food, and water and headed out into the middle of the Pacific Ocean. They had more than 2,000 miles to go before they would reach the Hawaiian island of Kauai (Howe, 2006). Ultimately, archaeological evidence suggests that by 1280 AD, the Polynesians had settled the vast Polynesian triangle with its northern corner at Hawaii, the eastern corner at Easter Island, and the southern corner in New Zealand (Lowe, 2008).

What was their motive? Were they trying to colonize or to escape famine, drought, or overpopulation? Were they exploring? No one really knows, of course, but given the great dangers and unknowns about the trips, we can at least conclude their actions reveal an adventuresome spirit, a yearning for travel.

Muhammad's Early Empire: Relaxation

Muhammad, which means "praised one," was the founder of the religion of Islam and one of the most influential people of all time. Within 100 years of his death, in 632 AD, Muslims had carried his teachings into parts of the Middle East, North Africa, Europe, and Asia. Today, Islam is the second largest world religion with 1.6 billion followers, or 23% of the world's population (Pew Research Center, 2013).

Included in the teachings of Muhammad is another meaning of leisure that is still expressed today. Early Muslims learned Muhammad's philosophy of leisure through one of his sayings: "Recreate your hearts hour after hour, for the tired hearts go blind' (from the Hadith). In the Qur'an (the Islamic holy book), paradise for the faithful is envisioned as a verdant garden where chosen men recline on beautiful carpets next to rippling water and delight in the fragrance of flowers.

This vision of relaxing was practiced by ancient wealthy Muslims, who spent hours among lush landscapes of pools, pavilions, and fountains. During the day, they conversed with friends and played chess. At night, musicians provided entertainment, and dancers performed until dawn. Women from this period were segregated from men, but the wives and other female relatives and children of the wealthiest men lived similarly relaxing lives within the palace in a special place called the harem.

Medieval Europe: The Work Ethic

The Middle Ages, or medieval period of human history, describes the era between ancient and modern times in Western Europe, extending from the end of the Roman Empire (about 400 AD) to the 1500s. The former Roman Empire was divided into large estates called kingdoms and ruled by wealthy landowners. Later, this evolved into the system of **feudalism**, which fostered another meaning of leisure.

Feudalism: Fragmented political and economic power in which people worked and fought for nobles who gave them protection and the use of the land in return

Feudalism produced an individual, power-based meaning of leisure according to distinctions between lords and vassals. Because the lords owned the land and the vassal protected the lords in exchange for use of the land, leisure expression could be bartered. As well, because protection of the kingdoms often required battling intruders, leisure was commonly expressed through violence. For example, as practice for defending the kingdom, lords and their vassals were particularly interested in hunting and sport contests as means to keep their fighting skills and strategies sharp (Labarge, 1965). Pastimes within the kingdom also included performing minstrels (musicians, acrobats, jugglers, and storytellers all in one); games of backgammon, checkers, and chess; brawling sports such as cockfighting, bull baiting, and wrestling; and also social drinking, gambling, and theatrical performances.

As you might already suspect, however, the story of leisure during the Middle Ages includes a subtext. Life was difficult for everyone. People lived only an average of 30 years. Very few could read or write, and much superstition surrounded daily life. In the midst of this context, the Catholic Church became the main civilizing force, and according to church doctrine, the way to a better afterlife was through hard work, good deeds, and self-deprivation. This is why this period of human history is often considered to be the birth of the **work ethic**.

Work ethic: A cultural norm placing a positive moral value on hard work and self-deprivation

The Renaissance: Humanism

By about 1300 AD, medieval Europe began to give way to a period in history called the **Renaissance.** Renaissance is a French word meaning "rebirth," and in this 300-year period, it meant changes in ways of experiencing leisure. This was the age of Michelangelo, Leonardo da Vinci, William Shakespeare, and Cervantes. Art, music, drama, and other literary forms flourished. This was also the age of adventure; people were fascinated with the world and other people. Books about travel began to flood England, and it became wide-spread practice for young gentlemen to complement their education with lengthy travel (Hudman, 1980).

Renaissance: The transitional era between medieval and modern times in Western Europe that is marked by a humanistic revival of the arts

Under the sponsorship of wealthy nobles and royalty, theaters and opera houses were constructed, and formal balls, exhibitions, banquets, and masquerades were arranged. The middle classes also participated in festivities, and children's activities stressed creative pastimes such as studies in music and science (Bucher, Shiver, & Bucher, 1984).

Humanism. A philosophy emphasizing the capacities and worth of human beings

This Renaissance emphasis on rediscovery and expression of literature and the arts is the basis of a contemporary philosophy known as **humanism**. Although today within both religious doctrine and individual beliefs there are many interpretations, humanism includes the idea of happiness as its own justification. Like leisure, life is to include freedom of expression and awareness of beauty, and to harmoniously combine personal satisfaction with self-improvement.

Colonial America: Practical Pastimes

As one recent theory goes (Raghavan et al., 2015), North America was originally populated by people of Siberian origin who migrated there about 13,000 years ago. Later, in the 1400s, large waves of people, mostly from Europe, sailed across the Atlantic Ocean to North America. Among them were British colonists, who settled on the east coast between what are now the states of Maine and Georgia. They came in search of opportunities for wealth, power, freedom, and adventure.

Yet these settlers did not find great riches at first; instead, they found rugged wilderness. The earliest colonists suffered from starvation and disease as they worked to harness America's abundant resources. Little time and energy could be squandered when there was so much work to be done to survive. Idleness was dangerous. As well, because some were motivated to cross the Atlantic by a belief in "divine mission," a calling that rebelled against the conspicuous pleasures of the privileged class of the English aristocracy, idleness was believed by some to be unholy.

History has suggested, therefore, that the early American colonists did not enjoy themselves. However, this reading of history ignores that in spite of the hard work to be done and religious reforms, early colonial life embraced many examples of leisure practices, including reading, singing, dancing, archery, shooting, hunting, fishing, vaulting, wrestling, nine-pins, tennis, horse-racing, billiards, backgammon, card games, and a lot of drinking at most every social occasion (Johnson, 2009).

Figure 1.6. Actors in costumes depict colonial life at Colonial Williamsburg, a living history museum in Virginia.

Box 1.3
In Profile

The New England Puritans

The Puritans were a group of 16th and 17th century English Protestants who sought to purify the Church of England from all Roman Catholic practices. Many left for the New England region of North America beginning in 1630, founding the Massachusetts Bay Colony and other settlements. The Puritan culture of New England was distinctive in its attitude toward leisure. For example, you may be familiar with the long-held reputation of the Puritans as being against all forms of recreation and play. According to Johnson (2009), however, this is an ahistorical understanding and not at all true.

New scholarship suggests the Puritans saw all honorable work as a means of glorifying God, and respected a lifestyle, including leisure expression, that was pious. For example, the Puritans of the New England colonies abolished the observation of Christmas, not because it was a celebration, but because it was a symbol of the Catholic Church. They replaced all Catholic holy days with holidays celebrating humiliation and thanksgiving (Borsay, 2006).

In fact, according to Hunnicutt (2013), the New England Puritans believed that wholesome leisure expressions were a way to find the kingdom of God. Thus, ordinances banning gambling and other "lascivious" behavior were not decreed because of an anti-play bias, but rather because these pursuits were contrary to leading a virtuous life. By extension, by the way, this interpretation of history has rendered some current American pastimes to be associated with guilt, sanctimony, and hypocrisy, too (Daniels, 1995).

Painting depicting Puritans celebrating the first Thanksgiving. Source: Public domain

The unique aspect of early colonial American pastimes, however, is their frequent connection to practicality. Many leisure pursuits were expected to serve a purpose. In addition to enabling the attainment of a pious life for the Puritans, leisure also enabled the achievement of getting the work of settlement done. For example, celebrations while sewing a quilt or building a barn, made it possible for many hands to help with the task. The New England colonists took great pains to distinguish "lawful" recreation as contributing to the greater good.

In the southern colonies, as well, early settlers linked recreational pursuits to practicality. But as the land became productive for their owners, and once slaves were brought in from the Caribbean and Africa in the early 1600s, leisure for European colonists in the south became based more on lavish entertainment and hospitality. Weddings and funerals, as well as horse races, dances, parties, and barbecues brought people together. Gambling was celebrated with cards, dice, coin tossing, and lotto. Some scholars have drawn a similarity between the nature of leisure in the southern colonies and that of the ancient Greeks. That is, what enabled such an aristocratic meaning of leisure for the antebellum South was an economic system based on slavery.

Yet, for those who were indentured to the plantation owners, leisure was differently expressed. Brought with them from their homelands, the customs that thrived in their harsh lives included music, storytelling, and dance. The slaves typically worked from sunrise to sundown six or seven days a week. Only during the Christmas season did owners allow a few days for feasting and games.

The Industrial Revolution: Leisure as Problem Solver

Beginning in Great Britain during the 1700s, and spreading to other parts of Europe and to North America in the early 1800s, the development of industrialization brought major changes in leisure's meaning. So significant were the changes to societies that historians refer to this period as the **Industrial Revolution.** Widespread by midcentury, industrialization created an enormous increase in the production of many kinds of goods because of the introduction of power-driven machinery.

Industrial Revolution: The complex and radical socioeconomic changes from extensive mechanization of production

Figure 1.7. During the Industrial Revolution, children were often used as laborers. Their smaller size allowed them to move in tight spaces in factories or mines where adults couldn't fit. Also, children were considered to be easier to manage than adult workers and could be paid less. Source: The U.S. National Archives, Lewis Hine, photographer, December 1908

Some people were able to amass huge fortunes through industrialization. By 1900, there were about 3,000 millionaires in the United States (a million dollars then is equivalent to about $30 million today), compared to only 20 in 1850. American author Mark Twain called this the Gilded Age, describing the leisure-based culture of the newly rich. Attending operas and horse races, holding balls and parties, yachting, and relaxing at luxurious resorts were common for the members of this elite group.

However, for the middle and lower classes of people, industrialization had a different impact. For starters, industrialization changed the nature of work itself by taking it out of the home and workshop and into the factory. Women and men were now separated for most of the day. For those who tended the machines life was harsh. Jobs became specialized, so the work was monotonous. Wages were as low as 20 cents an hour and workers put in at least 60-hour workweeks (Fourastie, 1951). Children, many under age 10, worked up to 14 hours a day, at only a small fraction of these wages.

Meanwhile, housing in the growing industrial cities of New York, Chicago, and others could not keep up with the migration of workers from rural areas and other countries. Overcrowding resulted along with poor sanitation and inadequate diets, making people vulnerable to disease. As an obvious consequence, some came to believe that social reforms were needed. Individuals and social welfare groups set up charities. Demands went out for more humane working and living conditions, and workers' strikes for better wages and shorter work schedules erupted. In the United States reformers such as Dorothea Dix (treatment of mental illness), Horace Mann (better schools), and Sarah and Angelena Grimké (abolition and women's rights) worked tirelessly for better lives for workers and families.

Most meaningful from our perspective were those efforts using leisure. Such reformers as Joseph Lee, Janie Porter Barrett, Juliette Low, Stanton Coit, Jane Addams, and Ellen Starr believed wholesome and enriching leisure expressions would solve the problems of industrialization. We will use as examples two of the leisure-based **social movements** of the time: settlement houses and **playgrounds.**

Social movement: A significant change in the social conditions and patterns of behavior in a society

Settlement House: An institution in an inner city providing various community services

Copying the British model of Toynbee Hall in London, for example, **settlement houses** were established in the United States as a way to help the urban poor. The settlement house objective was to improve living conditions in cities, particularly for new immigrants. To accomplish this, they offered educational classes, nurseries, play apparatus for young children, sport activities and social clubs for older children, cultural arts programs for adults, as well as civil rights and fair employment advocacy. Stanton Coit established the first settlement house in 1886 in New York City, and three years later, Jane Addams and Ellen Starr established a settlement house in Chicago that became famous as the Hull House.

Box 1.4
In Profile

The Hull House

In 1889, Jane Addams and Ellen Gates Starr, college educated, upper middle-class women, using their own money, founded the Hull House in Chicago and quickly made it a model for nationwide efforts to improve the lives of people coping with poverty. When the heir of Charles Hull granted Jane and Ellen a rent-free, 4-year lease on his large, dilapidated old home that had become surrounded by deteriorating immigrant slums of Chicago's 19th Ward, they quickly moved in and made it the center of activity.

A day care center and kindergarten were available in the morning. In the afternoon, classes and clubs for teens were provided, and adult education programs were held in the evening. Nearby buildings were acquired and converted into a coffeehouse, a gymnasium, and a playground. Classes were offered in pottery, rhythm and dance, photography, and chorus. Concerts, dramatic readings, art exhibits, and lectures were weekly events. These carefully supervised programs were central to helping people resist the negative effects of the city around them (McBride, 1989).

Figure 1.8. Janie Porter Barrett wanted to teach life skills to neighborhood African-American girls in Hampton, Virginia. What began in 1889 as a sewing class for a few girls in her home on Tuesday afternoons soon became known as the Locust Street Social Settlement. Courtesy of Hampton University Archives

Meanwhile, another use of organized play to solve social problems at the time was the establishment of playgrounds. In the United States, this reform was represented initially by the public-spirited members of the New England Women's Club. Their project was the establishment in 1885 of The Boston Sand Garden, giving the city's children huge piles of sand in which to play. Later, strides to promote playgrounds in Boston were made by Joseph Lee, who helped create a model playground that included an area for small children, a boys' section, a sports field, as well as sand gardens. Other playgrounds sprang up elsewhere. Jacob Riis initiated the movement for publicly sponsored playgrounds in New York City, and Philadelphia moved ahead with full playground programs in the summer.

There were other initiatives using leisure as problem solver at this time as well. For example, Sir Robert Baden-Powell of Great Britain started the Boy Scout movement in 1907, and 6,000 girls registered, too. As he "could not have girls traipsing about over the country after his Boy Scouts," he got his sister Agnes Baden-Powell to form the Girl Guides program in Britain in 1909 (Schultz & Lawrence, 1958). Their first law was that they must not even speak to a Boy Scout if they saw him in uniform. A few years later, while visiting Britain, Juliette Gordon Low met the Baden-Powells and became fascinated with their organizations. When she returned to her home in Savannah, Georgia, she brought the idea with her. Changing the name to Girl Scouts, she held the first troop meeting in her home on March 12, 1912.

Other efforts at the turn of the last century to use leisure as problem solver included the establishment of therapeutic recreation services in state hospitals, the expansion of the national park system, the beginnings of the organized camping movement, the establishment of private athletic clubs, and the offering of college-level professional training for recreation leaders. Ultimately, the effort was so sweeping that it involved city, state, and federal governments, as well as private and voluntary welfare agencies, all relying on leisure as a tool. This "leisure movement" continues today. (See Chapter 13.)

Box 1.5
What Do
You Say?

Tragedy of the Commons

The beginnings of the city park in the United States are obscure. Some historians assert the plaza in St. Augustine, set aside by the Spanish in 1565, should be considered the first city park, whereas others refer to the Boston Common, established in 1634 by the British, as the first. Regardless, both had similar uses; people had unlimited access to the commonly held land for whatever they wanted. As cities grew and open space became scarce, the common and the plaza became important universally held resources.

However, consequences of this idea have been unintended, claims Garrett Hardin (1968)—referring to this as "the tragedy of the commons." Hardin in his essay asks us to imagine a pasture that is fixed in size and accessible to all the livestock owners of a village. Each herdsman naturally wants to maximize his use of the pasture by grazing as many cattle as possible. Therefore, he expands the size of his herd, recognizing the benefits from this will be his alone, whereas any costs for the increased grazing will be shared among all the village members. What each herdsman fails to recognize, claims Hardin, is that every other herdsman in the village is following the same logic, and the cumulative effect of their independently rational action ultimately destroys the pasture.

Later, in their own essay, Dustin, McAvoy, and Schultz (1982) asked us to imagine this tragedy of the commons another way. Consider an urban resident who wishes to escape the heat, congestion, and noise of the city on a summer weekend. She gathers the family, packs the car, and heads for the public beach. In fact, thousands of other city dwellers are making the same logical decision. So, instead of a cool, quiet, and refreshing leisure experience, they are treated to a beach with traffic jams, noise, and crime, to the ultimate destruction of the beach itself.

1. What is meant by the tragedy of the commons concept?
2. Is Hardin's logic applicable to recreation settings as Dustin et al. suggest? If so, what other examples can you cite of this?
3. Visit a public recreation area in your community or campus. Can you find traces of the tragedy of the commons there? What are these?

Today's Meanings

By tracing the meanings of leisure in the humanities and through history, we can see the term means many things depending on the place, the time, and the people. So what are the legacies of all these meanings for today? Our contemporary definitions are also a matter of perspective: individual experiences and cultural biases continue to define leisure in multiple ways. As described in a study by Watkins and Bond (2007), today's leisure meanings are a "continuum of experiences that reflect high levels of contextual diversity and flexibility" (p. 287).

This means that today, leisure is achievement of the highest ideal, idle hours and entertainment, mass spectacle, relaxation, a good time, relief from work, humanism, political expression, utilitarian, and a problem solver. It is an experience, but in context; it is a form, but not defined by form; and it takes place in time, but is not defined by time (Kelly & Freysinger, 2004). Therefore, as we now consider the contemporary connotations of leisure, we need to be aware that clear boundaries are not possible.

Yet, when taken altogether, many of today's leisure meanings can be broadly categorized in three ways: free time, recreational activity, and a special state of mind or spirit (Table 1.1).

Table 1.1
Contemporary Themes in Leisure's Meanings

Free Time	Time free from obligations	"To me, leisure is the weekend."
Recreational Activity	Nonwork kinds of experiences	"To me, playing golf and watching TV are leisure."
Spirit	A self-actualized attitude about life	"To me, getting the most zest out of my day is leisure."

Leisure as Free Time

An often-heard connotation today is that leisure is the time available after obligations. That is, leisure is a time frame within which you can make your own personal choices about how to spend it. Often referred to as **discretionary time**, leisure as free time divides life into separate spheres, such as work, study, sleep, eating, and leisure. Life, then, is all about prioritizing these "boxes of life" within time according to importance. The free time definition of leisure, then, suggests leisure is leftover time, or spare time, and thus of lower status. Furthermore, leisure defined as free time suggests that its purpose is to fill vacant time.

Discretionary time: Time that is free of obligation

This means that leisure is quantifiable and it is possible to refer to differing amounts of it. For example, we often look forward to weekends and holidays because we will have more free time than usual.

This also means that leisure as free time is comparative. For example, according to Ray, Sanes, and Schmitt (2013), the United States is the only advanced economy in the world that does not guarantee its workers any paid vacation and holidays. In contrast, European countries have established legal rights to at least 20 days of paid vacation and holidays per year (in Austria it is 35 days), while workers in Australia are guaranteed 28 days, Canadian employers are required to give workers 19 days, and 10 days is the mandate in Japan.

Kelly and Freysinger (2004) have also compared free time across demographic groups in North America. They found that teens have more free time than do middle-aged adults, single men have more than married men, and single mothers employed outside the home have the least free time of all.

Leisure as Recreational Activity

A second common meaning of leisure today is based on participation in nonwork activities. That is, we define leisure according to the form of our recreational pursuits. Riding a bike, knitting a scarf, playing a video game, and throwing a Frisbee are leisure according to this definition. And, according to many sources, the overwhelmingly most participated in recreation activity is watching television.

Box 1.6
By the
Numbers

Top Recreation Activities for American Adults

		Amount of day spent
1.	Watching television	2 hours, 49 minutes
2.	Socializing and communicating (i.e., texting)	38 minutes
3.	Playing games on the computer	27 minutes
4.	Reading	19 minutes
5.	Other leisure activities (gardening, playing music, etc.)	18 minutes
6.	Relaxing and thinking	17 minutes
7.	Participating in sports, exercise	17 minutes

Source: U.S. Bureau of Labor Statistics, 2014

Recreation activity experiences are of great benefit to us. According to Dumazedier (1974), for example, through recreation activities, we often achieve relaxation, diversion, and refreshment. Some contemporary scholars have pointed out a problem with leisure defined as recreation, however. For example, in considering thc benefit of relaxation, can't we achieve this by sleeping in on Saturday morning? Is the activity of sleeping, then, considered leisure?

Another curiosity in defining leisure as recreational activity can be demonstrated with the sport of tennis. Is tennis leisure when played at the local park with friends, and when played as part of a required physical education class, and when competing in the professional tennis circuit?

As with the free time definition, leisure defined as recreational activity means it can be counted and compared across different population groups. For example, in Australia, participation in sports and physical activities differs according to gender, with women more likely to walk for exercise, attend aerobics and fitness programs, and swim, while men are more likely to cycle, jog, and play golf (Australian Bureau of Statistics, 2011).

Leisure as a Special Spirit

Defining leisure as time left over after obligations and as recreational activity helps us to understand leisure objectively. That is, we can observe, count, and compare it. But as you can guess from our humanities and history journeys earlier in the chapter, there is more to it than this. Thus, a third way of defining leisure today is as a special attitude, or state of mind.

Although subjective, this third definition asserts that time and activities are irrelevant, that only personal feelings are meaningful. That is, leisure is a psychological condition by the meaning it holds for us, as our own spirit about living. This spirit often entails feelings of freedom, happiness, self-enrichment, and personal fulfillment. Leisure is a state of feeling satisfied, "a feeling of luxurious well-being" (Ryken, 1995). Leisure, then, is a state of mind that fosters a peaceful and productive co-existence with one's environment (Veal, 2004). Accordingly, leisure is a(n)

- decision, integral to its nature;
- act, whole and complex with its own history, emotion, and interpretation;
- creation, a product of decision and action;
- process, not fixed but developing it its time and place; and
- situation, constructed in an ever-new context. (Kelly, 1987, p. 49)

Box 1.7
In Your Own Experience

Definition Interviews

Why not discover the complexity of leisure meanings today for yourself? Here's one way:

1. Randomly ask at least 20 friends and family members what leisure means to them. Ask them to give you one-word definitions. Record every definition you are given.
2. Next, select for longer interviews two people you don't know very well and who are different from you. For example, you might choose someone from another country, a person quite a bit older or younger, or a person of a different race than you. Ask them what they like best about leisure? Least about leisure? How do they experience leisure? What does leisure mean to them?
3. Compare the results from both the quick and more extensive interviews. In an essay, discuss the multiple meanings of leisure and their context.

What We Understand About Leisure's Meaning

Leisure is a complex concept. To understand its contemporary meanings, this chapter explored definitions from three perspectives: the humanities, the histories of past societies, and current connotations. After studying this chapter, you should know the following:

1. Leisure is contextual. That is, its meaning depends on the place, the time, and the people.
   Give and contrast two examples of this from the chapter:

   ____

   ____

2. Literature, art, and music offer interpretations of leisure as integral to the human experience.
   Give an example of three different interpretations, one each from literature, art, and music:

   ____

   ____

3. In past societies, leisure has meant many things and has varied in its importance.
   Discuss one of the historical societies presented in the chapter and describe the meaning of leisure to it. Also, what is the legacy from this past society for today?

   ____

   ____

4. Our contemporary themes of leisure's meaning include free time, recreational activity, and a special spirit.
   Which of these connotations is most valid for you? Why?

   ____

   ____

References

Angelou, M. (1971). Harlem hopscotch. In *Just give me a cool drink of water 'Fore I die*. New York, NY: Random House.

Association of American Publishers. (2015). Book stats. Retrieved from http://www.publishers.org/press144/

Australian Bureau of Statistics. (2011). Participation in most popular sports and physical recreational activities, by sex. Retrieved from www.abs.gov.au/ausstats/abs@nsf

Borsay, P. (2006). *A history of leisure: The British experience since 1500.* New York, NY: Palgrave-Macmillan.

Brewer, D. J., & Teeter, E. (2007). Ancient Egyptian society and family life. In D. J. Brewer & E. Teeter (Eds.), *Egypt and the Egyptians* (2nd ed., pp. 110–126). Cambridge, UK: Cambridge University Press.

Bucher, C. A., Shiver, J. S., & Bucher, R. (1984). *Recreation for today's society.* Englewood Cliffs, NJ: Prentice-Hall.

Butler, J. (1971). *The theatre and drama of Greece and Rome.* San Francisco, CA: Chandler.

Daniels, B. C. (1995). *Puritans at play: Leisure and recreation in colonial New England.* New York, NY: St. Martins.

Dumazedier, J. (1974). *Sociology of leisure.* New York, NY: Elsevier North–Holland.

Dustin, D. L., McAvoy, L. H., & Schultz, J. H. (1982). *Stewards of access, custodians of choice: A philosophical foundation for the park and recreation profession.* Minneapolis, MN: Burgess.

Fitzgerald, F. S. (1920). The camel's back. *Tales of the jazz age.* New York, NY: Charles Scribner's Son.

Fourastie, J. (June 1951). Productivity and economics. *Political Science Quarterly, 66*(2), 216–225.

Godbey, G. (2008). *Leisure in your life: An exploration* (7th ed.). State College, PA: Venture.

Hamed, A. E. A. (2015). Sport leisure: Artistic perspectives in ancient Egyptian temples (Part II). *Recorde: Revista de Historia do Esporte, 18*(1) 1–28.

Hardin, G. (December 13, 1968). Tragedy of the Commons. *Science, 162,* 1243–48. Retrieved from http://www.garretthardinsociety.org/articles_pdf/tragedy_of_the_commons.pdf

Hemmingway, J. L. (1988). Leisure and civility: Reflections on a Greek ideal. *Leisure Sciences, 10,* 179–191.

Herbert, R. L. (1988). *Impressionism: Art, leisure, and Parisian society.* New Haven, CT: Yale University Press.

Howe, K. R. (2006). *Vaka Moana: Voyages of the ancestors, the discovery and settlement of the Pacific.* Albany, Auckland: David Bateman.

Hudman, L. E. (1980). *Tourism: A shrinking world.* Columbus, OH: Grid.

Hunnicutt, B. K. (2013). *Free time: The forgotten American dream.* Philadelphia, PA: Temple University Press.

Ibrahim, H. (1991). *Leisure and society: A comparative approach.* Dubuque, IA: Wm. C. Brown.

Ice Age. (2016). In Dictionary.com. Retrieved from http://www.dictionary.com/browse/ice-age

International Federation of Phonographic Industry. (2016). Key statistics. Retrieved from http://www.ifpi.org/global-statistics.php

Johnson, K. E. (2009). Problematizing Puritan play. *Leisure/Loisir, 33*(1), 31–54.

Kamakau, S. M. (April 1992). *Ruling chiefs of Hawaii* (Revised ed.). Honolulu, HI: The Kamehameha Schools Press.

Kelly, J. R. (1987) *Freedom to be: A new sociology of leisure.* New York, NY: Macmillan.

Kelly, J. R., & Freysinger, V. J. (2004). *21st Century leisure: Current issues.* State College, PA: Venture.

Labarge, M. W. (1965). *A baronial household of the thirteenth century.* New York, NY: Barnes & Noble.

Lowe, D. J. (2008). Polynesian settlement of New Zealand and the impacts of volcanism on early Maori society: An update. In Lowe, D. J. (Ed.), *Guidebook for pre-conference North Island Field Trip A1 "Ashes and Issues"* (28-30 November, 2008). Australian and New Zealand 4th Joint Soils Conference, Massey University, Palmerston North. New Zealand Society of Soil Science, pp. 142–147.

McBride, P. (1989). Jane Addams. In H. Ibrahim (Ed.), *Pioneers in leisure and recreation* (pp. 35–37). Reston, VA: American Alliance for Health, Physical Education, Recreation and Dance.

Metrolyrics. (2016). Gang of Four lyrics for "Natural's Not In It." Retrieved from http://www.metrolyrics.com/naturals-not-in-it-lyrics-gang-of-four.html

Otterman, S. (July 17, 2010). At camp, make-believe worlds spring off the page. *The New York Times.*

Pausanias. (1918). *Description of Greece* (vols. 1-4). (W. H. S. Jones & H. A. Ormerod, translators). Cambridge, MA: Harvard University Press.

Pew Research Center. (June 7, 2013). Global Religious Landscape Report. Retrieved from http://www.pewforum.org/2012/12/18/global-religious-landscape-exec/

Raghavan, M., Steinrucken, M., Harris, K., Schiffels, S., Rasmussen, S., DeGiorgio, M., …Cornejo, O. (August 2015). Genomic evidence for the Pleistocene and recent population history of Native Americans. *Science, 349* (6250). doi: 10.1126/science.aab3884

Ray, R., Sanes, M. & Schmitt, J. (May 2013). *No-vacation nation revisited.* Center for Economic and Policy Research, Washington, DC. Retrieved from www.cepr.net

Roberts, V. M. (1962). *On stage: A history of theatre.* New York, NY: Harper & Row.

Ryken, L. (1995). *Redeeming the time: A Christian approach to work and leisure.* Grand Rapids, MI: Baker Books.

Schultz, G. D., & Lawrence, D. G. (1958). *Lady of Savannah: The life of Juliette Low.* Philadelphia, PA: J. B. Lippincott.

Scott, J. L. (2008). Leisure remix: Hip hop's impact on reframing leisure. Master's Thesis. University of Tennessee, Knoxville. Retrieved from http://trace.tennessee.edu/utk_gradthes/441

Sylvester, C. (1999). The classical idea of leisure: Cultural ideal or class prejudice? *Leisure Sciences, 12,* 3–16.

Tierney, J. (2011, April 25). A new generation's vanity, heard through hit lyrics. *The New York Times.* Retrieved from http://www.nytimes.com/2011/04/26/science/26tier.html

U.S. Bureau of Labor Statistics. (2014). American time use survey. Retrieved from http://www.bls.gov/TUS/CHARTS/LEISURE.HTM

Veal, A. J. (1992). Definitions of leisure and recreation. *Australian Journal of Leisure and Recreation, 2* (4), 44–48, 52.

Watkins, M., & Bond, C. (2007). Ways of experiencing leisure. *Leisure Sciences, 29*(3), 287–307.

Wilford, J. N. (June 14, 2012). With science, new portrait of the cave artist. *The New York Times.* Retrieved from http://www.nytimes.com/2012/06/15/science/new-dating-puts-cave-art-in-the-age-of-neanderthals.html

CHAPTER 2

Why Leisure Is Vital

Is it important to have fun?

Even though we may casually think of leisure as "just having fun," philosophers and scientists have taken the matter quite seriously.

What do we gain from leisure?

Leisure is important because it gives us freedom, intrinsic reward, happiness, pleasure, play, humor, relaxation, ritual, solitude and silence, commitment, spirituality, risk, and other benefits.

Does leisure provide all of these benefits?

For any single leisure expression some of these benefits result, yet not usually all of them. In a different leisure experience, another set of benefits may result.

Are you having fun? Although this may seem a trivial question, much of our life is spent in pursuit of a good time. And while just having fun is often what we casually think of when considering leisure, almost everyone wants it. Why? What is it that makes leisure so coveted? That is, what are the benefits of leisure?

In this chapter, we consider the nature of leisure by characterizing its expression. We go beyond the definitions of leisure explored in the previous chapter and focus on the variety of ways it is of value to us.

Freedom

Foremost, leisure makes us feel free. We are having fun when we freely choose what we're doing. In fact, scholars suggest leisure cannot exist at all when our perception of freedom is curtailed, as the amount of **perceived freedom** we experience is one of the most basic values of leisure.

Perceived freedom: Believing that you are in charge of your leisure expression

For example, as shown in Figure 2.1, how much freedom of choice we have in a pursuit categorizes the type of leisure it is (Neulinger, 1981). Neulinger referred to these categories as "states of mind." The first state of mind represents the purest form of leisure: an expression freely chosen for its own sake. Neulinger's states of mind not only classify leisure according to the amount of perceived freedom in the experience, but also the degree of intrinsic reward. We focus on the first quality here and feature the second quality in the next section.

Meanwhile, another leisure scholar, John Kelly (2009, 2012), refers to this freedom state of mind as ideal leisure, which is also somewhat similar to the leisure ideal of the ancient Greeks. That is, ideal leisure requires freedom from external control. Like Neulinger's pure leisure, Kelly's ideal leisure also is the result of another quality—intrinsic reward.

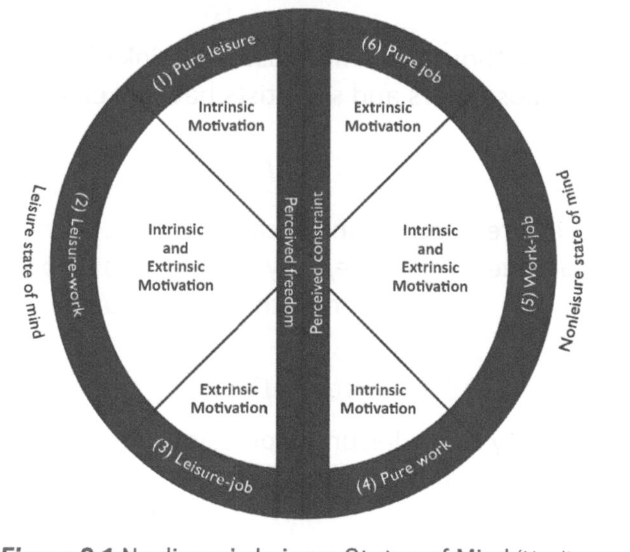

Figure 2.1 Neulinger's Leisure States of Mind (Neulinger, 1981)

The pure/ideal leisure quality suggests two different understandings of freedom. These are the distinctions between leisure as freedom "from" and leisure as freedom "to." First, leisure is temporary freedom from the necessary routine of life. That is, leisure frees us from obligations and provides a relief from work, such as when we take a vacation. Leisure as freedom "from" is considered a less satisfying experience because it carries the connotation that leisure must first be earned through work. For example, is leisure as freedom "from" possible for someone retired from a paying job?

On the other hand, leisure as freedom "to" is considered more satisfying. Here the focus is on freedom to experience a particularly personal expression. This means in order to experience leisure, we must claim our choices and expand beyond the limits of the present toward truly fulfilling possibilities. Freedom "to" is what Neulinger and Kelly had in mind with the idea of pure/ideal leisure.

How, then, do we acquire more leisure as freedom "to" in our lives? According to the investigations of Bregha (1991), freedom in leisure is a matter of

- possessing personal qualities,
- having the means, and
- receiving permission.

First, freedom "to" in leisure requires having the knowledge, physical ability, personality, and other personal qualities required for a successful experience. This means having information about what is available, as well as knowledge about oneself, including the consequences of our actions. For example, you cannot choose to go sculling if you do not know how to locate a boat, oars, and a waterway, or if you do not understand your own physical and mental readiness for it. Similar to the ancient Greek ideal, this means leisure requires the ability to choose with intelligence and responsibility.

Second, for Bregha (1991) leisure involves having means. Throughout history, wealth has always been considered a factor in experiencing leisure. In fact, during the 19th century in Western cultures, the wealthy were tagged "the leisure class" because they had the means for it. This link still exists today as many forms of recreational activity require expensive fees, equipment, clothing, transportation, and instruction. For example, with a one-day admission price of $95 (as of 2016), is SeaWorld in Orlando equally accessible to everyone?

Finally, the ability to freely choose leisure requires permission. Because few forms of leisure, except perhaps daydreaming and contemplation, can be experienced without at least the passive consent of our family, neighbors, or civic authorities, leisure expressions require sanction from others. For example, there are city ordinances against making too much noise at an outdoor party, restaurants are open only at specific times, and we must have prior permission from the owner to jog on private property.

So, it is possible to conclude that leisure is perhaps our most precious expression of freedom because while it affords us freedom to choose, our choices require capability, means, and authority. In other words, leisure's freedom is qualified.

Figure 2.2. Many societies have developed accommodations for persons with disabilities so that everyone can express the freedom "to" qualities in leisure. © Ruth V. Russell, 2016

Intrinsic Meaning

Another, often considered basic, value from leisure is intrinsic meaning, or intrinsic reward (Kelly, 2009). **Intrinsic meaning** comes from doing something for its own reason. Cross-country skiers, for example, often exclaim about sensations of peacefulness while gliding along; potters typically value working with clay on the wheel because of the elastic and smooth response of the clay in their hands; and dancers have described dancing as moving to a rhythm within (Csikszentmihalyi, 1975). Having fun, then, can also mean experiencing something for its own sake—for the joy and personal fulfillment of it.

Intrinsic meaning: Doing something for its own reason

Back to the ideas of Neulinger and Kelly: Pure/ideal leisure occurs when an experience or expression is also intrinsic. That is, pure leisure is not only the experience of high amounts of perceived freedom, but also lots of intrinsic reward. The experience is freely chosen for its own sake. To clarify, let's review each of Neulinger's leisure and nonleisure categories (see Figure 2.1 again).

1. **State of Mind One.** This represents the purest form of leisure—an expression freely chosen for its own sake. That is, "pure leisure" requires freedom from external control, and it brings intrinsic rewards. Thus, a particular pastime can be explained as the highest form of leisure if both of these ingredients are present in your state of mind.
2. **State of Mind Two.** This leisure situation explains a wide range of experiences, all of which are freely chosen yet are both extrinsically and intrinsically rewarding. For example, perhaps you are refinishing a piece of antique furniture because it not only provides you with a creative feeling but also because the result will look nice in your house. Neulinger referred to this as "leisure-work."
3. **State of Mind Three.** This situation is "leisure-job" according to Neulinger. It explains a type of leisure you engage in without coercion, but the satisfaction comes only from external payoffs. For some, playing cards for money (when they don't need the money) might fit this state of mind. The experience is leisure because of perceived freedom to pursue it, but like a job in that it is only extrinsically rewarding.
4. **State of Mind Four.** Neulinger's idea holds that the first three states of mind describe leisure. The fourth through sixth states of mind are considered nonleisure (see Figure 2.1). That is, without freedom of choice, we can't have leisure. Thus, the fourth state of mind is not considered to be leisure because even though it is done for intrinsic reasons, it is under the perceived constraints category. Neulinger called this "pure work." An example might be doing your homework because you are interested and even enjoyably involved, but which you would not choose to do unless the teacher made the assignment.
5. **State of Mind Five.** This is "work-job," namely, activities engaged in under constraints and having both intrinsic and extrinsic rewards. The typical employment situation may match this state of mind. For example, in one study, the staff of a large municipal recreation and park department rated their jobs as highly meaningful and personally satisfying, but they also indicated on the survey they would quit or retire immediately if given the financial opportunity (Russell, 1993).
6. **State of Mind Six.** A state of mind in the "pure job" category is completely opposite pure leisure. It is an activity engaged in by necessity and under constraints. There is no reward in and of itself but only through a payoff resulting from it. Having to work at a job in its most negative connotation to earn a living only is categorized as pure job. It has no other redeeming qualities.

Extrinsic meaning: Doing something for another reason, such as for status or a reward

Another way to view this is that while intrinsic meaning describes the leisure value of doing something for its own sake, **extrinsic meaning** is the consequence of engaging in a pastime for reasons other than its own. For example, if we sign up for a group exercise class because we want to lose weight, not because we want to experience the exhilaration of moving our bodies, we do so for extrinsic rewards. In this case, our motivation is from the outside rather than from within us. Thus, Neulinger's first three leisure states of mind are also distinguished according to the mix of intrinsic and extrinsic meaning.

Obviously there is a hierarchical valuing of leisure implied here. That is, pure leisure (and Kelly's ideal leisure) is the ultimate expression because it is freely chosen and for intrinsic reasons, and leisure-job is least desired because while it is freely chosen, it is for extrinsic reasons. Leisure scientists and practitioners, therefore, are interested in how pure leisure can be encouraged. For example, in a study by Walker (2010), it was found that the possession of a personal sense of autonomy and competence fostered intrinsic motivation in leisure. Also, research has demonstrated (see Lepper, Greene, & Nisbett, 1973) that intrinsic motivation can be turned into extrinsic motivation in leisure if extrinsic rewards such as prizes are emphasized.

Happiness

Another benefit often available to us from our leisure is happiness. Also known as subjective well-being, high morale, life satisfaction, and positive life attitude, happiness in general is an indicator of the overall quality of our inner experience that typically comes from living well. For example, according to multiple polls, the citizens of Denmark are among the happiest in the world. What makes them so happy? What is happiness? We answer these questions from three perspectives: classical philosophies, research studies, and current popular ideas.

Box 2.1
By the Numbers

Rank Order of Happiest Countries

1. Denmark
2. Switzerland
3. Iceland
4. Norway
5. Finland
6. Canada
7. Netherlands
8. New Zealand
9. Australia
10. Sweden

(United States = 13th, Germany = 16th, United Kingdom = 23rd, Japan = 53rd, Russia = 56th, China= 83rd)

Source: The World Happiness Report, 2016

Thinking about what happiness is, and asking questions on how to have it, have occupied philosophers for hundreds of years. Explanations have ranged from happiness being free from worldly interest (Avicenna, 980–1037) to satisfying a wish (Schopenhauer, 1788–1860). To Aristotle, the question was how should the good life be lived? His answer was that a flourishing life comes from **eudaimonia**, which most translations today interpret as happiness or personal well-being (Sylvester, 1991). Unlike today's common understanding of happiness as an inner good feeling, via eudaimonia Aristotle meant something else. Eudaimonia was not determined by positive feelings but rather by good actions. Thus, for life and leisure to bring happiness, it must entail only moral and worthy activities, or unhappiness results.

Eudaimonia: Aristotle's idea of happiness; doing good things provides the good life

In even stronger syncopation with Aristotle, Immanuel Kant (1781) suggested we should not have happiness as our highest goal if it keeps us from doing the right thing. Ultimately, he argued, not doing the right thing destroys our happiness. Contrastingly, Bertrand Russell (1968) focused on how to avoid unhappiness. For example, he considered competition, boredom, fatigue, and envy the causes of unhappiness, while the cure for unhappiness is zest in life.

As well, over the years, scientists have carried out hundreds of studies seeking to answer the question of what makes us happy. A vast amount of data suggests correlations between happiness and various genetic, social, economic, and personal factors. Some have predicted, for example, that age is important —younger people and older people are happier than middle-aged people. Some studies suggest women are happier than men, and that having good health makes one happy. Having friends and family, enough money, a good education, a meaningful career, helpful coping strategies and life goals, a creative and nurturing personality, being an optimist and an extrovert, and even a genetic predisposition toward a positive attitude, have all been connected to happiness in research studies (Kovacs, 2007).

For example, Sonja Lyubomirsky concludes in her book, *The How of Happiness* (2007), that 50% of a given human's happiness level is genetically determined (based on twin studies), 10% is affected by life circumstances and situation (such as housing, marital status, and income), and a remaining 40% of happiness is subject to self-control. If this is so, what is the role of leisure within the 40% sector?

In fact, several studies have focused on leisure's role. For example, in one study (Larson & Richards, 1998), adolescents revealed their emotional high points were on Fridays and Saturdays, with their moods dropping on Sundays and staying low during the rest of the week. The researchers explained this as the distinction between adult structured time (Sunday through Thursday) and teen structured time (Friday and Saturday).

In another study (Putnam, 2000), the role of specific forms of leisure in adult happiness was examined. Results suggested attending club meetings, volunteering to help others, entertaining at home, and attending church regularly, were related to higher levels of happiness. However, the researchers also discovered a diminishing return; doing too many of these activities often reduced happiness.

In a study about vacation by Nawijin (2012), findings indicated unsurprisingly that vacationers are happier than nonvacationers, and that vacationers feel much better during vacation compared to everyday life. Surprising, however, was that people returned to their baseline of happiness immediately after returning from vacation, and vacation happiness did not impact overall life satisfaction. The researcher concluded that perhaps the idea of travel is more appealing than the actual travel.

The most vital link between leisure and happiness is most likely via the concept of **leisure satisfaction**. Leisure satisfaction is our perception of how satisfying our leisure experiences and expressions are. Several studies have found, for example, that experiencing leisure with an optimistic outlook, meaningful focus and commitment, a lot of perceived freedom and intrinsic reward, and a belief in being capable in the leisure event determine happiness (Kovacs, 2007).

Leisure satisfaction: Gratification and contentment with one's leisure experiences and opportunities

So what about the residents of Denmark? Why are they so happy? In the World Happiness Report (2016) prepared by the United Nations (see Box 2.1), numerous factors are evaluated and compared. These include life expectancy, environmental vulnerability, cancer rates, take-home pay, and many others, such as "leisure and personal care." This category highlights the role of such activities as walking, sports, entertainment, cultural activities, socializing, watching television, gardening, and so forth. In the report these are measured as the number of hours per day, that, on average, full-time employed people spend on them. And in Denmark, an average of 16 hours each day is devoted to leisure pursuits, as compared to 14 hours in the United States and Canada.

Pleasure

In almost all characterizations of leisure, pleasure is included. Listening to a well-performed orchestral piece, eating a handful of popcorn, petting the dog—these are all forms of pleasure, and all provide value to our lives. Indeed, it is thought that to be human is to be pleasure-seeking—that our brains are "hard wired" to be motivated by pleasure (Esch & Stefano, 2004).

Pleasure is difficult to distinguish from other leisure benefits. For example, pleasure has been described as a feeling of happiness and as a sense of freedom. We'll tease out some distinctions by first relying again on ancient Greek ideas, and then more recent typologies of the various kinds of pleasure resulting from leisure.

To the ancient Greeks, pleasure had multiple connotations (Goodale & Godbey, 1988). Cynicism, for example, suggested virtue rather than pleasure was life's goal. In contrast, the ancient idea of stoicism suggested people should be indifferent to both pleasure and pain. Even today, stoics accept good fortune without joy and misfortune without complaint: "You win a few, you lose a few!" But the two ancient ideas of Epicureanism and hedonism are what we most often associate with pleasure today. Epicureanism holds that pleasure should be experienced in moderation, and that the best pleasures are intellectual, such as contemplation and appreciation. According to epicurean understanding, the inferior pleasures are those that respond to the senses, such as sexual drives and hunger. Hedonism, on the other hand, suggests pleasure is the highest goal of life. Ancient followers of hedonism included the body, fame, power, and wealth as sources of pleasure.

All four of these ancient perspectives about pleasure have influenced contemporary ideas about leisure as pleasurable. For example, some consider certain forms of leisure, such as dancing, to be pleasurable because of sensations in the body (hedonism), while others consider such physical pastimes immoral because of their sensual nature (cynicism).

A more recent typology of pleasure contains sensory, expressive, and intellectual forms (Smith, 1991). **Sensory pleasures** are found in eating, listening to music, having sex, and playing sports. These expressions are pleasurable because they directly stimulate our senses. For example, by measuring people's physiological responses to musical tones using a facial electromyography technique, researchers found that tones of low intensity (75 dB) were more pleasing than tones of high intensity (95 dB and above).

Sensory pleasure: Pleasure from direct stimulation of the senses

Expressive pleasure: Pleasure from creativity

Intellectual pleasure: Pleasure from thinking

Expressive pleasures from leisure, on the other hand, are based on the use of creativity. As a result of an experience, something is produced and this gives us pleasure. To distinguish, listening to rap music may trigger sensory pleasure, whereas creating a rap song more likely offers expressive pleasure. Finally, **intellectual pleasure** from leisure comes from thinking activities. These might include fantasizing, daydreaming, solving puzzles, and even studying.

Figure 2.3. The sculpture "The Traveler" perhaps gave expressive pleasure to its creator, Duane Hanson, and gives intellectual pleasure to visitors in the Orlando, Florida airport. In fact, giving pleasure is an expressed purpose of the airport's public art program. © Ruth V. Russell, 2008

Regardless of exactly how pleasure is categorized, the most important conclusion about this leisure benefit is its usefulness to good health. Of course, pleasure is capable of promoting addictions and other dangerous behaviors, but in appropriate amounts and expressions, it is a positive life force. Scientists have shown, for example, that moderate pleasurable experiences are able to enhance what is referred to as our biological flexibility and complexity, and thereby provide a sort of health protection. This is because feelings of pleasure are naturally occurring health processes (Esch & Stefano, 2004, p. 245).

Play

A child once told me that play "is what I do when people stop telling me what to do." Perfect definition. Play is human nature itself, and like everything so essentially human, there are many different ways to individually express it. For example, we play a role on the stage, play the fish on the line, and play a musical instrument. We play along, play around, play down, play up, play fair, and play possum.

When children, adults, and animals play, defenses dissolve. We become spontaneous and expanded. We are in the moment—flexible, open, and delighted. All this serves many valuable purposes. It is a means by which we develop and maintain physical, intellectual, emotional, social, and moral capacities. It is how we form and preserve friendships. It provides a state of mind that, in adults as well as children, is uniquely suited for high-level reasoning, insightful problem solving, and all sorts of creative endeavors.

Box 2.2
The Study Says

The Games Animals Play

Charles Darwin wrote in his 1872 classic, *The Descent of Man*, "happiness is never better exhibited than by young animals ... when they are playing together" (p. 47). Since this observation, scientists have been keenly interested in the games animals play.

Horses: Baby horses have been observed playing within two hours of birth. They especially enjoy exaggerated galloping and playfully nipping at their mothers. After a few weeks, they frolic with other foals and chase and circle each other, while also tossing around objects such as sticks and rags. At one month of age, colts and fillies develop different play styles, in preparation, scientists believe, for the gender roles they will adopt later in life: colts spend much of their time playfully fighting and mounting others; fillies mostly engage in galloping play and mutual grooming.

Most dogs enjoy interacting with each other in play that extends into adulthood.

Fish: Many researchers have reported that, even when no predators are in sight, fish playfully jump over everything from twigs to turtles. While proof that fish play is far from conclusive, some experts believe this leaping behavior constitutes play because it takes place during the calmest days, when fish are not concerned about food, mates, or safety.

Mice: According to biologists, mice start playing at about 15 days of age, with leaping, jumping, twisting, and shaking peaking at days 19 to 25. This timeline corresponds closely with the development of synapses in their brain's cerebellum, which plays a critical role in muscle movement and coordination.

Source: Dugatkin & Rodrigues, 2008

Susanna Millar, in her classic book, *The Psychology of Play*, suggested that "perhaps play is best used as an adverb, not as a name of a class of activities ... but to describe how and under what conditions an action is performed" (1968, p. 21). As an action, playfulness is an attitude of throwing off the physical, emotional, social, and intellectual constraints that hold us back from high spiritedness, a lightness of heart, enthusiasm, and readiness for surprise. As also suggested in 1938 by Dutch anthropologist Johan Huizinga, play is an action that is fully absorbing, includes elements of uncertainty, involves a sense of illusion or exaggeration, and most importantly, exists outside of ordinary life (Huizinga, 1955).

Let's use the playing of games to illustrate all this. The English word *game* is related to the old German word *gaman*, which means glee. Thus, the original meaning of game was not far from that of play. While games vary considerably in the nature of winning, the rules, the number and roles of players, and the particular equipment and amount of time required to play, they are at heart in some way artificial. They take place as a synthetic counterpart to real life. The chess match, for example, is the artificial enactment of a medieval war. Monopoly is the counterfeit experience of capitalism.

Box 2.3
In Profile

Board Games Are Back!

Are you a "gamer?" In answering, I bet you are thinking of the latest PC and console blockbusters descriptive of video gaming. However, the past decade has seen unexpected growth in an industry assumed to be redundant in the era of screens. In the past 4 years, tabletop board game purchases have risen by between 25% and 40% annually. Thousands of new titles are released each year, and the top ones sell millions of copies.

All this is perhaps the result of an approach to game design that considers the creation of shared social experiences to be important. For example, "Pandemic" casts players as a team of medics trying to rid the world of four deadly infectious diseases. "Dead of Winter" challenges a group of survivors to stay alive in a world overrun by zombies. "Freedom – The Underground Railroad" gives players a chance to examine the history of the U.S. abolitionist movement, as they shelter runaway slaves.

Source: Duffy, 2014

In the outside-of-reality world of games, the types of play can be categorized. For French intellectual Roger Caillois (1961), four types of play in games are distinguished: agon, alea, mimicry, and ilinx. Agon games are competitive and require some skill. These include most sports. Alea games, such as Bingo, require luck and winning is a matter of fate. Mimicry games, typically video and table-top board games, involve role-playing, and ilinx games are more sensory in nature, such as drinking games. Some games, of course, involve more than one of these forms of play. For example, playing the card game of poker likely involves both agon and alea play.

One enduring question for scientists and philosophers has been about why we play. Since the 18th century, at least 15 different theories explaining play have been considered, based on studies from biology, psychology, sociology, and anthropology. In reviewing the more common of these theories, we'll use this classification system (Ellis, 1973): first the older theories, then the more recent theories, and finally the most contemporary explanations. (See Table 2.1.)

One of the oldest and most often quoted theories of play is the surplus energy theory. It claims play serves as a pressure valve for burning up stored physical energy. Another early theory viewed play as preparation for adulthood. This biologically based theory explains that children play because of instinctual urges required for survival. Finally, the relaxation theory explains play as an action that provides recuperation from fatigue and stress. Opposite the surplus energy explanation, the relaxation perspective claims play restores energy.

These and other older theories, which date back to the late 19th and early 20th centuries, are often labeled "armchair" theories because they have limited research support. More recent theories represented attempts to make the explanation of play more scientific. For example, the catharsis theory is similar to the surplus energy theory, except it focuses on pent-up emotional energy rather than physical energy. Play is viewed in this theory as a socially acceptable way to purge negative feelings. Another more recent theory is the behaviorist explanation, which labels play as a form of learning. Based in the work of behavioral psychologists such as B.F. Skinner, play is connected with the stimulus-response mechanisms. That is, play is considered a pleasurable activity that receives praise and recognition; thus, it is learned and repeated. Finally, the psychoanalytic explanation, first discussed by Sigmund Freud, viewed many forms of play as symptoms of psychological illness. That is, play was a method of mastering disturbing events or thoughts.

Table 2.1
A Brief Comparison of Play Theories

Theory	Definition	Example	Critique
Surplus energy	Burning up excess energy	Children chasing each other around the playground	Helps justify the role of physical play for problem youth; doesn't explain nonphysical play
Preparation	Practice for adult life	Children playing house or doctor	Doesn't explain adult play
Relaxation	Recuperation	Playing solitaire as a study break	Doesn't explain play that is similar to work
Catharsis	Letting off emotional steam	Working out on a punching bag after an argument	Has intuitive appeal, yet aggressive behavior often increases aggressive behavior
Behavioristic	A response to a pleasurable stimulus	Playing basketball just after your team won a tournament	Overlooks the role of individual differences, yet has boosted play as appropriate to study
Psychoanalytic	Mastering disturbing events or thoughts	A child yelling at her stuffed animals after a scolding from a parent	Initiated the practice of careful observation of play; play therapy
Arousal seeking	Seeking optimal stimulation	Bored student counting a professor's mannerisms in class	Has more research support
Competence-effectance	Having an effect on things	Making snow angels in the backyard	Requires more research testing

While these more recent theories have been substantiated by research data, they remain credible as only partial explanations of why people play. The most contemporary explanations, in fact, have often been composites of these earlier theories. For example, the arousal-seeking theory claims the main goal of play is both intellectual and physical stimulus. That is, play serves to generate complexity as a guard against boredom. And, the competence-effectance theory refers to the need to produce effects—to be a cause of things taking place or being produced.

Each of these contemporary theories of play, as well as others such as attribution theory, conflict-enculturation theory, and recapitulation theory, contain an element of truth, yet none fully explain all aspects of why we play. Yet, maybe this is as it should be. Perhaps play does not occur because it is accountable. Perhaps it is simply an enchanted place outside ordinary life.

Humor

"Angels fly because they take themselves lightly," says an old Scottish proverb. And researchers have reported that this "lightening up" is good medicine. It aids digestion, stimulates the heart and lungs, lowers blood pressure, strengthens muscles, improves the immune system, and reduces pain (Jones, 1992). For example, in some hospitals there are laughing rooms where patients are encouraged to watch funny movies and read humorous books, which are believed to decrease their need for pain medication. Other hospitals have instituted comedy carts and Clown Care units.

As well as physical benefits, humor improves our mental and social health. For example, having a good laugh helps to relieve stress, improve mood, ease anxiety and fear, and improve resilience. Further, humor helps us make friends, diffuse conflict, and promote group bonding (Smith & Segal, 2016).

Box 2.4
In Your Own Experience

How to Lighten Up!

How much humor do you feel you have in your daily life? Want to add more? Here's your to-do list:

- Search for humor in the every day.
- Try laughter yoga.
- Turn off the TV news, and watch a funny movie or a comedy channel instead.
- Post a picture of someone laughing on your bathroom mirror.
- Hang out with children and funny people.
- Be mindful of when you are and are not smiling and increase the smiling ratio.
- Learn how to tell a joke.

What is humor? Jokes, cartoons, caricatures, parodies, puns, silliness, imitations, wisecracks, and tall tales provide pleasant psychological shifts that usually result in an audible physiological expression of laughter. When we laugh we experience two physiological phases: the arousal phase—when the heart rate increases, and the resolution phase—when the heart rests. Our heart can reach up to 120 beats per minute when laughing. Unfortunately, we don't always take advantage of this. For example, on average, children laugh 400 times per day, while adults only laugh about 15 times per day (Roach, 1996).

Humor is a benefit of leisure. In addition to making us happy and being pleasurable, there are other connections. For example, along with make-believe, fantasy, and daydreaming, humor can be considered a form of daily-life play (Martin, 1996).

A study by Martin and Kuiper (1995) found that laughter tends to occur throughout the day, although it is more frequent in the evening when we are more likely to be around other people. Thus, other studies have shown that humor is primarily a social experience. For example, using a humor diary and mood measures, research by Mannell and McMahon (1982) examined the frequency and types of humorous experiences of university students and their relationship to psychological well-being during a day. Mass media, such as television, provided the fewest incidents of humor (18%), while social interactions generated the largest number (56%). Also, increases in positive moods and decreases in negative moods were associated significantly with greater numbers of incidents of humor and overt laughter.

Figure 2.4. Do animals laugh? According to the National Geographic organization, apes and mice are the only animals to get the giggles (Langley, 2015).

Relaxation

A child drawing pictures in the beach sand that a wave immediately erases, a tourist wandering without an itinerary, and two friends rocking in silence on the front porch are relaxing, and through relaxation, they are experiencing being "leisurely." An early proponent of this leisure benefit was Josef Pieper, a German scholar who declared, "Leisure is not the attitude of the mind of those who actively intervene but of those who are open to everything; not of those who grab hold, but of those who leave the reins loose and who are free and easy themselves" (1963, p. 41). To Pieper, leisure was defined as an "attitude of nonactivity," of not being busy, but letting things happen. Doug Kleiber, a contemporary American scholar, agrees, and claims true leisure is simply being appreciative, contemplative, and peaceful. He writes, "Leisure is most essentially a position of relaxation, of faithful openness to immediate reality …" (2000, p. 83).

The importance of this quality of leisure may be difficult for us to grasp because we live in societies that celebrate effort and accomplishment, and idleness is considered supremely nonproductive. But modern living suggests there could be no greater circumstance for ensuring that we take the time to do nothing at all. Thomas Merton, a Catholic writer and mystic, perhaps struck a chord with millions by not just noting that "Man was made for the highest activity, which is, in fact, his rest" (1948, p. 32), but by also acting on it, leaving the rat race for a Cistercian cloister.

While most of us won't need to take such a drastic step to relax, there are at least two positions from which to argue its importance. First, relaxation is of value for its ability to recharge us to be productive later. It relieves stress, improves the immune system, and generally restores us for our work or school tasks. This is the logic often used when we decide to take a vacation. For example, Pulitzer Prize winner Nicholas Carr, who in the book, *The Shallows* (2010), points to research that demonstrated that after spending time relaxing in quiet rural settings, subjects exhibited greater attentiveness, stronger memory, and generally improved cognition.

But relaxation can also be revered as an end in itself. In *Freedom and Destiny*, psychoanalyst Rollo May (1981) refers to it as "the pause," which is important because it interrupts the routine and habits of our lives with imagining, reflecting, wondering, and pondering. The pause has become increasingly sought today. For example, the recent popularity of yoga, tai chi, and meditation, as well as such relaxation techniques as autogenic relaxation, progressive muscle relaxation, hot stones massage, and aromatherapy perhaps support this perspective.

Solitude and Silence

Often when we relax, we do so alone and silently. Spending time alone is an integral part of living well. Brief periods of solitude can return us to ourselves by providing opportunities for growth and creativity (Storr, 1988). While many people fear being lonely, when voluntarily chosen, being alone provides a time and space to be ourselves, accountable only to ourselves, and free of obligations. When this is the experience, we are at leisure.

In a sense, the leisure benefit of solitude is a form of narcissism. In leisure's solitude, we are allowed to return to ourselves. For example, May Sarton, an American poet and novelist, referred to solitude as the "richness of self." In a journal entry, she wrote:

> I am here alone for the first time in weeks, to take up my 'real' life again at last. That is what is strange—that friends, even passionate love, are not my real life unless there is time alone in which to explore and to discover what is happening (Sarton, 1973, p. 3).

Often silence is a companion of solitude. Yet society makes both solitude and silence difficult to attain. Traffic and construction noise, working with and around other people, and perhaps especially personal communication devices see to it that we have no quiet privacy. For example, the average office worker today has no more than 3 minutes at a time at his or her desk without interruption (Iyer, 2011). And smartphone users check their devices on average every 6.5 minutes, which works out to around 150 times a day (Nguyen, 2015).

An example of combating this is the Intel Company, which experimented in 2007 with conferring 4 uninterrupted hours of quiet time every Tuesday morning on 300 engineers and managers. During this time, workers were not allowed to use the phone or send e-mail, but simply had the chance to clear their heads and hear themselves think. A majority of Intel's trial group recommended that the policy be extended to others (Iyer, 2011). Another example is the rising demand in travel for "black-hole resorts," which charge high prices precisely because there is no television and you can't get online in the rooms.

Box 2.5
By the Numbers

Top 10 Benefits of Silence and Solitude

1. Bypassing burnout
2. Heightened sensitivity to sights and sounds
3. Dissolving tomorrow's problems
4. Improves memory
5. Strengthens intention and action
6. Increases self-awareness
7. Improves the ability of the brain to process information
8. Boosts creativity
9. Builds self-discipline
10. Releases emotional turbulence

Source: Nguyen, 2015

Ritual

Does your family celebrate Thanksgiving in much the same way year after year? Do you always watch the annual Super Bowl football game on television with the same group of friends? These are examples of ritualized leisure. Ritual is a set of everyday acts with their sequence established by tradition. Perhaps born from the human need for regular and mutual affirmation (Ibrahim, 1991), an everyday pattern may begin at the individual level and then evolve into collective patterns.

Holidays provide rich illustrations of this in all cultures. Today we ritualistically experience patriotic holidays, as well as holidays considered seasonal or religious. In addition, people establish unofficial holidays that inspire specific rituals, such as Friendship Day (first Sunday in August) and Buy Nothing Day (the day after the American Thanksgiving). Some holidays have rich traditions that trace ancient origins, often having no contemporary basis in their original meaning. Groundhog Day, for example, was originally celebrated as Candlemas Day, an ancient European festival marking the mid-point of winter by bringing all the candles to be used for the coming year into the church to be blessed (Godbey, 2003).

Figure 2.5. Tourist visiting Machu Picchu in Peru.

Many illustrations of leisure as ritual can also be found in tourism. For example, anthropologist Dean MacCannell (1999) claims modern international sightseeing possesses its own rituals that morally structure tourist behavior. His point is that guided tours are extensive ceremonial agendas involving long strings of obligatory rites. If you go to Europe, you must see Paris, and if you go to Paris, you must see the Louvre Museum, and if you go to the Louvre, you must see the Mona Lisa.

MacCannell declares this ritual attitude of the tourist originates in the act of travel itself, which in turn originated as a pilgrimage to holy places. In anthropology, a special term has been identified for the tourist ritual: **sight sacralization**. A particular destination becomes a tourist attraction because for social, historical or cultural reasons it represents something morally good. The next time you're visiting the Mona Lisa, for example, notice how reverent the other museum visitors are in its presence.

Sight sacralization: A tourist destination is considered sacred

Holiday and tourism rituals share certain common characteristics. Typically, both involve intrinsic reward, having meaning in and of themselves. As well, much of the ritual of leisure is of the type labeled by Goffman (1959) as decorum. **Decorum** is nonessential, as is decoration, but is practiced because it enhances social interaction. The game of golf, for example, is considered one of the most decorum-rich sports. Where to stand while others are playing, how to mark the ball on the green, and whose turn it is can intimidate a new player unaware of the ritual.

Decorum: Socially useful behavior

Box 2.6
Web Explore

Burning Man

For a unique illustration of ritual in leisure check out "The Burning Man" event at:

http://burningman.org/

https://en.wikipedia.org/wiki/Burning_Man

https://www.youtube.com/burningman

Commitment

Do you know anyone who is so committed to a particular pastime that it holds absolute primacy in his or her life priorities? For example, after being asked, "How bad would it be if you were unable to downhill ski anymore?," a 57-year old man responded, "It would be very bad. Skiing is an important part of my life. Not just of my leisure life, but of my real life. It is who I am. I cannot imagine living without skiing" (Russell, 2000).

For many people, leisure supplies the main source of personal identity and meaning in life. For them, a particular pastime is taken very seriously. There are several ways to consider this leisure benefit. For starters, commitment in leisure could mean devoting energy and resources to perfecting the skills and knowledge needed to do an activity well. Also, someone who has consistently and regularly pursued a pastime from childhood through old age demonstrates a commitment.

The focus of numerous research studies has combined these ideas into the concept of "serious leisure." **Serious leisure** is the "systematic pursuit of an activity that participants find so substantial and interesting that, in the typical case, they launch themselves on a career centered on acquiring and expressing its special skills, knowledge, and experience" (Stebbins, 1992, p. 3).

Serious leisure: The substantial and systematic pursuit of a pastime

In other words, it is high-investment leisure. According to Stebbins (2011), serious leisure is a particular leisure quality that is contrasted with "casual leisure" (watching television and hanging out with friends) where little or no commitment is required to enjoy it, and with "project leisure," which includes intense yet short-term commitment. This distinction depends on the degree and focus of the commitment, with serious leisure requiring the highest commitment.

Serious leisure is independent of the actual recreational activity. It can be almost anything from participating in triathlons to knitting. What makes the pursuit serious leisure is high amounts of what Stebbins (2011) considers the characteristics of serious leisure:

- A high standard of performance (effort)
- Participation for the experience of it (intrinsic motivation)
- A set of values, resources, and schedules constructed around the activity (career)
- Involvement in groups engaged in the same activity (unique ethos)
- Self-identification with the activity (durable benefits)
- Need to persevere (consistency)

Such committed leisure can be both good and bad. For example, in a study by Cheng and others (2016), a high degree of commitment in a leisure pursuit usually means the quality of the pursuit is enhanced. On the other hand, overcommitment—to the point of addiction—can be harmful. In exercise addiction, for example, a habitually exercising individual loses control over his or her exercise habits and acts compulsively, exhibits dependence, and experiences negative consequences to health as well as in his or her social and professional life (Veale, 1995).

Risk

Ocean cruising is an exotic way of life. Cruisers sail the oceans of the world for years just for fun. They forsake the security and safety of land-based life for the formidable challenges of the high seas. Their lifestyle requires effort and expensive resources in the face of danger. Are cruisers a special case?

Formerly viewed as fringe activities, high-risk recreation is now globally popular. Since 2009, for example, participation has increased over 25% (Gilbertson & Ewert, 2015). Also referred to as extreme sport and adventure recreation, the increased popularity of risk in leisure is mirrored by the increase in media coverage that glorifies it. Once the domain of esoteric enthusiasts, such as ocean cruisers, participants now come from a wide range of age, income, and education levels (Olivier, 2006).

Risky leisure includes bungee jumping, rock climbing, surfing, whitewater and sea kayaking, rafting, parasailing, cave diving, free diving, mountaineering, storm chasing, gliding, and paragliding. Risk as a leisure value pertains to an experience of excitement and danger, with the certain potential of loss, injury, illness, and even death. Leisure that provides for sensation-seeking—for varied, novel, and complex sensations, in spite of or because of physical and psychological risks, is the point.

We are not limited, however, to consider risky leisure only on rock faces and in whitewater rapids. Other high-risk pursuits might include gambling, having a poem you've written read aloud to an audience, and baking a cake for friends using a new recipe. In these activities, the risk is not of physical harm, but they require emotional and/or social risk.

So why do we do these things? What is the value? Well, the reward is the risk itself. Risk in leisure gives us a feeling of exhilaration. We feel competent. We find an escape from the ordinary routines of our lives. For example, Paxton (1998) measured gains in ability to consider oneself as able to produce intended results, labeled self-efficacy, from risky forms of leisure and concluded these gains lasted for at least one year after the experience. A study by Priest and Bunting (1993) similarly found that participation in a three-day whitewater canoeing trip resulted in increases in feelings of competence, which also lasted for at least one year after the experience. As well, Gilbertson and Ewert (2015) concluded from their investigation of motivations for adventure activities (rock climbing, whitewater kayaking, sea kayaking, and canoeing) that over time participation became more based on social and escape reasons, while self-image and sensation-seeking reasons remained constant.

Figure 2.6. Popular worldwide, BASE jumping is one of the riskiest leisure pursuits. Base jumping from the KL Tower in Kuala Lumpur, Malaysia.

Box 2.7
What Do
You Say?

Is Risky Leisure Morally Right?

Extreme pastimes are very popular. Yet, there is some criticism about their potential negative costs. The heart of the discussion is, as the number of people participating in risky leisure increases, so do the number of serious injuries and death.

Taking BASE jumping as an example, at least 250 conventional free-fall skydives are usually recommended before attempting a BASE jump. The main reason for this is that initiation of the jump can be lower than the parachute opening height for conventional skydiving, with jumpers having only seconds to deploy their parachutes. Also, unpredictable side drafts can force the participant into the structure that was jumped from.

Considered an "underground" activity with fatality statistics difficult to confirm, between 1978 and 2016, there were an estimated 282 known BASE jumping deaths worldwide (BLiNC, 2016). Other criticisms include the costs to rescue teams, and the emotional impact on participants' friends and family. Further, use of such natural resources as rock faces and icefalls can have an irreparable negative impact on the resource itself. While there are attempts to manage the risk of BASE jumping, such as thorough training and better equipment, there is always a risk of harm.

1. Have you participated in what you'd consider to be risky leisure? For what reasons did/do you choose to participate?
2. What are some reasons for you personally that taking a risk of being seriously injured or even killed is worth it? Also, what might be some justifications for not taking the risk?
3. Some participants have concluded that mature, rational individuals ought to have the right to pursue activities that have potentially harmful consequences for them. What do you think? Is this morally right?

Spirituality

Everyone's life draws on some form of inspiration. This is a good thing because spirituality is considered a requirement for good health (Heintzman & Mannell, 2003). Not only does a belief system provide important coping resources for dealing with stress, but it also fosters a "sense of inner wholeness" (Walsh, 1999, p. 6). Living spiritually can give us hope, forgiveness, a sense of meaning, and a feeling of unity with the world around us.

Some even refer to spirituality as a kind of intelligence. For example, Zohar and Marshall (2001) consider spiritual intelligence (SQ) to reflect our capacity to vision, value, and believe; it is what we use to place our actions and lives into a wider, richer context. That is, when we have high spiritual intelligence, we are able to satisfy a longing for something that gives us and our actions a sense of meaning. SQ is an ability to let go of the confines of our ego, and according to Zohar and Marshall, is a necessary foundation for the effective functioning of both our intellectual and emotional intelligences.

How does leisure benefit us spiritually? Let's consider two particular pastimes to illustrate this: skiing and snowboarding. In a study by Marsh (2007), interviews were conducted with people who had been skiing and snowboarding in the region of Teton Pass, Wyoming, a backcountry area with more than 400 inches of annual snowfall. They were asked about the meanings they perceived experiencing from their adventures in the backcountry. Most frequently expressed meanings were a transcendent experience, increased awareness, connection to others, reflection, tranquility, appreciation of beauty, and mental and physical exercise. The study concluded that these leisure pursuits provided a means for participants to find an inner wholeness.

Other scholars have linked leisure and spirituality in similar ways. For example, Lehman (1974) suggested leisure is a sense of being that helps us attain enlightenment, and for Pieper (1963), leisure is a meditative state in which we discover God and the true meaning of life. Some consider the practice of such spiritual activities as prayer to be leisure-like.

Another perspective suggests leisure may have a spiritual quality because it connects us with others. Through shared leisure, we may grow to better understand and get along with each other. This can be illustrated through celebrating festivals and holidays. Pieper (1963), for example, declares that celebration is the soul of leisure. He argues that people celebrate with each other that which is good.

What We Understand About Leisure's Value

There is no debating that the experience of leisure is important to us. To demonstrate, this chapter presented several examples of the benefits. After studying this chapter, you should know the following:

1. We all need leisure in our lives because it provides us with the benefits that make us human.
   Give and contrast two examples of this from the chapter:

   ____

   ____

2. These benefits include freedom, intrinsic reward, pleasure, happiness, solitude and silence, ritual, humor, play, commitment, relaxation, commitment, risk, and spirituality.
   Select two of these benefits and give examples for each on how leisure provides for them:

   ____

   ____

3. We don't need all of these benefits at the same time and in the same pastime, but we do need some of them at least some of the time.
   Which of leisure's benefits are most important to you and how does leisure provide them in your life?

   ____

   ____

References

BLiNC Magazine. (April 20, 2016). Fatality statistics. Retrieved from http://www.blincmagazine.com/forum/wiki/Fatality_Statistics

Bregha, F. J. (1991). Leisure and freedom reexamined. In T. L. Goodale & P. A. Witt (Eds.), *Recreation and leisure: Issues in an era of change* (pp. 47–54). State College, PA: Venture.

Caillois, R. (1961). *Man, play, and games.* Glencoe, IL: Free Press of Glencoe.

Carr, N. G. (2010). *The shallows: What the Internet is doing to our brains.* New York, NY: W.W. Norton.

Cheng, M.-T., Hung, S.-H., & Chen, M.-T. (2016). The influence of leisure involvement on flow experience during hiking activity: Using psychological commitment as a mediate variable. *Asia Pacific Journal of Tourism Research, 21*(1), 1–19.

Csikszentmihalyi, M. (1975). *Beyond boredom and anxiety.* San Francisco, CA: Jossey Bass.

Duffy, O. (2014). Board games' golden age: Sociable, brilliant and driven by the Internet. *The Guardian.* Retrieved from https://www.theguardian.com/technology/2014/nov/25/board-games-internet-playstation-xbox

Dugatkin, L. A., & Rodrigues, S. (Spring 2008). Games animals play. *Greater Good Magazine.* Retrieved from http://greatergood.berkeley.edu/article/item/games_animals_play

Ellis, M. J. (1973). *Why people play.* Englewood Cliffs, NJ: Prentice-Hall.

Esch, T., & Stefano, G. B. (2004). The neurobiology of pleasure, reward processes, addiction and their health implications. *Neuroendocrinology Letters No. 4, August, Vol. 25,* 235–251.

Gilbertson, K., & Ewert, A. (November 2015). Stability of motivations and risk attractiveness: The adventure recreation experience. *Risk Management, 17*, 276–297.
Godbey, G. (2003). *Leisure in your life: An exploration* (6th ed.). State College, PA: Venture.
Goffman, E. (1959). *The presentation of self in everyday life*. New York, NY: Doubleday.
Goodale, T., & Godbey, G. (1988). *The evolution of leisure: Historical and philosophical perspectives*. State College, PA: Venture.
Heintzman, P., & Mannell, R. C. (2003). Spiritual functions of leisure and spiritual well-being: Coping with time pressure. *Leisure Sciences, 25*, 207–230.
Huizinga, J. (1955). *Homo ludens: A study of the play element in culture*. Boston, MA: Beacon Press.
Ibrahim, J. (1991). *Leisure and society: A comparative approach*. Dubuque, IA: Wm. C. Brown.
Iyer, P. (December 31, 2011). The joy of quiet. *The New York Times*. Retrieved from http://www.nytimes.com/2012/01/01/opinion/sunday/the-joy-of-quiet.html?_r=0.
Jones, S. S. (1992). *Choose to live peacefully*. Berkeley, CA: Celestial Arts.
Kant, I. (1781) First edition of the *Critique of Pure Reason*. (published later in multiple editions and translations).
Kelly, J. R. (2009). Work and leisure: A simplified paradigm. *Journal of Leisure Research, 41*(3), 439–451.
Kelly, J. R. (2012). *Leisure* (4th ed.). Urbana, IL: Sagamore.
Kleiber, D. A. (2000). The neglect of relaxation. *Journal of Leisure Research, 32*(1), 82–86.
Kovacs, A. (2007). The leisure personality: Relationships between personality, leisure satisfaction, and life satisfaction. Unpublished doctoral dissertation, Indiana University, Bloomington.
Langley, L. (June 13, 2015). Do animals laugh? Tickle experiments suggest they do. *National Geographic*. Retrieved from http://news.nationalgeographic.com/2015/06/150613-animals-laughter-apes-evolution-science/
Larson, R., & Richards, M. (1998). Waiting for the weekend: Friday and Saturday night as the emotional climax of the week. In A. C. Crouter & R. Larson (Eds.), *Temporal rhythms in adolescence: Clocks, calendars, and the coordination of daily life* (pp. 37–51). San Francisco, CA: Jossey Bass.
Lehman, H. D. (1974). *In praise of leisure*. Scottdale, PA: Herald Press.
Lepper, M. R., Greene, D., & Nisbett, R. E. (1973). Undermining children's intrinsic interest with extrinsic reward; A test of "overjustification" hypothesis. *Journal of Personality and Social Psychology, 28*(1), 129–137.
Lyubomirsky, S. (2007). *The how of happiness: A scientific approach to getting the life you want*. New York, NY: Penguin.
MacCannell, D. (1999). *The tourist: A new theory of the leisure class*. Berkeley, CA: University of California Press.
Mannell, R. C., & McMahon, L. (1982). Humor as play: Its relationship to psychological well-being during the course of a day. *Leisure Sciences, 5*(2), 143–155.
Marsh, P. E. (2007). Backcountry adventure as spiritual experience: A means-end study. Unpublished doctoral dissertation, Indiana University, Bloomington.
Martin, R. A. (1996). Humour as therapeutic play: Stress-moderating effects of sense of humour. *Journal of Leisurability, 23*(4), 45–61.
Martin, R. A., & Kuiper, N. A. (1995). Daily occurrence of laughter, stress, and moods: A naturalistic study. Paper presented at the annual meeting of the International Society for Humor Studies, Birmingham, England.
May, R. (1981). *Freedom and destiny*. New York, NY: W.W. Norton.
Merton, T. (1948). *The seven story mountain*. New York, NY: Harcourt Brace.
Millar, S. (1968). *The psychology of play*. London, UK: Penguin books.
Nawijn, J. (2012). Leisure travel and happiness: An empirical study into the effect of holiday trips on individuals' subjective wellbeing. Doctoral dissertation, Erasmus Universiteit Rotterdam.

Neulinger, J. (1981). *To leisure: An introduction.* Boston, MA: Allyn & Bacon.

Nguyen, T. (January 3, 2015). 10 important reasons to start making time for silence, rest and solitude. *The Huffington Post.* Retrieved frim http://news.nationalgeographic.com/2015/06/150613-animals-laughter-apes-evolution-science/

Olivier, S. (2006). Moral dilemmas of participation in dangerous leisure activities. *Leisure Studies, 25*(1), 95–109.

Paxton, T. S. (1998). Self-efficacy and outdoor adventure programs: A quantitative and qualitative analysis. Unpublished doctoral dissertation. University of Minnesota, Minneapolis-St. Paul.

Pieper, J. (1963). *Leisure: The basis of culture.* New York, NY: The New American Library.

Priest, S., & Bunting, C. (1993). Changes in perceived risk and competence during whitewater canoeing. *Journal of Applied Recreation Research, 18*(4), 265–280.

Putnam, R. D. (2000). *Bowling alone.* New York, NY: Simon & Schuster.

Roach, M. (September 1996). Can you laugh your stress away? *Health*, 92–96.

Russell, B. (1968). *The conquest of happiness.* New York, NY: Bantam.

Russell, R. V. (1993). *Employee perceptions of workplace barriers to change.* Technical report prepared for the Indianapolis, IN Department of Parks and Recreation.

Russell, R. V. (2000). Unpublished field notes.

Sarton, M. (1973). *Journal of a solitude.* New York, NY: W.W. Norton.

Smith, S. L. J. (1991). On the biological basis of pleasure: Some implications for leisure policy. In T. L. Goodale & P. A. Witt (Eds.), *Recreation and leisure: Issues in an era of change* (pp. 73–84). State College, PA: Venture.

Smith, M., & Segal, J. (April 2016). Laughter is the best medicine. Retrieved from http://www.helpguide.org/articles/emotional-health/laughter-is-the-best-medicine.htm

Stebbins, R. A. (1992). *Amateurs, professionals, and serious leisure.* Montreal, Quebec: McGill-Queen's University Press.

Stebbins, R. A. (2011). The semiotic self and serious leisure. *The American Sociologist, 42*(2-3), 238–248.

Storr, A. (1988). *Solitude: A return to the self.* New York, NY: Ballantine Books.

Sylvester, C. (1991). Recovering a good idea for the sake of goodness: An interpretive critique of subjective leisure. In T. L. Goodale & P. A. Witt (Eds.), *Recreation and leisure: Issues in an era of change* (pp. 441–454). State College, PA: Venture.

The World Happiness Report. (2016). Retrieved from http://worldhappiness.report/

Veale, C. D. (1995). Does primary exercise dependence really exist. In J. Anett, B. Cripps, & H. Steinberg (Eds.), *Exercise addiction: Motivation for participation in sport and exercise* (pp. 1–5). Leicester, UK: The British Psychological Society.

Walker, G. (2010). The effects of personal, contextual, and situational factors on the facilitation of intrinsic motivation: The case of Chinese/Canadians. *Journal of Leisure Research, 42*(1), 43–66.

Walsh, F. (1999). *Spiritual resources in family therapy.* New York, NY: Guilford.

Zohar, D., & Marshall, I. (2001). *SQ: Connecting with our spiritual intelligence.* New York, NY: Bloomsbury.

CHAPTER 3

Explaining Leisure Behavior

What determines our pastime choices and actions?

Because leisure behavior is complex and dynamic, there are many explanations, and thus we only have a composite understanding of the phenomenon.

What role do demographic characteristics play in explaining leisure behavior?

Factors such as our age, gender, ethnicity, race, income, education level, and residence shape our leisure choices and actions.

Are there theoretical explanations?

Many theories from fields such as psychology, sociology, and anthropology attempt to explain the conditions and functions of leisure behavior.

Are these theories supported by research?

Research demonstrates that theories explain some aspects of leisure behavior, yet more studies are needed to develop a comprehensive explanation.

Why did you choose to take a vacation last summer? How did you choose where to go and what to do after you got there? As you begin to answer this (or the alternate question of why you chose not to take a vacation), you quickly begin to realize your reasons are numerous and interrelated.

Perhaps this is what makes studying leisure so intriguing. Indeed, leisure has been the subject of scholarship by a wide range of investigators representing a broad collection of disciplines. Some of this study focuses on the causes of leisure behavior by particular life situation factors, such as age and level of education. Other explanations are derived from the development of theories that are then tested for validity through research studies. In this chapter we describe what we know about leisure behavior from both of these approaches.

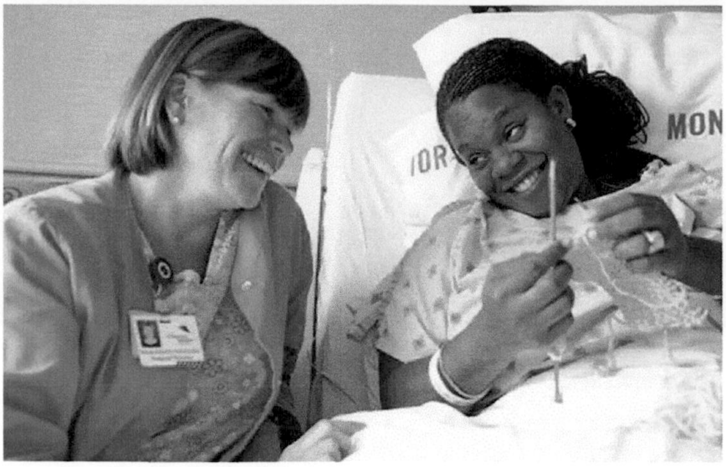

Figure 3.1. A knitting program helps hospital patients to pass time, get better, and learn a hobby that can last a lifetime. How? Our leisure interests, needs, choices, and behaviors are determined by many interrelated factors. Source: New York Daily News. FLORESCU, 2016

Demographic Explanations of Leisure Behavior

In explaining our leisure choices and actions, one important source of understanding is **demographic information.** Commonly studied demographics include age, gender, race, ethnicity, income, residential location, disabilities, availability of transportation, health status, educational attainment, home ownership, employment status, and occupation. All of these factors play a role in determining what, why, and how we pursue our pastimes.

Demographic information: Characteristics of a population

For example, one's age greatly affects leisure behavior. This is a frequently researched demographic characteristic, because age is an indication of not only maturation, but also historical experiences, social expectations, and social rights and privileges. To illustrate, in the U.S., state law determines minimum driving and alcoholic beverage consumption ages, and retirement status is usually reserved for older ages as dictated by federal entitlement programs and employer policy. Being able to drive, socially drink, and retire in turn are huge age-related factors in explaining leisure choices and actions.

There are many other illustrations of the effect of age. For example, in a U.S. Department of Labor *Time Use Survey of Americans* (2015) those aged 75 and over spent 8 hours a day on average engaged in leisure and sport activities—more than any other age group. Those 35 to 44 years old spent 4.1 hours—less than any other age group. For Canadians, according to national data (Human Resources and Skills Development Canada, 2010), social activities took up most of the leisure time until age 75, when the amount of time spent on cognitive activities (e.g., hobbies, games, puzzles) began to exceed that spent on social leisure.

As you know, gender is also a frequently cited distinction in our leisure choices and actions. In fact, age as a predictor of leisure expression often operates in tandem with gender. Although the term ***gender*** is commonly used interchangeably with the term *sex*, within the social sciences gender more specifically refers to social differences, including social expectations and roles, rather than biological distinctions.

Gender: Social expectations and roles

A great deal of research has also been done on gender and leisure behavior, most of it focusing on describing differences between men and women. However, while more recent studies in general suggest gender is a less limiting factor in leisure choices and actions, gender still matters (Ridinger & Funk, 2006). Let's consider the realm of sports to illustrate.

Box 3.1
In Profile

The Villages

The Villages is a community in central Florida. Ranked each year as one of the United States' fastest growing areas, as of 2016, its population was 157,000. Residents are 98% white, have a median age of 66 years, and less than 1% of households have children living there (United States Census Bureau, 2015). As a master planned retirement community, The Villages offers numerous forms of recreation. In fact, this abundance of leisure is the point of choosing to live there. Opportunities include golf courses (39); recreation centers (57), which feature swimming pools, bocce, shuffleboard, pickleball, and fitness centers; softball fields; a polo stadium; dog parks; and fitness trails. In keeping with the leisurely lifestyle promoted at The Villages, most residents use golf carts to get around the property via a specially designated network of paved paths and tunnels.

In one of the villages at the Villages.
Source: Owningthefence.com

Female athletic participation has surged in the U.S. since the enactment of Title IX in 1972, with a tenfold growth in the number of female high school athletes (Title IX, 2003). At the college level, 45% of all NCAA Division I student-athletes are women (NCAA, 2014). Not only are more girls and women playing sports, but also they are more involved as sports spectators. For example, U.S. women comprise about 45% of the fan base for the National Football League (NFL), Major League Baseball (MLB), National Basketball Association (NBA) and NASCAR (Sport Business Research Network, 2014).

Yet, such gains can also bring opposition. Research suggests that when women attempt to further their sport consumption and participation, they may still be met with resistance or indifference. Even with Title IX, girls and women do not experience full equity with men. For example, female high school and college athletes continue to lag behind males in the provision of resources such as scholarships, uniforms, and facilities (Women's Sport Foundation, 2011). Also, significant salary gaps exist between coaches of women's and men's collegiate teams (Ross, 2015). As well, women and men, girls and boys, often remain physically separated in organized sport participation, allowing for "differentness" to be maintained (Reskin, 1998). And, still today there is debate on the question of equity for women participating in the international Olympic Games, as well as their eligibility for membership in sporting clubs.

Our leisure is shaped not only by age and gender, but also by ethnicity and race, income, and residence. For example, the leisure preferences of different ethnic groups differ primarily because of cultural distinctions. Leisure choices according to race are also in large part economically defined. That is, many researchers have found similarities in leisure preferences between Black and White Americans who defined themselves as middle class (Shinew, Floyd, McGuire, & Noe, 1996).

Thus, the explanatory power of income on leisure choices seems obvious, especially for those pursuits that must be purchased. For example, as one study in tourism demonstrated, while income does not affect the choice of holiday destination, it does affect the mode of travel, such as air versus driving (LaMondia, Snell, & Bhat, 2010). Similarly, research by Mill (1986) found that tourists with higher incomes stay longer and spend more money per day than do those with lower incomes.

Where we live affects the nature and accessibility of pastime opportunities. Some pursuits are not universally available because of climate and topography. Also, if you live in an urban location, you are more likely to participate in commercial and cultural forms of leisure. Such pursuits as hunting are more likely to be found in rural areas, while apartment and condominium living more typically offers swimming, tennis, and fitness. Suburban locations are a good choice for organized youth sports.

Box 3.2 What Do You Say?

Going Solo

We're living in the middle of an amazing era of individualism. According to a book by Eric Klinenberg, *Going Solo*, published in 2012, more than 50% of American adults are single, and 28% of households consist of just one person. In large cities such as Denver, Washington, and Atlanta the proportion of one-person dwellings is even higher. In Manhattan, roughly half the households are solos. Nationwide, there are more single-person households than there are married-with-children households. Also, a few generations ago, most people affiliated with either the Republican or Democrat party; today more people consider themselves Independent. Also, a few generations ago, teens "went steady," but over the past decades, the dating relationship has been replaced by a more amorphous hook-up culture. Further, today the fastest-growing religious category is "unaffiliated."

1. Do you think these changes are positive or negative for leisure? How?
2. What might be causing the "going solo" phenomenon? An aging society? Women having more power and options? More affluence? The information technology revolution?
3. What do you think is the role of leisure for such an individualistic society?

These and other demographic characteristics explain our leisure behavior directly, as well as indirectly, via the concept of lifestyle. Our lifestyle can be considered a "stew pot" of demographic factors affecting our values, attitudes, and ultimately our interests, choices, and behaviors. **Lifestyle** is a pattern of living. For example, you may have heard of some typical lifestyles: retirement, luxury, family, party, healthy, and simple. Indeed, there are many lifestyle patterns that have been identified – all based on the mix of demographic factors. For example, the VALS (values, attitudes, and lifestyles) typology divides people into eight lifestyle types based mostly on age, income, education, values, and attitudes.

Lifestyle: A quality and custom of living

VALS is a proprietary tool used for segmenting consumer markets. It was originally developed in 1978 to guide companies in tailoring their products and services to people most likely to purchase them. Interestingly, such a consumer marketing tool has implications for understanding leisure behavior based on lifestyle as it features leisure actions and choices as a part of consumption actions and choices. For example, Table 3.1 outlines the eight VALS lifestyle types, with implications for leisure behavior.

Table 3.1
Lifestyle Types and Leisure According to the VALS

Lifestyle Type	Description	Leisure Implications
Innovators	Successful, sophisticated, take-charge people with high self-esteem and resources	Cultivated tastes for upscale, high image, and variety
Thinkers	Mature, satisfied, comfortable, reflective people with respect for the status quo	Centered on the home
Believers	Idealistic, conservative, conventional people with concrete beliefs	Established routines organized around home, family, and community traditions
Achievers	Busy, goal-oriented, career-committed people who value stability	Social lives structured around work
Strivers	Trendy, fun-loving people who care about others' opinions and having enough money	Active consumers of shopping as a social activity; easily bored
Experiencers	Young, energetic and motivated by self-expression; quickly cool to new ideas	Seek variety and excitement, savoring the offbeat and the risky
Makers	Practical people who have constructive skills and value self-sufficiency	Physical forms of recreation
Survivors	Live narrowly focused lives with limited resources; comfortable with the familiar	TV watching and other low-cost pursuits

Box 3.3
In Your Own Experience

What Is Your VALS Type?

After studying Table 3.1, make an initial estimate of which lifestyle type you think you are. Then take the actual VALS survey to see how close your estimate came. Go to the Internet site for Strategic Business Insights, http://www.strategicbusinessinsights.com/vals/presurvey.shtml and click on "Take the Survey." After answering all questions, hit "Submit," and in a few seconds your lifestyle profile will be reported. Were you surprised by the results? Why or why not? How does your lifestyle type relate to your leisure interests?

Theories Explaining Leisure Behavior

Theory: A plausible set of principles used to explain a behavior or event

Philosophy: Beliefs about morals, character, and behavior

Now we turn to theoretical ways of explaining leisure. What is theory? A **theory** is a set of interrelated, testable propositions. Theory attempts to explain why facts are what they are—asking how the world works. Sometimes we confuse theory with philosophy. **Philosophy** relates to a belief system about how the world should work (Henderson, Presley, & Bialeschki, 2004). Thus, theory "has to do with what is, not what should be" (Babbie, 2012, p. 26).

Numerous theories have been used to explain leisure behavior based on propositions in biology, sociology, psychology, anthropology, economics, the humanities, and other disciplines. Some of these theories are simple and are based on direct observation, whereas others are more comprehensive, involving extensive research testing. None of the theories available to us completely explain all leisure behavior for all people in all situations, however. Nonetheless, they remain useful, particularly for those professionals who provide leisure services, because they help predict the leisure needs and interests of clients. To illustrate, we'll discuss several of the more widely acknowledged theories about leisure behavior from psychology, sociology, and anthropology.

From Psychology

Psychology is interested in how our minds shape our behaviors. Over the years, many theories about leisure reflect a psychological perspective exploring such concepts as perception, emotion, motives, and personality. Essentially the psychological lens explains leisure behavior as an individual's motivation to be actualized. We'll mention three theories here: flow, self-as-entertainment, and reversal.

Flow. Perhaps one of the most widely understood theories about leisure comes from psychologist Mihaly Csikszentmihalyi (1975, 1990, 1997). Over more than 40 years, Csikszentmihalyi and his colleagues have studied thousands of people who experienced a feeling of energized focus, full involvement, and success in the process of an activity. Csikszentmihalyi referred to the feeling as "flow," athletes describe it as being "in the zone," religious mystics as being in "ecstasy," and artists and musicians as "aesthetic rapture."

Figure 3.2. According to the Flow Theory, leisure is at its best when we lose self-consciousness, merge action and awareness, have a sense of self-control, and an altered sense of time. © Patricia D. Setser, 2016

Csikszentmihalyi discovered people reached this optimal experience through different activities but in similar ways. Thus, while flow may be found when people climb mountains, play in a rock band, collect fossils, or play chess, the experience is the same. Flow is a subjective state we feel during an intense engagement in an activity. First, let's highlight its characteristics, and then we'll discuss its necessary conditions.

The emotional characteristics of this optimal experience include the following (Csikszentmihalyi et al., 2005):

Loss of self-consciousness. Feeling as though the boundaries of our being have been pushed forward without self-scrutiny. "My focus is always disrupted when I make a mistake and fall" – a figure skater (Jackson, 1992, p. 165).

Merging of action and awareness. Our attention is completely absorbed by the activity so that doing the activity becomes automatic. "You don't feel like you're doing something as a conscious being; you're adapting to the rock and becoming part of it" – a rock climber (Csikszentmihalyi, 1975, p. 86).

Sense of self-control. We feel in charge of what we are doing. "I felt really powerful, like I had the information in the palm of my hand and could mold it any way I wanted" – a high school student working on a paper (Larson, 1988, p. 153).

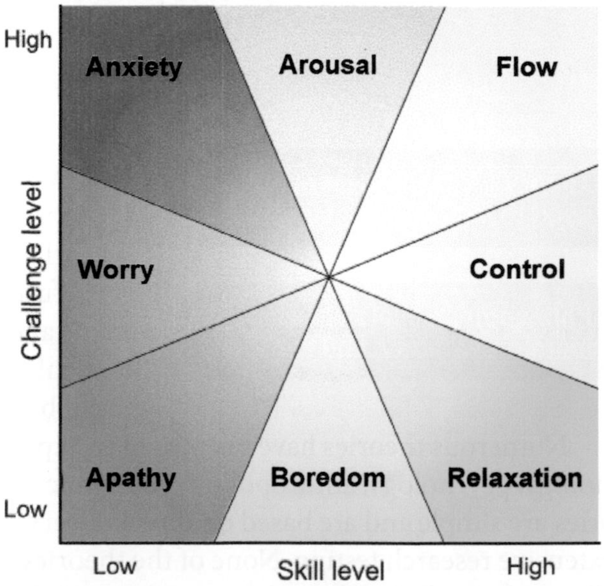

Figure 3.3. According to Flow Theory, one condition for an optimal experience is a balance of challenge and skill. Flow results when high challenges are matched with high skills (Csikszentmihalyi, 2000).

Altered sense of time. Time seems to pass much more quickly or we lose track of the passing time. "The next 20 minutes of my life passed in a pure bliss" – a performer in a rock band (Giovannoli, 2007, p. 2).

In addition to these characteristics of the flow experience, specific conditions are necessary for enabling flow. These include the following (Csikszentmihalyi et al., 2005):

Having a clear set of goals. The rules of action and success are clear and feedback is immediate.

Autotelic. We engage in the activity for its own reward; it is intrinsically motivating.

Balance between perceived challenges and perceived skills. We are able to achieve a fine match between what we can accomplish and what the activity requires we accomplish. (See Figure 3.3. Notice, as well, the conditions for boredom, anxiety, relaxation, and other emotions in leisure, when skill and challenge are out of balance.)

In other words, flow is more likely to be experienced when the activity provides clear goals and feedback, is intrinsically rewarding, and contains a balance of challenge and skill.

Box 3.4
Web Explore

More About Flow Theory

Learn more about flow theory from its author at

http://www.ted.com/talks/mihaly_csikszentmihalyi_on_flow?language=en.

Self-as-entertainment. Another theoretical perspective coming from the psychological perspective is the self-as-entertainment (S-A-E) construct developed by Roger Mannell (1984). It focuses on answering questions about leisure choices based on our personality. S-A-E reflects the capacity of people to fill their free time with activities that are personally satisfying and involving. People who are high on the S-A-E personality trait are able to fill free time satisfactorily. They do not experience time as "hanging heavily on their hands" or feel that their free time is "wasted." On the other hand, people who are low on the S-A-E trait perceive they have "too much free time" and there is frequently "nothing to do" (Mannell, 1984, pp. 232–233).

According to Mannell, there are three possible ways of coping with boredom: by the sheer perception that we are in control of how and what we do in our free time (self), by being able to use our mind through our own imagination and escape to fantasy to fill free time (mind play), or by going places and seeking out other people to share experiences (environment). Those who seek out their environment for entertainment, such as calling up a friend or watching television, are not relying on themselves, and are thus low on the S-A-E construct. For example, in a research study of college students (Barnett, 2006), it was found that those who thought they were good at entertaining themselves participated more frequently in performing arts. In contrast, those who more typically turned to their external environment preferred outdoor activities.

Reversal theory. Reversal theory is a way to explain leisure behavior that is based on emotion, personality, and motivation. It describes how people regularly shift between psychological states, reflecting their motivational style and the meaning they attach to a given situation at a given time (Apter, 1997). For example, sometimes a crowded lively restaurant seems exciting and fun; other times, it may make us anxious.

Reversal theory proposes that human behavior is organized into four domains. Each domain contains two opposite pairs of motivation, with only one condition in each pair active at a time (Apter, 2001, 2007). In leisure, we reverse between the motivation pairs for each domain depending on situational factors, including our inherent tendency (personality). Here are the four domains, and their pairs of motivation (Figure 3.4), using roller coaster riding to illustrate.

Means-ends. The two motivation states in this first domain are called "telic" (or serious) and "paratelic" (or playful). When we are in our telic state we are motivated by achievement and future goals; when we are in our paratelic state we are motivated by enjoyment in the moment. Thus, in order to successfully participate in roller coaster riding, we need to be in our paratelic state.

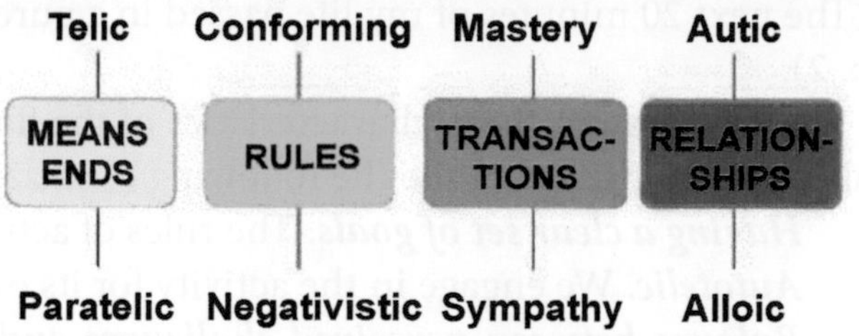

Figure 3.4. Reversal theory explains leisure behavior by way of a match between our motivations and the situation. Source: Reversaltheory.net

Rules. For this domain, the two states are "conforming" and "negativistic." Obviously, when we are in our conforming state, we enjoy operating within rules and expectations; when we are in our more rebellious state we wish to be free and push against the rules. Thus, in order to successfully participate in roller coaster riding, we must be in our rebellious state.

Transactions. In this domain, the two states are called "mastery" and "sympathy," which relate to whether we are motivated by transacting power and control, or by care and compassion. Probably a positive situation for enjoying a roller coaster ride requires a mastery state.

Relationships. The two states here are called "autic" (self) and "alloic" (other), referring to whether one is motivated by self-interests (personal accountability and responsibility) or by the interests of others (altruism and transcendence). Roller-coaster riding in an autic state would probably be more enjoyable.

Obviously, what is key in reversal theory is the concept of reversal. That is, by triggering a reversal between states (such as a toy can trigger the paratelic state or a park rules sign may invoke the conforming state), we can change the meaning and thus our enjoyment of a situation. What seemed serious before can suddenly feel exciting with the right change in situation or mindset.

Like the flow and self-as-entertainment theories already discussed, reversal theory has research support, particularly with sports performance and sport violence (Kerr, 2001, 2004), and high-risk adventure activities (Mackenzie, Hodge, & Boyes, 2011).

From Sociology

Sociology is interested in the social structures of people. Over the years, many theories about leisure have reflected a sociological lens, exploring such concepts as social networks, social class, social mobility, gender, family, religion, deviance, and other concepts. Essentially the sociological perspective explains leisure behavior as activity adapted to the constructions of society. We'll mention two theories here: compensation and spillover, and symbolic interactionism.

Compensation and spillover. For a long time, leisure choices have been explained as a reaction to the structures of work. That is, the nature of people's work directly influences their choice of pastimes. Illustrating this are the theoretical ideas of spillover and compensation. Whether leisure behavior is a spillover response to work, or a compensation response to work, depends on the nature of the work. That is, which explanation applies depends on the amount of satisfaction found in work.

When deprivations and dissatisfactions are experienced in work, leisure makes up for them. This compensation explanation claims people participate in those pastimes that satisfy needs they cannot satisfy at work. As described by Wilensky (1960), a person engaged in repetitive, low-skilled, and machine-paced work, will seek the opposite for leisure. This helps explain, perhaps, why people who perform physical work choose to spend their free time resting, or why those who work indoors prefer outdoor leisure pursuits.

In contrast, the spillover idea claims when people are satisfied and fulfilled in their work, leisure activities are chosen that mimic it. Leisure becomes an extension of the skills and attitudes used at work.

Work spills over into leisure (Wilensky, 1960). This helps to explain why some people participate in pastimes that have characteristics similar to their job tasks. For example, computer skills learned and used on the job may be used to socialize on social media Internet sites.

Research testing on this theoretical approach has been limited, and with contradictory findings (c.f. Burch, 2009). Also, because the basis of the explanation is work, compensation and spillover do not explain the leisure behaviors of those who do not work, such as those who are retired.

Symbolic interactionism. This sociological perspective focuses on the symbols of life—what these symbols mean and how people interact with each other via these symbols. An early proponent, George Mead in the 1920s, suggested that people attach meanings to symbols, and then they act according to their subjective interpretation of these symbols. Verbal conversations, in which spoken words are the symbols, are a primary example. Anything can serve as a symbol, however, just so long as it is outside the individual. Music, art, and sport also provide powerful examples of symbols that people use as a basis for communication, interpretation, and adjustment among themselves.

Box 3.5
Top Six

Symbols and Their Changed Meanings

Symbol	Current Meaning	Historical Origin
Swastika	Nazis	Prosperity to ancient Greeks, Egyptians, Romans, Celts
Peace Symbol	Hippy movement of 1960s	British nuclear disarmament
Devil Horns	A staple at heavy metal concerts	Ancient use to ward off evil
The Okay Sign	To Americans: "I'm fine." To other countries: "You are a Zero," or "anus"	In Buddhism and Hinduism: teaching and reason

There are three basic premises of symbolic interactionism (Armstrong, 2007). These are (a) people act toward things/experiences on the basis of the meanings those things/experiences have for them, (b) the source of the meanings for things/experiences are derived from social interactions with others, and (c) the meanings of things/experiences are modified through an interpretive process used by people.

Consider a basketball team as an example. Symbols might include uniforms and assigned numbers on the back, shoes, the ball and hoops, game rules, coaches, spectators, and perhaps even logos and slogans. Society attaches general meanings to these symbols, but individuals on the team (or in the stands) also maintain their own perceptions of what these and other symbols mean. For example, the phenomenon of the "home-team advantage" is often attributed to symbolic interactionism.

In fact, a great deal of the research on symbolic interactionism has been carried out on sport spectating. For example, Underwood et al. (2001) concluded that sport spectators comprise a distinct subculture whose consumption patterns via the meanings of certain activities or products attributed to a sport or team give meaning to their lives. Further, the behavior of sport spectators may be premised on the shared meanings they have created, such as being quiet (or not) when a member of the opposing basketball team is shooting free throws (Leonard, 1998).

From Anthropology

Finally, we explore a bit of what an anthropological lens might theorize about leisure behavior. Anthropologists try to holistically understand the complexity of human cultures, past and present, by drawing on knowledge from the social and biological sciences, as well as the humanities and physical sciences. This leads to primarily studying a particular place, problem, or phenomenon in detail over an extensive period of time. In explaining leisure, consequently, the anthropological lens is typically a cultural one, examining social patterns and practices across cultures.

One aspect of such patterns and practices is ritual. Let's conclude our theoretical journey by considering a theory of leisure behavior based on the idea of ritual: anti-structure theory.

Figure 3.5. "Flamingo Racing" at a Florida retirement neighborhood. Leisure situations provide one of he best ways to experience communitas. © Ruth V. Russell

Anti-structure theory. Proposed by Victor Turner, the idea is there are formal rituals that govern people's behavior both inside and outside everyday life (Turner, 1969, 1982). To Turner, leisure is the ritual that takes us outside everyday life. It does this by being antagonistic to everyday experiences. That is, leisure behavior can be seen as "anti," or opposite, structure.

It is easy to see the usefulness of this theory in explaining vacations and media-based forms of entertainment as these leisure situations have their own distinct realities for the express purpose of being removed from everyday routine. Research has also been carried out in the name of the anti-structure theory in sports. For example, Deegan (1989) studied the University of Nebraska football experience to confirm a great abundance of ritual events, inside the stadium and out.

Two concepts help to extend our understanding of leisure as anti-structure. These are *liminality* and *communitas*. Coming from Latin, meaning threshold, Turner uses the term **liminality** to refer to the transition from the everyday to outside the everyday. It is in this liminal phase where a purer form of play occurs because it is free of societal norms and structures. Its transitional nature creates an environment conducive to fun (Turner, 1982, p. 40).

Liminality: A transitional stage of ambiguity

Further, while people are in the liminal stage they tend to develop an intense comradeship with one another. Social distinctions that separated them before the ritual and that will separate them again afterward, become irrelevant. Turner called this liminally produced social relationship ***communitas***, by which he meant a loosely structured community of equal individuals. In thinking about the moshing research presented in Box 3.6, we can see how both liminality and communitas occur.

Communitas: A temporary sense of social camaraderie

According to the anti-structure theory, then, leisure is very important in life. In referring again to the Nebraska football study, Deegan (1989) states, "The ability to have something in common with strangers, to sing and yell and cry in public, to root for one's team, and to publicly participate and reaffirm one's values, are strong bonds that help us tolerate and give meaning to life" (p. 87).

Box 3.6
The Study Says

Moshing

A study (Riches, 2011) focused on the relationship between extreme metal music with moshing and liminality. It found that moshing, which is a kind of dance related to heavy metal music, allows fans to establish their own social order and foster a separate sense of community. The study concluded that women who participate in mosh pits consider it as a way to embrace and be a part of a domain which is considered a masculine leisure area.

What We Understand About Explaining Leisure Behavior

The many ways of explaining leisure help us understand our own and others' pastime choices and actions. In this chapter, we studied this by overviewing demographic factors that shape leisure behavior, as well as several theoretical perspectives. After studying this chapter, you should know the following:

1. Leisure interests and actions are complex and unique, and thus difficult to explain.
   Identify one of your leisure interests and then list all the demographic factors and theories that could possibly explain your choice. Which is correct?

   ____

   ____

2. Nonetheless, leisure behavior can be explained in part by lifestyle, which is shaped by multiple demographic characteristics, including age, gender, income, ethnicity, race, and residence.
   Select one of the demographic characteristics discussed and summarize how it influences leisure behavior:

   ____

   ____

3. Formal theories that explain leisure behavior come from the basic disciplines, including psychology, sociology, and anthropology.
   How do these different disciplines look at leisure differently?

   ____

   ____

4. These formal explanations include flow, self-as-entertainment, reversal, compensation and spillover, symbolic interactionism, and anti-structure theories.
   Select one of these theories and describe how leisure behavior and actions are explained accordingly:

   ____

   ____

5. Beyond the excitement of knowing for the sake of knowing, explaining leisure is also useful to managers of recreation businesses, facilities, and programs.
   How might this be so? Give an illustration from your own experience:

   ____

   ____

6. However, neither demographic characteristics nor the various theories are able to explain leisure behavior completely.
   Draw a conclusion about this based on your answer to the first summary statement above:

   ____

   ____

References

Apter, M.J. (1997). Reversal theory: What is it? *The Psychologist, 10*(5), 200–217.

Apter, M. J. (Ed.). (2001). *Motivational styles in everyday life: A guide to reversal theory.* Washington, DC: American Psychological Association.

Apter, M. J. (2007). *Danger: Our quest for excitement.* Oxford, UK: Oneworld Publications.

Armstrong, K. L. (2007). Self, situations, and sport consumption: An exploratory study of symbolic interactionism. *Journal of Sport Behavior, 30*(2), 111–130.

Babbie, E. (2012). *The practice of social research* (13th ed.). Belmont, CA: Wadsworth.

Barnett, L. A. (2006). Accounting for leisure preferences from within: The relative contributions of gender, race or ethnicity, personality, affective style, and motivational orientation. *Journal of Leisure Research, 38*(4), 445–474.

Burch, W. R. (2009). The social circles of leisure: Competing explanations. *Journal of Leisure Research, 41*(3), 313–335.

Csikszentmihalyi, M. (1975). *Beyond boredom and anxiety.* San Francisco, CA: Jossey-Bass.

Csikszentmihalyi, M. (1990). *Flow: The psychology of optimal experience.* New York, NY: Harper & Row.

Csikszentmihalyi, M. (1997). *Finding flow: The psychology of engagement with everyday life.* New York, NY: Basic Books.

Csikszentmihalyi, M. (2000). The contribution of flow to positive psychology: Scientific essays in honor of Martin E. P. Seligman. In J. E. Gilham (Ed.), *The science of optimism and hope* (pp. 387–398). Philadelphia, PA: Templeton Foundation.

Csikszentmihalyi, M., Abuhamdeh, S., & Nakamura, J. (2005). Flow. In A. J. Elliot & C. S. Dweck (Eds.), *Handbook of competence and motivation* (pp. 598–608). New York, NY: Guilford Press.

Deegan, J. J. (1989). *American ritual dramas: Social rules and cultural meanings.* New York, NY: Greenwood Press.

Giovannoli, D. (2007). The unconscious influence. Unpublished paper for the course HPER R160, Indiana University, Bloomington.

Henderson, K. A., Presley, J., & Bialeschki, M. D. (2004). Theory in recreation and leisure research: Reflections from the editors. *Leisure Sciences, 26*(4), 411–425.

Human Resources and Skills Development Canada. (2010). Indicators of well-being in Canada. Retrieved from http://www4.hrsdc.gc.ca/.3ndic.1t.4r@-eng.jsp?iid=51

Jackson, S. A. (1992). Athletes in flow: A qualitative investigation of flow states in elite figure skaters. *Journal of Applied Sport Psychology, 4*(2), 161–180.

Kerr, J. H. (2001). *Counseling athletes: Applying reversal theory.* London, UK: Routledge.

Kerr, J. H. (2004). *Rethinking aggression and violence in sport.* London, UK: Routledge.

Klinenberg, E. (2012). *Going solo: The extraordinary rise and surprising appeal of living alone.* New York, NY: Penguin.

LaMondia, J., Snell, T., & Bhat, C. R. (2010), Traveler behavior and values analysis in the context of vacation destination and travel mode choices: European Union case study. *Transportation Research Record,* 2156, 140–149.

Larson, R. (1988). Flow and writing. In M. Csikszentmihalyi & I. S. Csikszentmihalyi (Eds.), *Optimal experience: Psychological studies of flow in consciousness* (pp. 150–171). Cambridge, MA: Cambridge University.

Leonard, W. M. (1998). Specification of the home advantage: The case of the world series. *Journal of Sport Behavior, 21,* 41–52.

Mackenzie, S. H., Hodge, K., & Boyes, M. (2011). Expanding the flow model in adventure activities: A reversal theory perspective. *Journal of Leisure Research, 43*(4), 519–544.

Mannell, R. C. (1984). Personality in leisure theory: The self as entertainment. *Society and Leisure, 7,* 229–242.

Mill, R. C. (1986). Tourist characteristics and trends. In *Literature review: The President's Commission on Americans Outdoors.* Washington, D.C.: Government Printing Office.

NCAA. (October 15, 2014). Athletics participation rates continue to rise. Retrieved from http://www.ncaa.org/about/resources/media-center/news/athletics-participation-rates-continue-rise

Reskin, B. F. (1998). Bringing the men back in: Sex differentiation and the devaluation of women's work. In K. A. Myers, C. D. Anderson, & B. J. Risman (Eds.), *Feminist foundations: Toward transforming sociology* (pp. 278–298). Thousand Oaks, CA: Sage.

Riches, G. (2011). Embracing the chaos: Mosh pits, extreme metal music and liminality. *Journal for Cultural Research, 15*(3), 315–332.

Ridinger, L. L., & Funk, D. C. (2006). Looking at gender differences through the lens of sport spectators. *Sport Marketing Quarterly, 15*, 155–166.

Ross, T. F. (March 18, 2015). What gender inequality looks like in college sports. *The Atlantic.* Retrieved from http://www.theatlantic.com/education/archive/2015/03/what-gender-inequality-looks-like-in-collegiate-sports/387985/

Shinew, K. J., Floyd, M. F., McGuire, F. A., & Noe, F. P. (1996). Class polarization and leisure activity preferences of African Americans: Intragroup comparisons. *Journal of Leisure Research, 28*, 219–232.

Sport Business Research Network. (September 17, 2014). The growing significance of women in 2013 sports market trends. Retrieved from http://www.sbrnet.com/newsletter/september-17-2014.html

Title IX. (May 2003). Title IX after thirty years. National Association of State Boards of Education. *Policy Update, 11*(8), 1.

Turner, V. (1969). *The ritual process: Structure and anti-structure.* Chicago, IL: Aldine.

Turner, V. (1982). *From ritual to theatre: The human seriousness of play.* New York, NY: Performing Arts Journal Publications.

Underwood, R., Bond, E., & Baer, R. (2001). Building service brands via social identity: Lessons from the sports marketplace. *Journal of Marketing Theory and Practice,* 1–13.

United States Census Bureau. (2015). American FactFinder. Retrieved from http://factfinder.census.gov/faces/nav/jsf/pages/community_facts.xhtml

U.S. Department of Labor. (2015). American time use survey–2014 results. Retrieved from http://www.bls.gov/news.release/pdf/atus.pdf

Wilensky, H. (1960). Work, careers and social integration. *International Social Science Journal, 12*, 4.

Women's Sport Foundation. (2011). Title IX Myths and Facts. Retrieved from http://www.womenssportsfoundation.org/home/advocate/title-ix-and-issues/what-is-title-ix/title-ix-myths-and-facts

CHAPTER 4

Leisure and Health

What does leisure have to do with our health?

Leisure is necessary for growing and maturing, as well as for maintaining good health.

How does leisure help us to grow and mature?

Our lives are experienced both as continuous and as change. Leisure stimulates and eases the transitions of change yet also remains constant throughout life.

How does leisure help us acquire and maintain health?

Leisure contributes to our physical, social, intellectual, and emotional health.

Achieving well-being is perhaps the essence of human existence. Originally of concern to philosophers such as Aristotle, in recent years, wellness has become of interest to science. There is a rapidly growing body of research on what contributes to the quality of people's growth and maturation, and ultimately their life-long health. This has enabled a new understanding of the factors that influence and constitute well-being, and emerging is the primacy of the factor of leisure.

In this chapter, we explore leisure's role in our physical, social, emotional, and intellectual growth and health throughout our lives. To start, we lay forth foundational understandings of well-being and such building block concepts as life-span development and health.

Building Blocks of Well-Being

We begin with a broad definition of well-being. While academic debate continues about precisely how well-being should be understood, for our purposes, it is most usefully thought of as the dynamic process that ensures that people (New Economics Foundation, 2012):

- possess a sense of individual vitality;
- are able to undertake activities that are meaningful, engaging, and which make them feel competent and autonomous; and
- have a stock of resources to help them be resilient to changes and circumstances not under their immediate control.

Well-being is not only a process that gives people a sense of how their lives are going, but also provides for the resources to cope with difficult life circumstances as they come along. People who have high levels of well-being also contribute more positively to the quality of community life, and make the world a better place to live for others. This sounds, of course, rather lofty, but the consequences of low levels of well-being for both individuals and their surroundings are harmful and costly. This is why we are interested in leisure's role. But before we get to that, we have a few more foundational understandings to establish.

The dynamic process of well-being includes the building blocks of growth and development, as well as health. What do these mean? First, in this chapter, we consider growth and development from a **life span** perspective. That is, we begin young, we mature and grow older, and we die. A life-span understanding of this cycle means we view human life as an uninterrupted sequence. Thus, we use physical, emotional, intellectual, and social development across the life span as our markers for how leisure relates.

Life span: The changes and continuities of life from birth to death

Box 4.1
In Your Own Experience

Calculating Your Life Span

To illustrate the dynamic interrelationships among the well-being components of life span, health, and leisure, you can estimate your length of life using a variety of web supported calculators. For example, try this one: https://www.northwesternmutual.com/learning-center/tools/the-longevity-game, or go to https://www.livingto100.com/

Since our primary focus is leisure, let's introduce a leisure concept that illustrates the life span perspective. This is the idea of **core plus balance** (Kelly, 1999). What we are in leisure today is based in part on what we were yesterday, as well as how we will be different tomorrow. That is, the types of leisure activities we choose, our frequency of participation in these activities, and our motivations and benefits for and from them are both constant and change across our life span (Freysinger, 1999).

Core Plus Balance: There is both a persistent core and a balancing variety in our pastimes across the life span

That is, there is a persistent "core" of leisure interests that occupy most people most of their lives. These represent continuity in leisure. Our core pastimes are typically those activities that are easily accessible and low cost, such as watching television, taking walks, playing cards, and reading. Such core activities usually occupy the greatest amount of our free time.

Figure 4.1. The Core Plus Balance concept maintains that there is a persistent core in our pastimes across the life span (such as a love of going to the circus) balanced by changes in our pastimes across the life span (such as making model circuses). That's exactly the story of the creator of this model (Howard C. Tibbals) displayed at the Ringling Museum in Sarasota, Florida. © Patricia D. Setser

On the other hand, our lives also include a variety of pastimes that change over time. This is our "balance" of leisure expressions that shift as we grow older. To balance out our core pastimes, we seek variety. For example, as a child you may have been involved in playing saxophone in the school band, and as a young adult, your weekends were devoted to whitewater kayaking. Then, as an older adult, you may throw yourself into flower gardening. Meanwhile, what has been consistent throughout your life is enthusiasm for reading fiction.

Finally, when we use the word *health* as it relates to leisure, what do we mean? To answer, we consult the World Health Organization (WHO), that since 1948 has declared health to be "a state of complete physical, mental, and social well-being and not merely the absence of disease or infirmity" (2015a, p. 1). Here it seems that the meaning of health is similar to the meaning of well-being, but considering it less broadly, health is the level of functioning for a person—the general condition of a person's mind, body, and spirit, usually meaning to be free from illness, injury, or pain.

According to these basic understandings of well-being, life span, and health, let's now focus on the specific roles of leisure.

Box 4.2
In Profile

Champs Keep Going

Larry Johnson, age 95, keeps busy in his retirement with a 90-minute indoor cycling class three times a week and upper-body workouts on the alternate days. In the winter, he goes into the mountains above his Albuquerque, New Mexico, home to ski at least once a week.

Jack Hicken grew up riding horses in rural Alberta, Canada, and now at 78 still ropes calves in the senior rodeo. This means jumping off a moving horse after roping a calf, and then tying it up.

Ethel Lehmann played softball when she was young and just decided not to stop. Now, at 85, retired in Largo, Florida, she plays infield for the "Kids and Kubs" team; she is the only woman on an elite 75-and-older men's team.

According to Emilio Pardo, president of Life Reimagined, a division of AARP, 38% of men 55 and older, and 33% of women in that age category play competitive sports regularly. Sporting venues and companies are quickly adapting to this demographic change.

Source: Strauss, 2015

Leisure and Physical Well-Being

The importance of leisure's role in physical development and healthy functioning remains strong throughout our life span, but the nature of its role changes. The physical benefits from leisure shift from developing motor control in children, to sustaining health during the middle years, to reducing the decline in physical capabilities in older adulthood.

Today, in the United States, the average life expectancy is 79 years for all races and both genders, which is ranked 34th in the world. Japan has the highest average life expectancy (84 years), followed by Spain (83 years), Singapore (83 years), and Australia (83 years) (World Health Organization, 2015b). How does leisure assist us in achieving this average? Well, basically, if you live a healthy lifestyle, including regular participation in active leisure pursuits, you can expect to actually add up to 10 quality years to these expected years. Here's how.

In the beginning, the newborn's mission is to master her or his own body, and play provides an important tool for this. Early learning is the result of seemingly random movement, and an infant's individualistic play provides the platform for this learning. By 2 years of age, the child has developed basic motor skills, such as running and jumping, and such nonmotor skills as pushing, pulling, and kicking. Early play experiences are crucial for the development of these skills, as well as for learning muscle control and coordination. For example, through repetitious play, children teach themselves to crawl, stand, and walk.

Box 4.3
What Do
You Say?

Sport Training for Babies

Gymtrix.net is a fitness service for babies and young children (6 months to 11 years) that coaches in the development of the physical skills needed for organized sport success. For example, the company offers a library of videos starting with training for babies. Parents are encouraged to work with their babies on jumping, kicking, and in one exercise, something that looks like baseball batting practice. The growing competition in baby sport DVDs includes companies such as Athletic Baby (athleticbaby.com) and Baby Goes Pro (babygoespro.com). The Baby Goes Pro "Discover Sports" video covers five sports: baseball, basketball, golf, soccer, and tennis. The Little Gym (thelittlegym.com), based in Scottsdale, Arizona, begins classes for children at 4 months old. At Lil' Kickers (lilkickers.com), with franchises in 28 states, parents can enroll children at 18 months in soccer training, complete with soccer jerseys.

1. What is your opinion about sport training for babies and toddlers? Would you enroll your child in one of these programs? Why or why not?
2. In an era when we worry about the decline in physically active children, is this solution right, or does it go overboard? Why?

Between the ages of about 6 and 12, the amount of muscle tissue doubles and flexibility increases, thus physical play continues to be a necessary developmental tool, particularly for promoting normal bone growth. Playing with ropes, mastering climbing and balancing equipment, and learning to control balls give children opportunities to expand their neuromuscular coordination and strength as well. Overall, and to put it bluntly, children would not grow up without play. Increased motor control does not occur automatically; the child's body develops in large part from the physical demands placed on it. Further, childhood activity levels are strong predictors of physical activity later in life (Taylor, 1999).

Yet, according to a 2015 National Academy of Medicine report, only about half of America's kids and teens get enough activity to meet current guidelines. The recommendations call for kids to participate in at least 60 minutes of vigorous or moderately intense physical activity every day. Yet, in the U.S. more than 30,000 schools have eliminated recess to make more time for academics. And, from 1997 to 2003, children's time spent outdoors fell 50%. Meanwhile the number of minutes children devote each week to passive leisure, not including watching television, has increased from 30 minutes to more than three hours (Hofferth, 2009). It is no surprise, then, that childhood obesity is now considered an epidemic (Elkind, 2008).

Many have studied about childhood obesity. For example, according to the Centers for Disease Control and Prevention (2012a), American childhood obesity has more than tripled in the past 30 years. In 2016, 12.7 million children and adolescents were obese, or 17% (American Academy of Child and Adolescent Psychiatry, 2016). This is a significant long-term health problem. Not only does it mean an increase in body fat, but also losses to muscular strength, cardiorespiratory fitness, and bone mass. Obese children are also more likely to have pre-diabetes, high blood pressure, sleep apnea, and social and psychological problems. For example, one research study (Chang & Hayga, 2010) demonstrated an inverse relationship between obesity and happiness. That is, due to a loss of self-esteem, the more overweight the child, the more likely he/she is to feel unhappy.

Figure 4.2. Many things contribute to childhood obesity, including poor diet and lack of sleep. However, lack of active play is always a major causal factor.

Physical change is the major initiator of a wide-ranging passage from childhood to adulthood, and leisure's role in the physical development of adolescents is significant. The word **adolescence** is Latin and means to grow up, and the physical changes experienced (growth spurts, changing body proportions, hormone increases, etc.) are large and rapid. These changes, and the accompanying traumas, can affect concepts of self that go beyond the physical. Thus, if appropriately selected, active forms of leisure can help teens cope with their social and psychological awkwardness as well.

Adolescence: The transition from childhood to adulthood, describing both the development of physical and sexual maturity, as well as psychological and economic independence

For example, competitive sport participation by teens not only provides exercise for developing strength and motor control, but can also improve self-confidence and social status. As found in one research study, playing on a sports team is linked to higher life satisfaction in both boys and girls due to increasing school connectedness, social support, and bonding among friends (Zullig & White, 2010).

When we enter the workforce or attend college in late adolescence and early adulthood, our physical capabilities and energy are usually high. Some of us seek a wide assortment of active forms of recreation, with participation in strenuous sports continuing from youth. Interest in high-risk activities, such as skiing and rock climbing, begin to develop fully as well.

Usually by our late 20s or early 30s, leisure and physical development begin to shift their relationship. Biological maturity, when bone density is greatest and most physical skills peak, occurs at about this time (Donatelle & Davis, 2011), while participation in strenuous and high-risk sports gradually begins to decrease. As a counterforce, however, the high-level skill development that has taken place through years of practice, makes some physical forms of leisure (such as golf) even more enjoyable.

Yet, for all phases in the life span leisure's most basic importance is in sustaining physical health. Indeed, the list of benefits is astounding. Active leisure provides for greater energy levels, a stronger immune system, improved cardiovascular function, reduced risk for type 2 diabetes and some cancers, an improved ability to manage stress, a more positive outlook on life, enhanced relationships with others, and a longer life expectancy (CDC, 2012b).

Box 4.4
By The Numbers

Causes of Death Worldwide (annually)

- Heart Disease (7.4 million)
- Stroke (6.7 million)
- COPD (3.1 million)
- Lower respiratory infections (3.1 million)
- Lung cancer (1.6 million)
- Diabetes (1.5 million)

Source: World Health Organization, 2014

Meanwhile, normal physical changes also affect our leisure as we continue to grow into advanced ages. As we age, our bodies gradually become less flexible and endurance is reduced. After about age 50, the number of muscle fibers steadily decreases. While sometimes these physical changes stimulate changes in leisure activity types and frequency, leisure can also be a means to slowing the age-related disability process. For example, even with up to 50% deterioration in many organ systems, by remaining physically vigorous through leisure, life's pleasures can continue. Even people who begin a regular fitness or sport program late in life can make significant improvements in their heart and lung capacity.

Box 4.5
The Study Says

The Right Amount of Exercise

We have always known that everyone needs physical activity. But, for adults, long-standing debate has wondered just how much is necessary for longevity. Two large-scale studies seemingly put this debate to bed. Using data from health surveys and death records they found the following:

- Adults who do not exercise at all are at the highest risk of early death.
- Those who exercise moderately (mostly by walking) for 150 minutes per week enjoyed greater longevity benefits with a 31% less risk of dying early.
- Those adults who exercise moderately for 450 minutes per week (a little more than an hour per day) had a 39% less risk of dying prematurely.

Sources: Arem et al., 2015; Gebel et al., 2015

Leisure and Social Well-Being

Infants are born into an environment rich with expectations, norms, and traditions. A full social heritage with standards of behavior awaits them. Thus, a rather dramatic series of changes takes place during their first two years as they become aware of their surroundings. Play, of course, is a prime teacher in a child's social development. From it they become aware of family relationships, themselves as girls or boys, and what is good behavior for getting along with others.

The importance of the **peer** group in teaching social skills has been well documented. As children become increasingly more effective at communicating and better at understanding the thoughts and feelings of others, the amount and quality of peer interaction increases. For example, studies of peer relations in children have charted the development of six different levels of social interaction in play (Hughes, 2009).

Peer: One who is of equal social standing, usually based on age and economic status

Table 4.1
Levels of Play According to Peer Interactions

Level of Play	Age	Peer Interaction
Nonsocial	Infant to 1 year	Unoccupied, unfocused. No peer interaction.
Solitary	Infant to 1 year	Child plays alone. No peer interaction.
Onlooker	2 years	Child's interaction with peers is limited to just observing other children.
Parallel	2-3 years	Children play alongside each other but do not interact much with each other.
Associative	4-5 years	Some interaction; children play in separate activities but interact (exchanging toys and commenting on another's behavior).
Cooperative	6-7 years	Fully interactive with peers; children's actions are directed toward a common goal.

Source: Adapted from Conger & Peterson, 1984

As indicated in Table 4.1, these levels of interactive play predominate at certain ages, yet what matters most is children are given opportunities to experience them all in order to develop such social skills as empathy, role taking, self-control, and sharing. At older ages, recreational activities also help children to learn how to make decisions, take turns, set boundaries, and understand rules.

Gender identity: A person's private sense of, and subjective experience in, their own gender

Gender identity is a particular example of the role of play in social development. Although the formation of **gender identity** is not completely understood, many things have been suggested as influencing it. Included are such factors as gender messages conveyed by family, mass media, and other institutions (Henslin, 2001). Of particular importance are the different ways parents play with male and female babies, including what toys they are given and whether gender-specific play activities are encouraged (Craig & Baucum, 2001).

For example, fathers' play with male babies tends to be physical and arousing rather than intellectual, as it is with mothers' play with female babies (Berk, 2012). Parents often allow boys more freedom to display aggressive behavior and to be more vigorous with toys. Boys also tend to receive more gross motor stimulation, whereas girls receive more verbal stimulation. For older children, parents, teachers, peers, and even television characters reinforce gender stereotypes. These stereotypes can be problematic for social development because they provide arbitrary scripts for behavior.

For adolescents, changes in social interactions join those in physical development. If an adolescent is to become truly adult and not just physically mature, he or she must fit into a social world, achieve independence from parents, and establish enduring healthy relationships with others. This means the development of **autonomy** is central, and social experiences provide an important context for this.

Autonomy: Independence from others in thoughts and actions; ability to self-govern

The way this works is primarily through social groups to which most teens are attached. Whereas during middle and late childhood, peer relationships center around informal neighborhood play groups, for the teenager, the world widens, and social groups become more highly organized with special membership requirements and rituals.

Many teens experience almost all of their leisure within these social groups. Further, the leisure context provided by these peer relationships is a strong factor in successful negotiation through adolescence and into responsible adulthood (Feinstein, Bynner & Duckworth, 2005). In especially social recreation experiences within peer groups, youth learn to manage their own encounters, have personal control over their environments, establish social negotiation skills, and become autonomous in their actions

(Caldwell & Darling, 1999). Exactly how productive these skills become for adulthood depends on the nature of the peer group.

In particular, social media sites and the profiles they contain provide teens (and young adults) a reference point in the process of developing their social identity. There they interact with their peers, their most important reference group, and by looking at each other's profiles, get a sense of what types of presentations of self are socially appropriate for their group (Herring & Kapidzic, 2015).

Box 4.6
In Profile

Play for Peace

Founded in 1999 by two former corporate consultants seeking to re-evaluate their lives, *Play for Peace* is a nonprofit organization that promotes peace through children's play. The program, which receives some funding from the U.S. Department of Education and the United Nations, has sites in areas where cross-cultural tensions are common: including the U.S., Guatemala, India, Northern Ireland, South Africa, and the Middle East. With over 1.5 million children having participated so far, *Play for Peace* is open to youth from different cultural backgrounds who work together to create their own play activities. There's only one rule: every activity is nonviolent and noncompetitive. See http://www.playforpeace.org/.

A program in Kundpur, India

Upon leaving school, young adults are propelled into more adult social roles related to the social institutions of family, community, and the economy. For many, these can be exciting times of exploring and filling new social identities. For example, some young adults choose life partners and the impact of this transition on leisure depends on whether residence, employment, and family size change as well. Most likely leisure will be expressed primarily with a partner, which becomes an important context for building the relationship. This may also mean involvement in some pastimes formerly experienced separately will decrease. Young adults are also taking on more work roles, thus leisure is predominantly commercial, taking place in bars, clubs, restaurants, and apartment complexes.

If children are added to the family, the time and money spent for leisure tend to be restructured. Typically, the first change in leisure new parents realize is that engaging in spur-of-the-moment pastimes outside the home becomes more difficult. As well, at-home pastimes become more interrupted and crowded. As for the old adage, "the family that plays together stays together," research suggests this is both true and false. For example, a study by Freysinger (1994) found leisure experienced between children and their parents was satisfying for fathers. For mothers, experiencing leisure with children can be perceived as just another duty of daily care giving. On the other hand, a study by Agate et al. (2009) found family leisure involvement is positively related to satisfaction with family life for both parents and children.

Families today can face challenges: changing member combinations, potential unemployment, poverty, job-mandated geographic separation, family violence, and crime. Yet, in spite of the changing nature and types of families today (Powell et.al, 2010), the family remains a fundamental unit in society. Further, family is a major context of leisure. It is within families that children first learn leisure skills, interests, attitudes, and behaviors, and there is typically a continuity of leisure interests learned in childhood and adolescence across the life span. In addition, family members are common and frequent leisure companions throughout life.

As children leave the family and assume their own lives more completely, their middle-aged parents change, although exactly how varies. Three different leisure patterns seem to be the main options for "empty-nest" adults. First, some use their new freedom to turn back to the partnership or marriage for leisure. For them, leisure may become more important as some of the pursuits laid aside during parenting are taken up again. Others turn outward and seek new and separate social groups and activities. This can also be a renaissance time for middle-aged adults who have not reared children, as their careers stabilize and become financially rewarding. Finally, some pour themselves into greater work engagement by launching new careers or increasing civic responsibilities, thus continuing the restrictions on their leisure time.

Of course, there is another possible scenario for this stage of life. Labeled the "failure to launch syndrome" (after the 2006 movie), it is estimated that about 1/5 of those young adults in the millennial generation (aged 24 to 34) remain dependent on their parents, including living at home. Demographers have explained this as the result of more years spent in education (and thus more debt), delayed age of first marriage, higher housing costs, parenting styles, and lack of intrinsic interest in living on their own (Soergel, 2016). Implications of this for leisure have yet to be studied.

As we grow into old age, the nature of our social roles and relationships changes again. Spouses and partners may die, and socializing with coworkers on the job disappears with retirement. The way older people interact in their social worlds of family, friends, and neighbors is affected by physical, situational, and even economic changes. Above all, keeping socially connected is important because older adults who are part of well-defined friendship groups tend to have higher morale (Searle et al., 1995).

Figure 4.3. When older adults do maintain social relationships with family members, the nature of the relationship often changes, depending on the presence of children living at home and the care needs of older parents. Leisure can enable these new relationships. © Ruth V. Russell, 2016

In fact, some research has demonstrated friends are more important than family for life satisfaction at older ages (cf. Adams, 1986). One explanation of this might be given from a leisure perspective. That is, friendship is more rewarding because it is not obligatory, and leisure often provides the context for friendship. One of the primary benefits of living in age-segregated retirement communities (such as the Villages in Florida), for example, is the availability of potential friends to have fun with.

Leisure and Intellectual Well-Being

Cognitive skills: The ability to process information, reason, remember, and relate

It has long been understood that one of the main contributions from child's play is the development of **cognitive skills**. This is especially true of the purest form of play: the unstructured, self-motivated, imaginative, independent kind, where children initiate their own games and even invent their own rules.

For example, in infancy and early childhood, play is the activity through which children learn to recognize colors and shapes, tastes and sounds—the very building blocks of reality (Elkind, 2008). Also, babbling is a self-initiated form of play through which infants create the sounds they need to learn the language of their parents. A 2007 report from the American Academy of Pediatrics documents that play promotes brain growth as well. Children who received an enriched, play-oriented early childhood program had significantly higher IQs at age five than did a comparable group of children who were not in the program (105 vs. 85 points).

Further, several studies by Hirsch-Pasek and colleagues (2009) have compared the performance of children attending academic preschools with those attending play-oriented preschools. The results showed no advantage in reading and math achievement for children attending the academic preschools. But there was evidence that those children had higher levels of test anxiety, were less creative, and had more negative attitudes toward school than did the children attending the play preschools.

One of the earliest documenters of the relationship between play and intellectual development in children was the Swiss psychologist Jean Piaget. His research about this consumed most of his life, and included the constant study of his own three children. His work led him to conclude children pass through four developmental stages of thinking ability.

First, according to Piaget (in Mussen, 1983), during the *sensorimotor stage* from birth to 2 years, children obtain a basic knowledge of objects they play with through their senses. Next, they enter the *preoperational stage*. From about ages 2 to 7, they use language and imagination to help build some facsimile of the outside world. For example, young children take dolls out for walks and line up toy trucks in the right direction. From about 7 to 11 years of age, children begin to think logically. This *concrete operational stage* is when they begin to use symbols. For example, whereas younger children require props to be similar to the real object for pretend play, older children can play with only abstract representations, such as a stick for a gun. Finally, in Piaget's fourth stage of intellectual development, *formal operations*, which lasts from about 11 to 15 years of age, children begin to reason realistically by imaging all the possibilities. Their thought is richer, broader, and more flexible.

Figure 4.4. Jean Piaget (1896–1980). According to his theory of cognitive development, the give and take in play and imitation is one way that children learn about their world. Source: Public domain

If unstructured play is so crucial to intellectual development, why is it disappearing? In American society over the last two decades, children have lost 8 hours of free, self-initiated play per week (Elkind, 2008). Increasingly, children are placed into leader-led organized play programs with prescribed behaviors, start and stop times, and expected outcomes. Due perhaps to increasing numbers of single parents working (83%) and both parents working (81%) (Bureau of Labor Statistics, 2016), children's play is being outsourced to coaches, teachers, and play leaders.

This problem is mirrored for adults, as well. Stereotypes about inevitable intellectual decline as we grow older have been largely refuted by many studies. "We used to think that the adult brain couldn't grow," says neurologist Jay Lombard (as cited in Merrell, 2003, p. 143). Yet, as with children, given the appropriate stimulus, some mental abilities improve well into old age.

As for the role of leisure in this, there is a surprisingly large literature suggesting that older persons who engage in a variety of leisure expressions (including playing games, working crossword puzzles, and having hobbies) actually show improvement on cognitive tests (Park et al., 2007). In one study, for example, Oxford University researchers taught 24 older adults to juggle and found that after six weeks the intraparietal sulcus region of the brain had a higher density of white matter (the fibers that let neurons communicate). They concluded that any novel activity that is practiced intently, such as tennis or guitar playing, will likely have this effect (Scholz et al., 2009).

Box 4.7
Web Explore

Where in the Brain Is Leisure?

One morning, a blood vessel in the brain of 37-year-old Jill Bolte Taylor exploded. As a brain scientist, she realized she had a ringside seat to her own stroke. She watched as her brain functions shut down one by one: motion, speech, memory, self-awareness. Amazed to find herself still alive, Taylor spent eight years recovering her ability to think, walk, and talk. Since then, she has become a spokesperson for stroke recovery and for the possibility of coming back from brain injury stronger than before. In her case, although the stroke damaged the left side of her brain, her recovery unleashed a torrent of creative energy from her right side. Watch a talk she gave at a TED conference and see if you can't discover where leisure is in the brain:

https://www.ted.com/talks/jill_bolte_taylor_s_powerful_stroke_of_insight?language=en.

Even under extreme circumstances of brain dysfunction, leisure continues to be important in maintaining health. For example, an experiment at nursing care facilities in the U.S. uses music, dancing, massage, and pastimes the patient was enthusiastic about at younger ages to replace large doses of antipsychotic drugs in calming agitation and aggressive behavior in elderly dementia sufferers (Lagnado, 2007).

Leisure and Emotional Well-Being

We spend our entire lifetime learning how to manage our feelings. Some are very good feelings, such as joy, affection, thankfulness, and sensuality. Others, such as anger, fear, anxiety, and frustration, are not pleasant at all. Leisure itself is often considered a type of emotion, a positive state of mind; thus, its role in the development of emotional health is particularly intriguing. Let's begin with children.

Young children have all the basic emotions of adults, but their expression is typically immediate, impulsive, and direct. Most children grow up learning to manage their emotions so their expression is more controlled and socially appropriate, and play is the primary teacher. For example, two of the negative emotions children must learn to grow from are fear and anxiety. Freud (1955) argued play helps children master these emotions, and children not allowed to deal with them through play can become psychopathic adults. Later studies by Barnett (1984) similarly supported the importance of fantasy play to neutralize the anxieties children feel. These researchers observed that children use fantasy play to reenact sources of emotional distress, often by changing the outcome or by reversing roles to achieve a more pleasant result.

Another way leisure aids in the emotional development of children is through a concept called locus of control. **Locus of control** is our own perception about the source of power in our life. When we have an external locus of control, we perceive that we have no control, that we are merely pawns moved by forces outside of us. With internal locus of control, we perceive we are the origin of our own life events. Internal locus of control is important to emotional maturity.

Locus of control: The extent to which individuals believe they can control events that affect them

As for the role of leisure, we know the more time children spend in a supervised, child-centered play program, the more internal their locus of control becomes. An example of this is the "play-work" or adventure playground (Brown, 2002). The concept originated in Europe after World War II when a playground designer studied children playing in cement playgrounds. He found they preferred playing in the dirt and with lumber from the postwar rubble. He realized children have the most fun designing and building their own equipment and manipulating their environment themselves. On an adventure playground, this means children are encouraged to play creatively. They climb on the forts, boats, and towers they themselves have built. They ride a zip line or hammer, saw, and paint.

Figure 4.5. **The formula for adventure playgrounds includes earth, fire, water, and lots of raw materials.** © Berkeley California Parks and Recreation Department

In growing from childhood to young adulthood, adolescents often display a curious combination of different levels of emotional maturity. Describing this often awkward mixture is typically the description of adolescence itself. Primary is the emotional task of answering the question, "Who am I?" and leisure provides a context for experimenting with one's identity, particularly in the more relaxed setting of the playing field, band room, Scout meeting, and even the mall.

Older adolescents, such as college students, are also engaged in discovering their identity. At this stage in the life span, leisure continues to provide a vital context for breaking with personal identities associated with family and home community. Several emotional transitions occur, such as the emergence of a focused sexuality, and confidence in greater social and economic independence from parents (Kelly, 1982).

Colleges and universities aid in this process by providing real-world simulations. For example, students can participate in politics through student government and in a profession through practicums and internships. Social events, intramural sports, spring break trips, hobby clubs, and other campus activities are crucial in increasing emotional maturity. They provide ways of experimenting with attitudes of influence, dissent, and cooperation. They also play an important role in reducing stress. For example, researchers Ragheb and McKinnney (1992) found the more students participated in campus recreation activities, the less academic stress they experienced.

The years from about 35 to 45 have been called the "deadline decade," or the time of the "midlife crisis." Divorce and career changes occur with increasing frequency. Predictable at this point in life is a feeling of stagnation. Again, leisure offers a context for coming to terms with the often tumultuous struggles adults experience within themselves. For example, in a study of 1,400 adults by researchers at the University of Pittsburgh School of Medicine (Pressman et al., 2009), participation in a variety of leisure activities were able to lower levels of depression and negative feelings. "When one is under stress, the usual thing is to cut back on enjoyable activities because you're feeling uncomfortable and you need more time to deal with the stress. But these data suggest that is the wrong thing to do and that continuing multiple activities can be helpful" (p. 729).

Meanwhile, the decade of our 50s has been labeled the reintegration period (Rapoport & Rapoport, 1975). Emotionally, this is when we reevaluate ourselves, and the meaning and worth of our life commitments. This includes questioning whether our pastimes are producing the fulfillment they once promised. As we approach the retirement years, the free-choice nature of leisure makes it a prime medium for life evaluation. Often new pastimes can be tried with minimal changes to family and work responsibilities.

As well, during retirement, increased free time brings a life stage in which former leisure interests can be renewed, often taking on more intrinsic motivation, as we do these activities more for their own sake. (See Table 4.2.) Yet, retirement can bring both positive and negative emotions. Some look forward to this life phase exactly because they will have more time for leisure. Others worry they'll feel at loose ends without the structure of employment.

Table 4.2
Leisure Before and During Retirement

Leisure Before Retirement	Leisure During Retirement
Restricted, mostly to evenings, weekends, and vacations	Abundant
Is often about relaxation and destressing	Often about engagement, connection, and activity
Goal is to escape from structure	Retirees often desire to balance both structure and nonstructure in leisure
Health less likely to be a constraint	Health is more likely to be a constraint
More income, but less time is a major limiting factor	Some have more limited income, but all have more free time
Technology for work interferes (people can't unplug)	Technology enhances leisure through social connection
Travel is often short	Travel can be longer and more immersive

Source: Bank of America / Merrill Lynch Survey, 2016

Alongside these uncertainties is continuity as people generally continue the pastimes of previous years. If they have had fulfilling leisure experiences outside of work, this will be a time of joy. Without leisure interests that are personally meaningful, however, the adjustments of retirement may be emotionally difficult, bringing feelings of loneliness and apathy. Expanding favorite leisure interests can aid in these emotional adjustments. In fact, determining one's leisure "career" should be part of retirement preparation decisions.

What We Understand About Leisure and Health

The cycle of life is both certain and uncertain, constant and changing. In this chapter, we emphasized that leisure is necessary for successfully growing, maturing, and reaching old age. Though the nature of its role may change, leisure is constantly helping us become and stay healthy. From studying this chapter, you should know the following:

1. Leisure helps children develop motor skills, and in the middle and later years it helps sustain physical capabilities.
   Discuss one example of leisure's role in physical health:
   ____
   ____

2. Through leisure, children are able to acquire skills for meaningful social interaction, and for adults, leisure is often the sole connection to the social world.
   Discuss one example of leisure's role in social health:
   ____
   ____

3. For children, leisure is a tool for learning; for adults, leisure is important in maintaining previously acquired cognitive abilities, as well as developing others more fully.
   Discuss one example of leisure's role in intellectual health:
   ____
   ____

4. Although leisure itself is often considered an emotional state, it also plays a role in the development of positive emotions and in the maintenance of emotional health throughout life.
   Discuss one example of leisure's role in emotional health:
   ____
   ____

References

Adams, R. G. (1986). A look at friendship and aging. *Generations, 10,* 40–43.

Agate, J. R., Zabriskie, R. B., Agate, S. T., & Poff, R. (2009). Family leisure satisfaction and satisfaction with family life. *Journal of Leisure Research, 41*(2), 205–223.

American Academy of Child and Adolescent Psychiatry. (No. 79, April 2016). Obesity in children and teens. Retrieved from http://www.aacap.org/AACAP/Families_and_Youth/Facts_for_Families/FFF-Guide/Obesity-In-Children-And-Teens-079.aspx

American Academy of Pediatrics. (2007). Child development: Bright futures. Guidelines for health supervision of infants, children, and adolescents. Retrieved from brightfutures.aap.org/pdfs/.../3-Promoting_Child_Development.pdf

Arem, H., Moore, S. C., Patel, A., Hartge, P., Berrington de, G. A., Visvanathan, K., … Mathews, C. E. (June 2015). Leisure time physical activity and mortality: A detailed pooled analysis of the dose-response relationship. *Journal of the American Medical Association, 175*(6), 959–967.

Bank of America/Merrill Lynch. (2016). Leisure in retirement: Beyond the bucket list. Retrieved from www.ml.com/retirementstudy

Barnett, L. A. (1984). Young children's resolution of distress through play. *Journal of Child Psychology and Psychiatry, 25,* 477–483.

Berk, L. E. (2012). *Child development* (9th ed.). New York, NY: Prentice Hall.

Brown, F. (2002). *Playwork: Theory and practice.* Buckingham, UK: Open University.

Bureau of Labor Statistics. (April 22, 2016). Employment characteristics of families summary. Retrieved from http://www.bls.gov/news.release/famee.nr0.htm

Caldwell, L. L., & Darling, N. (1999). Leisure context, parental control, and resistance to peer pressure as predictors of adolescent partying and substance use: An ecological perspective. *Journal of Leisure Research, 31*(1), 57–77.

Centers for Disease Control and Prevention (CDC). (2012a). Childhood obesity facts. Retrieved from http://www.cdc.gov/healthyyouth/obesity/facts.htm

Centers for Disease Control and Prevention (CDC). (2012b). Physical activity and health. Retrieved from http://www.cdc.gov/physicalactivity/everyone/health/index.html

Chang, H. H., & Hayga, R. M. (2010). Childhood obesity and unhappiness: The influence of soft drinks and fast food consumption. *Journal of Happiness Studies, 11*(3), 261–275.

Conger, J. J., & Peterson, A. C. (1984). *Adolescence and youth: Psychological development in a changing world.* New York, NY: Harper & Row.

Craig, G. J., & Baucum, D. (2001). *Human development.* Englewood Cliffs, NJ: Prentice-Hall.

Donatelle, R. J., & Davis, L. G. (2011). *Access to health* (12th ed.). New York, NY: Benjamin Cummings.

Elkind, D. (Spring 2008). Can we play? *Greater Good, 4*(4). Retrieved from http://greatergood.berkeley.edu/author/david_elkind/

Feinstein, L., Bynner, J., & Duckworth, K. (2005). Leisure contexts in adolescence and their effects on adult outcomes. *Wider Benefits of Learning Research Report No. 15.* Centre for Research on the Wider Benefits of Learning, Institute of Education, London.

Freud, S. (1955). Beyond the pleasure principle. In J. Strachey (Ed.), *The standard edition of the complete psychological works of Sigmund Freud* (Vol. 18, pp. 280–292). London, UK: Hogarth.

Freysinger, V. J. (1994). Leisure with children and parental satisfaction: Further evidence of a sex difference in the experience of adult roles and leisure. *Journal of Leisure Research, 26,* 212–226.

Freysinger, V. J. (1999). Life span and life course perspectives on leisure. In E. L. Jackson & T. L. Burton (Eds.), *Leisure studies: Prospects for the twenty-first century.* State College, PA: Venture.

Gebel, K., Ding, D., Chey, T., Stamatakis, E., Brown, W. J., & Bauman, A. E. (June 2015). Effect of moderate to vigorous physical activity on all-cause mortality in middle-aged and older Australians. *Journal of the American Medical Association, 175*(6), 970–977.

Henslin, J. M. (2001). *Essentials of sociology.* Oxford, UK: Taylor & Francis.

Herring, S. C., & Kapidzic, S. (2015). Teens, gender, and self-presentation in social media. In J. D. Wright (Ed.), *International encyclopedia of social and behavioral sciences* (2nd ed.). Oxford, UK: Elsevier.

Hirsch-Pasek, K., Michnick, G. R., Berk, L., & Singer, D. (2009). *A mandate for playful learning in preschool.* New York, NY: Oxford University Press.

Hofferth, S. L. (2009). Changes in American children's time: 1997–2003. *Electronic International Journal of Time Use Research, 6*(1), 26–47. Retrieved from http://www.ncbi.nlm.nih.gov/pmc/articles/PMC2939468/

Hughes, F. P. (2009). *Children, play, and development.* New York, NY: Sage.

Kelly, J. R. (1982). *Leisure.* Englewood Cliffs, NJ: Prentice-Hall.

Kelly, J. R. (1999). Leisure and society: A dialectical analysis. In E. L. Jackson & T. L. Burton (Eds.), *Leisure studies: Prospects for the Twenty-first century.* State College, PA: Venture.

Lagnado, L. (December 20, 2007). Nursing homes look for ways off drugs. *The Wall Street Journal,* pp. A1, A14.

Merrell, K. (November 2003). Get smart: Science has found new strategies to help our sharp minds keep their edge. *Real Simple,* 143–147.

Mussen, P. (Ed.). (1983). Piaget's theory. *Handbook of child psychology, Vol. 1.* (4th ed.). New York, NY: Wiley.

National Academy of Medicine. (June 10, 2015). Physical activity: Moving toward obesity solutions—Workshop in brief. Retrieved from http://nationalacademies.org/hmd/reports/2015/physical-activity-wib.aspx.

New Economics Foundation. (2012). What is well-being? Retrieved from http://www.nationalaccountsofwellbeing.org/learn/what-is-well-being.html

Park, D. C., Gutchess, A. H., Meade, M. L., & Stine-Morrow, E. A. L. (2007). Improving cognitive function in older adults: Nontraditional approaches. *Journals of Gerontology, 62B,* 45–52.

Powell, B., Bolzendahl, C., Geist, C., & Steelman, L. C. (2010). *Counted out: Same-sex relations and Americans' definitions of family.* New York, NY: Russell Sage Foundation.

Pressman, S. D., Matthews, K. A., Cohen, S., Martire, L. M., Scheier, M., Baum, A., & Schulz, R. (2009). Association of enjoyable leisure activities with psychological and physical well-being. *Psychosomatic Medicine, 71*(7), 725–732.

Ragheb, M. G., & McKinnney, J. (1992). Campus recreation and perceived academic stress. Paper presented at the Leisure Research Symposium, National Recreation and Park Association, Cincinnati, OH.

Rapoport, R., & Rapoport, R. N. (1975). *Leisure and the family life cycle.* London, UK: Routledge & Kegan Paul.

Searle, M. S., Mahon, J. J., Iso-Ahola, S. E., Sdrolias, H. A., & van Dyck, J. (1995). Enhancing a sense of independence and psychological well-being among the elderly: A field experiment. *Journal of Leisure Research, 27*, 107–124.

Scholz, J., Klein, M. C., Behrens, T. E. J., & Johansen-Berg, H. (2009). Training induces changes in white-matter architecture. *Nature Neuroscience, 12*(11), 1370–1371.

Soergel, A. (May 9, 2016). Failure to launch: Young adults increasingly moving in with Mom and Dad. *U.S. News and World Report.* Retrieved from http://www.usnews.com/news/articles/2016-05-09/failure-to-launch-young-adults-increasingly-moving-in-with-mom-and-dad

Strauss, R. (April 14, 2015). Odds of being a champ at 95? Not bad. *The Herald-Tribune*, Sarasota, Florida, p. 30E.

Taylor, W. C. (1999). Childhood and adolescent physical activity patterns and adult physical activity. *Medicine and Science in Sports and Exercise, 31,* 118–123.

World Health Organization. (1948). Preamble to the Constitution of the World Health Organization as adopted by the International Health Conference, New York, 19–22 June, 1946; signed on 22 July 1946 by the representatives of 61 States (Official Records of the World Health Organization, no. 2, p. 100) and entered into force on 7 April 1948.

World Health Organization. (2014). Top ten causes of death worldwide. Retrieved from http://www.who.int/mediacentre/factsheets/fs310/en/

World Health Organization. (2015a). Mental health. Retrieved from http://www.who.int/topics/mental_health/en/

World Health Organization. (2015b). Global health observatory data repository. Retrieved from http://apps.who.int/gho/data/node.main.688?lang=en

Zullig, K. J., & White, R. J. (2010). Physical activity, life satisfaction, and self-rated health of middle school students. Applied research in quality of life. Retrieved from http://www.springer.com/about+springer/media/springer+select?SGWID=0-11001-6-1000421-0

PART 2

Leisure as a Cultural Mirror: Societal Context

Leisure also helps define who we are as a civilization.

Leisure is significant to us not only individually but also collectively. Like a mirror, how we express ourselves through our individual pastimes helps define who we are as a community, a society, and a world.

Chapter 5

Discusses leisure's cultural significance according to anthropology.

Chapter 6

Presents the expression of leisure as geographically determined.

Chapter 7

Debates the boon and bane of leisure in a technological society.

Chapter 8

Explores popular culture, the most typical pastimes of the majority of people.

Chapter 9

Portrays cultural leisure expressions that are considered taboo due to law, custom, or belief.

CHAPTER 5

Leisure's Anthropology

What is leisure's cultural significance?

Leisure is so much a part of the patterns of our collective life that it can describe how cultures are characterized, compared, and changed.

Did the earliest human cultures have leisure?

Leisure was a part of human culture before civilization itself.

How is leisure unique in developing cultures?

Leisure can be used as a tool for cultural development. As such, leisure is also typically changed by development.

How does modernity affect a culture's leisure?

Leisure in modern societies is more commercial, diverse, sped up, and technologically oriented. Is it better?

Leisure and culture mutually shape each other. In this chapter, we tell this story from the lens of cultural anthropology: how leisure is formed by culture and in turn helps to form culture. **Cultural anthropology** is the study of human society that incorporates ideas from archeology, the social sciences, and the humanities. So, when we consider leisure anthropologically, we are interested in how leisure and human societies are reciprocal forces.

Cultural anthropology: The comparative study of human groups and their development

First, let's explore basic concepts about culture. Then we'll trace the likely role of leisure for humans in the earliest cultures. Finally, we'll contrast leisure's expression today in relation to cultural development and modernity.

Leisure and Culture

Culture is a complex and flexible concept, so there are many definitions for it. Broadly the term denotes the set of distinctive spiritual, material, intellectual, and emotional features of a society or social group. Markers of these features are typically found in art, literature, sport, lifestyles, value systems, traditions, and beliefs (UNESCO, 2009). Culture, then, includes the collective expression of leisure. This means our individual leisure expressions fit within what our culture considers important. There are two basic concepts about culture that are important to understanding leisure's role: culture characteristics and cultural change.

Culture: The distinct ways the people in different social groups live

Figure 5.1. The Olympic Games celebrate not only athletic performances but also the nations that participate. Summer Olympics, London, 2012. Source: Reuters/Mike Blake

Characteristics of Culture

Through comparisons of many different cultures, cultural anthropologists are able to differentiate the basic characteristics of all cultures (Table 5.1). As a result, we are able to understand how leisure functions as a cultural mirror. The basic characteristics of culture are: shared, learned, integrated, and has symbols.

The first characteristic is culture is shared (Haviland et al., 2014). That is, culture is a set of shared ideas and standards of behavior. Because they share a common culture, the actions of individuals are understandable and people can predict how others are most likely to behave in given circumstances. For example, in the United States children are likely to participate in basketball, whereas children in Chile consider soccer their more popular sport, and children in Malaysia will likely learn to play sepak takraw.

Figure 5.2. Sepak takraw as played in Malaysia. Source: Reuters/Issei Kato

Table 5.1
Characteristics of Culture

Characteristic	Defined	Leisure Example	Related Concept
Shared	Values and standards of behavior are held in common.	Football to Americans is different than football to Germans.	Subcultures based on leisure
Learned	We learn our culture by living in it.	In some social groups, it is considered rude to be late to a party.	Enculturation
Integrated	All parts of a culture are interrelated.	When and where people take their summer vacation affects transportation, hospitality, and attraction services.	Example in Poland
Symbols	Cultural "currency" is based on representations.	The scoring system for strikes and spares in bowling.	Whorfian hypothesis

Box 5.1
By The Numbers

The #1 Sport in Selected Countries

United States	American Football
Australia	Australian Football
Bulgaria	Football Soccer*
Venezuela	Baseball
Israel	Basketball
Nicaragua	Boxing
India	Cricket
Canada	Ice Hockey
New Zealand	Rugby
Bahamas	Tennis
Korea	Martial Arts

*Football soccer is the most popular participation and spectator sport in the world with 57 countries identifying it as its top sport.

Source: ChartsBin, n.d.

Just because culture is shared, doesn't mean everyone in a culture is the same, however. Within American culture, for example, people listen to a wide variety of music, including country, jazz, classical, and rap. In fact, we can categorize people into subgroups, or subcultures, based on their specific musical tastes. This demonstrates that while a **subculture** can be based on such demographic factors as race, geographic region, religion, or social class, it can also be based on leisure interests. Examples of leisure-based subcultures include biker gangs, Trekkies, backpackers, and the poker club.

Subculture: A subdivision of culture, often having beliefs or interests at variance with those of the larger culture

A second characteristic of culture is that it is learned (Haviland et al., 2014). The idea that culture is learned, rather than biologically inherited, prompted anthropologist Ralph Linton (1936) to refer to it as our social heredity. We usually learn our culture by first growing up with it, but this learning process is needed for anyone new to a culture. For example, Tsai (2000) studied Chinese immigrants in Australia and found that only after the immigrants sufficiently learned their new culture were they able to participate in the leisure expressions there.

Enculturation: The process by which cultural understanding is transmitted to new members

The process whereby culture is learned is called **enculturation.** An established culture teaches an individual new to the culture accepted norms and values by repetition so that the individual can become an accepted member of the group and find a suitable role. Most importantly, enculturation establishes a context of boundaries and correctness that dictates what is and is not permissible within that group.

For example, the appropriate time of day to eat varies from culture to culture, and through enculturation we learn what time this is. When we eat may not have anything to do with when we're hungry, but rather we eat when our culture tells us to. For example, the evening meal in the United States is served generally between 6 p.m. and 7 p.m. In Spain, supper commonly begins at 10 p.m.

Box 5.2
The Study Says

Cross-Cultural Comparisons

In 2011, the Organisation for Economic Cooperation and Development (OECD) published the results of multiple studies comparing social indicators across countries of the world. Data collected from time use diaries included comparisons for free time and recreational activity participation:

- **Preferred Leisure Activity.** Watching television is the most popular activity across all countries, with Americans watching the most (44% of total free time) and New Zealanders watching the least (25% of total free time); there is twice as much sport participation in Spain as there is in most other countries; and visiting or entertaining friends is more popular in Turkey than in other countries.
- **Daily Time Spent Eating and Drinking.** 140 minutes in France; 95 minutes in Korea; 75 minutes in the U.S.; 70 minutes in Canada.
- **Daily Time Spent Sleeping**. 530 minutes in France; 520 minutes in the U.S.; 495 minutes in Germany; 485 minutes in Norway.
- **Percentage Free Time in Average Day.** 27.7% in Belgium; 24% in U.S.; 21.3% in Japan; 15.8% in Mexico.

Source: OECD, 2011

The third characteristic of culture is that it is integrated (Haviland et al., 2014). This means all aspects of a culture relate to one another, so that changes to one seemingly unimportant part of a particular culture can reverberate throughout the entire culture and affect all other aspects.

An example of this characteristic as related to leisure is what occurred in Poland with the demise of communism. Formerly, under the communist system, government-owned companies in Poland were required to generate cultural funds to be used to subsidize holidays and trips for employees; recreational services for employees' children; book purchases for company libraries; and tickets for the theater, cinema, and concerts. When the country shifted away from a communist political system in 1980 by implementing market-oriented economics, one essential feature was the privatization of these government funds for leisure (Jung, 1992).

This meant not only that some establishments formerly used for recreation had shifted to other uses, but also that with commercialization, recreation services were now available only to more wealthy consumers. Thus, with one change in the political system, changes were also felt in the economic system, which in turn had an impact on leisure resources and how leisure services were made available in Polish culture.

The fourth characteristic of culture is that it is based on symbols (Haviland et al., 2014). Anthropologist Leslie White (1959) insisted all human behavior originates in the use of symbols. For example, art, religion, and money all involve the use of symbols—the visual image in art, the icon in religion, and the credit card in money. The most important symbolic aspect of culture is language—the substitution of words for objects (Haviland et al., 2014).

One way of thinking about leisure relative to this characteristic is to consider the word *leisure* itself. According to deGrazia (1962) "leisure cannot exist where people don't know what it is" (p. 3). That is, one must have a symbol (word) for leisure in order to have it. For example, while conducting research with the Sherpa people of the Khumbu region of Nepal in the 1980s, I realized many people were unable to understand my question "What do you do for leisure?" because they did not have a readily translatable word for the English word leisure.

This idea is labeled the Whorfian hypothesis. Named for one of the early anthropologists who studied the phenomenon (Benjamin Lee Whorf in the 1950s), the idea suggests that language not only provides a way of communicating among people, but it also becomes the nature of behavior within the culture. The Whorfian hypothesis, however, has received only limited and confusing research support, even though many commonly agree with it (Chick, 1995). As I discovered in my own study, the Sherpa people indeed had a life experience characterized by many of the qualities we identify with leisure, even though their word for it does not translate exactly to the English word.

Box 5.3
In Profile

The Tango

One of the most fascinating of all dances, the Tango is a sensual ballroom form that originated in South America in the early nineteenth century. Brought by Spanish settlers, Tango initially took hold in working-class Buenos Aires. The popularity of Tango has increased over the years. From Argentina, the dance spread quickly through Europe during the 1900s, then moving into the United States, where it began gaining popularity in New York City around 1910. Tango has again become very popular in recent years, in South America as well as Europe, the United States, and Japan. As it has spread, different styles have emerged: Argentine, French, Gaucho, American, and International. While some aficionados lament foreign interpretations of Tango and a possible loss of authenticity for the dance, the dance's intimacy and creativity remain its distinct character.

Cultural Change

One outcome from the characteristics of culture we've just discussed is that cultures change. All cultures change over a period of time, sometimes gently and gradually, without altering any of the fundamental ways underlying the core of the culture. At other times, the pace of change may be dramatically fast, causing radical cultural alternation in a short period of time, sometimes to the disadvantage of the culture. Regardless, certain mechanisms are at work in cultural change having implications for leisure. These mechanisms of cultural change are innovation, diffusion, loss, and acculturation (Haviland et al., 2014).

Innovation: A chance discovery that gains widespread acceptance

Innovation as a mechanism of cultural change refers to any new practice, tool, or principle that gains widespread acceptance. A significant example of how innovation changes cultural expressions of leisure is television. Indeed, television has changed just about everything, almost everywhere. When television was introduced in the 1940s, very few homes could afford the "box." By 1950, only 9% of American homes had it, but its popularity grew quickly, and five years later, TV was in 65% of households (Nielsen Media Research, 2009). In the 2016/2017 season, Nielsen (2016) estimated there were 118.4 million "TV homes" in the United States, which is not counting all the mobile ways people watch television as well.

Initially the impact of this innovation was felt in the role of TV as an advertising medium. As well, it was nearly a perfect expression of suburban leisure as it celebrated domesticity in the situation comedy, or "sit-com" programming format, and warned of urban dangers in the action-adventure shows (Cross, 1990). Since then, the impact of television has been widely and thoroughly studied and commented about. Table 5.2 summarizes some of the changes to leisure resulting from the innovation of TV.

Table 5.2
Cultural Changes Since the 1950s Invention of Television

- Less socializing in the family, neighborhood, and community and increased social isolation.
- Television characters used as role models.
- Freakishness and sensation treated with solemn importance.
- Expansion of such forms of leisure as the arts, cooking, travel, and sports.
- Development of new forms of leisure, such as extreme sports.
- A more homogenized expression of leisure across all members of the culture, as well as across cultures themselves.
- Conversion of some leisure forms into competitions (i.e., cooking and travel).

Diffusion: The spread of customs from one culture to another

Diffusion is another mechanism of cultural change. Diffusion is the spread or borrowing of customs or practices from one culture to another. So common is diffusion that anthropologist Linton suggested that borrowing accounts for as much as 90% of any culture's content (Haviland et al., 2014). One major example of cultural change brought about by diffusion is McDonald's restaurants. What began as a single establishment in Des Plaines, Illinois, in 1955 has now expanded to more than 14,350 restaurants in the United States, and 21,908 restaurants in international locations (McDonald's, 2014). Yet, while global in its market, the company also encourages local operators to tailor menu items to local tastes, such as the Ebi Filet-O Burger (shrimp) in Japan and the McLaks (salmon and dill sauce) in Norway.

The mechanism of diffusion doesn't always cause major cultural change. This is because people are choosy about their borrowing and pick only those things that are compatible with their existing culture. For example, particular songs, sports, dances, and art forms introduced in one culture spread to others and are often changed in accordance with the dominant values of the receiving culture. Heider (1977) described a game of physical skill developed in Java, Indonesia, and later introduced in a highland New Guinea tribe. New Guinean culture valued noncompetitiveness, so when they played the Javanese game, they disregarded scorekeeping and rules to be more in keeping with their own cultural values (Chick, 1995).

As our discussion has led us so far, most often we think of cultural change as an accumulation of innovations and borrowings; new things are added to those already in a culture. This is not always the case, of course, and frequently the acceptance of an innovation or borrowing leads to loss in a culture. This is **cultural loss** (Haviland et al, 2014).

Cultural loss: Change resulting in the loss of a cultural tradition

Acculturation: A merging of cultures as a result of prolonged contact

A final mechanism of cultural change is acculturation. **Acculturation** occurs when different cultures come into intensive firsthand contact, with subsequent changes in the original cultural patterns of one or both (Haviland et al., 2014). Acculturation implies a mutual influence in which elements of the two cultures mingle and merge. It has been hypothesized that in order for acculturation to occur, some relative cultural equality has to exist between the giving and the receiving cultures. Acculturation is a complex cultural change concept, with different anthropologists proposing different outcomes. For example, J.W. Berry (1986) suggested there are four possible outcomes of the acculturation process: assimilation, integration, rejection, or marginalization.

Box 5.4
What Do You Say?

UNESCO Preserves Djenné, Mali

Djenné, Mali, is one of the oldest towns in Sub-Saharan Africa. Inhabited since 250 B.C., the area is an ensemble of nearly 2,000 houses, a mosque, and other civic buildings that over many years have represented typical Islamic architecture in sub-Saharan Africa. Characterized by the intensive and remarkable use of earth, the architecture of the entire town, with a distinctive style of buttresses and intricate facades, contains great monumental and religious value. Excavations carried out in 1977, 1981, 1996, and 1997 revealed an extraordinary page of human history—of a long-gone pre-Islamic civilization. So significant is this ancient city that to protect it from harm, in 1988, the United Nations Educational, Scientific, and Cultural Organization (UNESCO) declared Djennéa a World Heritage Site.

Abba Maiga stood in his dirt courtyard in Djenné, seething over the fact that his 150-year-old mud house is so culturally precious he is not allowed to update it—no tile floors, no screen doors, no shower. This is because the guidelines established by UNESCO demand that any reconstruction not substantially alter the original. "But we want development, more space, new appliances, things that are modern" (from MacFarquhar, 2011). He and his fellow Djenné residents feel their lives are frozen in time like pieces in a museum so that visitors can come and gawk.

1. What are the goals of the World Heritage Site program? Check out the site http://whc.unesco.org and read about the current list of sites and the criteria for being on the list.
2. What do you think are the advantages and disadvantages of the program? Can the disadvantages be reduced or eliminated and still maintain the advantages?
3. How is Djenné an example of cultural loss? Can you think of areas near you where tourism is an example of cultural loss?

Assimilation is the first outcome from acculturation. While assimilation can happen at the individual level, here we are referring to the process whereby a minority group gradually adopts the customs and attitudes of the prevailing dominant group. For example, in considering mass tourism, in order to succeed, sometimes the tourism hosts (in this case a minority group) must adopt the expectations and attitudes of the tourists (the majority group).

Assimilation: To adopt the ways of the main culture

Figure 5.3. Even wildlife has needed to assimilate to the world of the tourist.

Integration is another way a culture can change as a result of acculturation. When integration results, there is a merging of the two cultures. This is the "melting pot" idea. We usually refer to integration as the

Integration: Combining parts so they form a new whole

bringing of people of different racial or ethnic groups into unrestricted and equal association. For an example, consider the leisure organizations to which you belong. Are they integrated? The word integration comes from the Latin word *integer*, meaning whole; thus, another way of thinking about integration of cultures is to describe them as becoming whole and unified.

Rejection, on the other hand, is directly opposite of integration. When rejection results from the prolonged contact between two cultures, each individual culture reaffirms its own traditions and ways, rejecting those of the other culture. One example might be the Amish groups in North America that maintain a principled rejection of modernity. As distinct from the majority cultures of North America, Amish leisure, for the most part, is not commercialized and remains connected to nature. It is almost always community oriented, revolving around family and friends.

Rejection: Denial and avoidance of others

Marginalization: To relegate to an unimportant or powerless position within a group

Finally, **marginalization** is the label applied to relegating a group to a lower or outer edge. Common examples of marginalized groups in our societies have been persons living with disabilities, women, racial minorities, the poor, children, the elderly, single parents, and even white men. Yet, marginalization does not only refer to groups of people; we can also find examples in other types of groups.

Let's consider works of art as an example. If you visit galleries and museums in North America, you'll notice an illustration of marginalized art. The Metropolitan Museum of Art (2008) in New York City, for instance, was having difficulties with its considerable yet undercataloged and minimally displayed holdings of Islamic art. This collection was closed in 2003 for renovation and expansion as a way to correct this marginalization. The new galleries reopened in 2011 featuring art of the Arab Lands: Turkey, Iran, Central Asia, and South Asia. Of course, the former treatment of the collection was not only the museum's fault, as Western audiences also hold a cultural bias against appreciating the aesthetic of traditional Islamic art forms like ceramics, textiles and calligraphy. Western museum visitors see these as decorative arts, and prefer the high art of three-dimensional sculpture and easel painting.

Hunches About the Earliest Human Cultures

In Chapter 1, we mentioned the artistic legacy of human cultures dating back 45,000 years ago. What else do we know about these ancient cultures that might illuminate our understanding of the leisure of present human cultures? Let's pinpoint the Paleolithic Period, because it covers the greatest portion of all humanity's time, roughly 99%. Paleolithic refers to the cultural period of the Stone Age, beginning with the earliest chipped stone tools, about 750,000 years ago, until the beginning of the Mesolithic Period, about 15,000 years ago. During this time, humans in mostly what today is Africa and Asia were grouped together in small-scale societies and subsisted by gathering plants and hunting or scavenging wild animals. Archeologists believe they ate what was available and then moved on, building shelters only if there was enough food in an area to last awhile.

Due to a lack of written records from this time period, nearly all of our knowledge of Paleolithic human culture and way of life comes from anthropological comparisons to more recent hunter-gatherer cultures. Accordingly comes one of the more fascinating conjectures about leisure at this time. For example, a standard anthropological view is that because they were constantly on the move in search of food for subsistence survival, Paleolithic people must have lacked free time. Yet, there is an alternative view. Marshall Sahlins (1988), an American anthropologist, has suggested Stone Age people were in fact the original leisure society.

Sahlins based his claim on two suppositions. First, Paleolithic people may not have spent as much time hunting and gathering food as formerly assumed. Second, Paleolithic people had comparatively few material goods and thus were free from the efforts of protecting and maintaining them. Let's ponder each suggestion in turn.

First, Sahlins cited research about two hunter-gatherer groups living in Australia in the 1960s as examples of what life could have been like for Paleolithic people. The results are surprising. As shown in Figure 5.4, the number of hours per day spent by one of the groups in hunting and gathering activities was not that much. The average length of time each person spent per day collecting and preparing food was three to four hours. The most obvious conclusion Sahlins drew from these data was the people did not have to work hard to survive, particularly by contemporary standards. What might they have done in the time remaining? As indicated in Figure 5.5 much of the time freed from the necessities of survival could have been spent in rest and sleep. According to Sahlins, other free-time activities may have included chatting, gossiping, and general sociability.

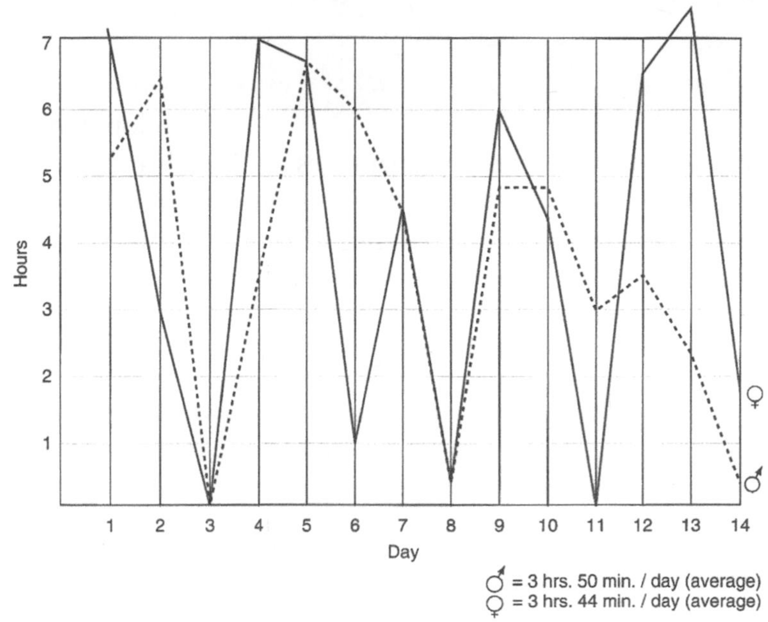

Figure 5.4. The hours per day spent in hunting and gathering activities by one of Sahlins' groups.

Sahlins' second supposition about the leisure of Paleolithic cultures has to do with what we might call materialism. In contrast to affluent societies today, with their focus on the acquisition of stuff, early people possessed very little. Most likely their possessions included a few pieces of clothing, portable housing materials, a few ornaments, spare flints, some medicinal quartz, a few tools and weapons, and a skin bag to hold it all. In contrast to the amount of possessions we have today, and the time we spend purchasing, repairing, cleaning, putting away, transporting, sorting, finding, protecting, and storing it all, Sahlins reasoned Paleolithic people were comparatively free. Although many might consider this prehistoric culture poor, another view is to think of them as rich in leisure.

Day	Men's Average		Women's Average
1	2' 15"		2' 45"
2	1' 30"		1' 0"
3		Most of day	
4		Intermittent	
5		Intermittent and most of late afternoon	
6		Most of the day	
7		Several hour	
8	2' 0"		2' 0"
9	50"		50"
10		Afternoon	
11		Afternoon	
12		Intermittent, afternoon	
13	--		--
14	3' 15"		3' 15"

Figure 5.5. Amount of daytime devoted to sleep. According to Sahlins' hypothesis, free-time activities could have also included chatting and general sociability.

Cultural Development and Leisure

The story of humankind after these prehistoric times is one of cultural development. **Development** simply means the extent to which the resources of a group have been brought into full productivity. In common usage, cultural development refers to economic growth and modernization. Today, cultures can be identified according to the extent of their development. In this final section of the chapter we discuss what cultural development means to the expression of leisure. The conclusion is there are both advantages and disadvantages.

Development: The process of improving the material conditions of people through the use of knowledge and technology

Developing was the term U.S. President Harry S. Truman introduced in 1949 as a replacement for *backward*, the unflattering reference then in use. Since then, grappling with how to label world cultures according to the amount of development has continued. For example, various international organizations have started to use the term "less economically developed country" (LEDCs) for the poorest nations, which restricts the concept to just gross domestic product (Table 5.3).

Table 5.3
Annual Gross Domestic Product per Capita for Selected Countries, 2014 (World Bank, 2016)

More Than $55,000 (ranked highest to lowest)	Between $55,000 and $45,000 (ranked highest to lowest)	Less than $1,500 (ranked highest to lowest)
Qatar ($140,649)	United States ($54,629)	Ethiopia ($1,499)
Macao SAR, China	Saudi Arabia	Madagascar
Luxembourg	Ireland	Comoros
Singapore	Netherlands	Guinea
Kuwait	Austria	Mozambique
Brunei	Germany	Niger
United Arab Emirates	Australia	Liberia
Norway	Denmark	Malawi
Switzerland	Bahrain	Congo, Democratic Republic
Hong Kong SAR, China	Sweden	Central African Republic

In addition to GDP income per capita, today the development of a country is measured with other statistical indexes, including population growth, industrialization, environmental degradation, expenditures for education, life expectancy, rate of literacy, adolescent fertility rate, and many others.

Cultural Vitality

In fact, according to the United Nations, development is measured as a combination of three basic factors: economic, social, and demographic. Several international organizations have worked on using these factors to determine an overall "score" of cultural development.

For example, the Quality of Life Index, produced by the website *Numbeo* (2012) incorporates the indicators of cost of living, property prices, traffic, crime, health care, pollution, and others to determine that Switzerland, Germany, and Norway are the most highly developed cultures. Also, the OECD (2012) sponsors an interactive calculation for cultural vitality that is based on the indicators of housing, education, environment, civic engagement, health, life satisfaction, and work-life balance. Called the "Better Life Initiative," the goal is to understand what drives the well-being of people and nations, and what needs to be done to achieve greater progress through policy making. Uniquely, on the website, you can prioritize the indicators and 111 countries are ranked accordingly. As well, the "Human Development

Index (HDI)," sponsored by the United Nations, combines seven indicators into the three dimensions of health, education, and living standards to produce a composite score. For example, in 2015, Norway, Australia, and Switzerland ranked the highest for these criteria on the HDI.

Another way to interpret development is to notice how leisure relates to the quality of living cross-culturally. For example, in developing countries such as Thailand, Philippines, and Indonesia, leisure is richly laced with the traditions and folkways of the culture. Music, dance, and art forms are woven into the fabric of society in ways uncommon in more developed countries such as Australia and Canada.

One of the ways developing countries attempt to make progress and become more developed is to embrace new income-generating efforts that sometimes mean the ruin of traditions and folkways. On the other hand, traditional arts and crafts are possibly updated and exported as a result of development. As illustration, today, perhaps the single largest use of leisure as a development tool is tourism. In such countries as Malaysia, which over the past 25 years has raised its level of development, tourism is a leading foreign exchange earner and thus a prime motivator for enhancing the country's infrastructure.

Leisure relates to development in other ways, as well. Basically, leisure can be an important source of growth as it widens a culture's relationship to the environment, builds social identity and harmony, and contributes other provisions of well-being. For example, research by Ryff and Keyes (1995) found individual self-acceptance, positive relationships with others, autonomy, purpose in life, and personal growth to be associated with a culture's well-being. Also, Diener and Diener (1995) showed that individualism, human rights, and social equality were also decisive factors. These are all features that can be produced by a vibrant leisure culture.

Box 5.5
Web Explore

The Material World

In an unprecedented effort, 16 of the world's foremost photographers traveled to 30 nations around the globe to live for a week with families that were statistically average for that nation. At the end of each visit, photographers and families collaborated on a remarkable portrait of the family members, outside their home, surrounded by all of their possessions. The project was published in a book in 1995, so check it out for yourself to appreciate the role of leisure in cultural development. Study the photos on these websites for evidence of the changing nature of leisure between more and less developed countries: http://menzelphoto.photoshelter.com/gallery-collection/Material-World-A-Global-Family-Portrait-by-Country/C0000d0DI3dBy4mQ, or http://www.npr.org/sections/pictureshow/2010/08/10/129113632/picturingpossessions.

Modernity

Another way to explore leisure and cultural development is via the concept of modernity. **Modernization** is the transformation from a traditional, rural, agrarian society to a secular, urban, industrial society. It results in the multiplying of institutions as the simple structures of traditional societies are transformed into complex ones. This means that the process of modernizing is a progression through stages of increasing complexity of technology and social organization. Modernization can be considered the ultimate goal of cultural development.

Modernization: A transition involving the implementation of recent techniques, methods, or ideas

Unfortunately, this suggests that "becoming modern" carries a connotation of "becoming like us" because of the idea that modernization is a desired goal of underdeveloped societies. Accordingly, there is a clear implication that not being like us is to be antiquated and obsolete. We realize this perspective is an ethnocentric one, because it insists these other societies must be changed to be more modern, and like us, irrespective of other considerations, including traditional ways of life.

Box 5.6
In Your Own Experience

An Ethnocentric Perspective

Check those statements you think indicate an ethnocentric perspective:

[ ] When reading it is natural to read from left to right and from top to bottom.

[ ] On a toggle switch the universal position for "on" is up.

[ ] Placing an "X" in a box indicates acceptance of that item.

[ ] Using chopsticks at every meal to eat is silly.

[ ] In Britain, drivers drive on the wrong side of the road.

Answers: All statements reflect ethnocentricity. For example, in some countries the switch position for "on" is down, and in Japan placing an "X" in a box indicates nonacceptance.

Even though people in every culture, developed and undeveloped, have at least some feelings of **ethnocentricity**, it seems Western cultures are particularly good examples. Let's consider football. Across the world, there are several different versions of football. That played in Australia is different from that played in the U.S., and the football played in numerous other countries is labeled soccer by Americans—not football at all, according to their perspective.

Ethnocentricity: The belief that your own cultural or ethnic group is superior to that of another

Since an ethnocentric view of modernization is less useful, then, let's explore a more anthropologically sound one. The process of modernization may be best understood as made up of four sub-processes: technological development, agricultural development, industrialization, and urbanization (Haviland et al., 2014). These elements are interrelated and occur simultaneously. First, with modernization, traditional knowledge and techniques are replaced by scientific knowledge and techniques. Likewise, the culture shifts from an emphasis on subsistence farming to commercial farming. Industrialization occurs when work is done by machines rather than by humans and animals, and the population generally moves from rural settlements into cities.

Modernization suggests other changes, as well. For example, political parties and some sort of electoral system likely appears, along with a bureaucracy. There is also usually an expansion of learning opportunities and literacy increases. Typically, there are improvements in health care, yet the environment usually becomes more precious as industrial pollution renders the air and water and soil quality and supplies more fragile. People's daily lives change as a result of modernization too. With modernity we become busier as time efficiency becomes more important. In fact, one of the most noticeable signs of modernity is that efficiency becomes a very important cultural value (Godbey, 2006).

The impact of modernization can be extreme and dramatic, and cultures may not always be better off as a result. For example, as modernization increases within a society, the individual becomes that much more important, eventually replacing the family or community as the fundamental unit of society. This critique of modernization can be expressed in the concept of **postmodernism**. The term is very slippery to define because it can mean different things when applied to literature, art, philosophy, and even architecture.

Postmodernism: Skeptical reaction to modernism

Postmodernism in the sense we use it here is largely a reaction to the assumed certainty of modernity. It is based on the position that reality is not mirrored in human understanding of it, but is rather constructed as the mind tries to understand its own personal reality. Postmodernism is therefore skeptical of explanations that claim to be valid for all groups, cultures, traditions, or races, and instead focuses on the relative truths of each person.

In terms of cultural development, postmodernism refers to the undesirable changes wrought by modernization. We can all readily observe that in the last few decades the nature of modern societies has changed dramatically. Social theorists have commented about these changes by applying such labels as a "media society," a "society of spectacle," and a "consumer society." Today, modern cultures are indeed dominated by consumption, media, and flashiness. From a postmodern perspective this means we live in a fragmented way. Old identities and common interests have become diffused.

Figure 5.6. One event that perhaps argues against postmodernity is the weekly "drumming the sun down" informal gathering that takes place on many beaches on the west coast of Florida. This one is on Siesta Key Beach, Sarasota. © Patricia D. Setser, 2016

Indeed, much of what is written these days about postmodernism and leisure carries a negative tone, as though leisure has lost something as a result of modernism. Leisure in modern societies does appear to be more commercial, diverse, and sped up—to the detriment of community, family, and social group. Modern leisure is more of a competition to collect fun experiences and recreational equipment. As well, modern leisure is expected to be more concerned with individual self-fulfillment, self-reliance, and image. This, a postmodernist perspective maintains, renders modern leisure to be more cherished, as it has to compete with the busyness of work and responsibilities. For example, according to some scholars our modern "day-to-day lives have been reduced to sedentary, boring routines, largely devoid of excitement, challenge, and personal growth" (Kernan & Domzal, 2000, p. 79).

Not everyone agrees the condition of leisure in modern cultures is as described by postmodernism, however. Some continue to argue that leisure is largely unchanged by progress. For example, Crouch and Tomlinson (1994) suggest leisure is still lived in communities and in family and social groups, and is not dependent on commodities and media. Similarly, Kelly (1999) contends most leisure still takes place in and around the home and serves to integrate communities and personal relationships.

What We Understand About Leisure's Cultural Meaning

From the perspective of anthropology, leisure can be understood as a significant cultural phenomenon. That is, leisure helps shape a culture, and like a reflection in the mirror, leisure is a result of a culture's shape. After studying this chapter, you should know the following:

1. As a cultural prodigy, leisure is characterized as shared, learned, based on symbols, and integrated. **Describe how leisure is characterized by each of these four qualities:**

____

____

2. Leisure contributes to and is affected by the cultural change mechanisms of innovation, diffusion, loss, and acculturation.
   Give a leisure example of each of these four cultural change mechanisms:
   ____
   ____

3. Acculturation is a complex cultural change concept, with the possible outcomes of assimilation, integration, rejection, or marginalization.
   Give an example of how leisure relates to each of these four cultural change outcomes:
   ____
   ____

4. Contrary to the standard view, more recent data suggest prehistoric people had abundant free time and spent it relaxing.
   Explain this via the writings of Sahlens:
   ____
   ____

5. Leisure can contribute to cultural development. How?
   Give one example from your own community or campus:
   ____
   ____

6. Leisure is subject to the processes of modernization. The result may be both good and bad. How?
   Give an example for both the bad and good outcomes of modernization from your own community or campus:
   ____
   ____

References

Berry, J. W. (1986). The acculturation process and refugee behavior. In C. I. Williams & J. Westermeyer (Eds.), *Refugee mental health in resettlement countries* (pp. 25–37). New York, NY: Hemisphere.

ChartsBin. (n.d.). Most popular sports by country. Retrieved from http://chartsbin.com/view/33104>

Chick, G. E. (1995). The anthropology of leisure: Past, present, and future research. In L. A. Barnett (Ed.), *Research about leisure: Past, present, and future.* Urbana, IL: Sagamore.

Cross, G. (1990). *A social history of leisure since 1600.* State College, PA: Venture.

Crouch, D., & Tomlinson, A. (1994). Collective self-generated consumption: Leisure, space, and cultural identity in late modernity. In I. Henry (Ed.), *Leisure: Modernity, postmodernity, and lifestyles* (Publication No. 48, pp. 309-321). Brighton, UK: Leisure Studies Association.

deGrazia, S. (1962). *Of time, work, and leisure.* New York, NY: Twentieth Century Fund.

Diener, E., & Diener, M. (1995). Cross-cultural correlates of life satisfaction and self-esteem. *Journal of Personality and Social Psychology, 68,* 653–663.

Godbey, G. (2006). *Leisure and leisure services in the 21st century: Toward mid-century.* State College, PA: Venture.

Haviland, W. A., Prins, H. E. L., McBride, B., & Walrath, D. (2014). *Cultural anthropology: The human challenge* (14th ed.). Belmont, CA: Wadsworth.

Heider, K. (1977). From Javanese to Dani: The translation of a game. In P. Stevens (Ed.), *Studies in the anthropology of play.* West Point, NY: Leisure Press.

Human Development Report. (2015). Sustaining human progress: Reducing vulnerabilities and building resilience. HDRO (Human Development Report Office) United Nations Development Programme. Retrieved from http://hdr.undp.org/sites/default/files/2015_human_development_report.pdf

Jung, B. (Winter 1992). Economic, social, and political conditions for enjoyment of leisure in Central and Eastern Europe of 1992: The Polish perspective. *World Leisure and Recreation Association Magazine*, 8–12.

Kelly, J. (1999). Leisure and society: A dialectical analysis. In E. L. Jackson & T. L. Burton (Eds.), *Leisure studies: Prospects for the Twenty-first Century* (pp. 53–68). State College, PA: Venture.

Kernan, J. B., & Domzal, T. J. (2000). Getting a life: Homo ludens as postmodern identity. *Journal of Travel and Tourism Marketing, 8*(4), 79–84.

Linton, R. (1936). *The study of man: An introduction*. New York, NY: Appleton.

MacFarquhar, N. (January 8, 2011). Mali city rankled by rules for life in spotlight. *The New York Times*. Retrieved from http://www.nytimes.com/2011/01/09/world/africa/09mali.html?pagewanted=all.

McDonald's. (2014). The statistics portal. Retrieved from http://www.statista.com/topics/1444/mcdonalds/

Metropolitan Museum of Art. (2008). Introduction to Islamic art. Retrieved from http://www.metmuseum.org/Works_of_Art/islamic_art

Nielsen Media Research. (2009). Television audience report. Retrieved from http://blog.nielsen.com/nielsenwire/media_entertainment/more-than-half-the-homes-in-us-have-three-or-more-tvs/

Nielsen Media Research. (2016). Nielsen estimates 118.4 million TV homes in the U.S for the 2016–17 TV season. Retrieved from http://www.nielsen.com/us/en/insights/news/2016/nielsen-estimates-118-4-million-tv-homes-in-the-us--for-the-2016-17-season.html

Numbeo. (2012). Quality of life. Retrieved from http://www.numbeo.com/quality-of-life/

Organisation for Economic Cooperation and Development (OECD). (2011). Society at a Glance 2011: OECD social indicators. Retrieved from www.oecd.org/els/social/indicators/SAG

Organisation for Economic Cooperation and Development (OECD). (2012). Better life initiative. Retrieved from http://www.oecdbetterlifeindex.org/

Ryff, C. D., & Keyes, C. L. M. (1995). The structure of psychological well-being revisited. *Journal of Personality and Social Psychology, 69*, 719–727.

Sahlins, M. (1988). The original affluent society. In J. B. Cole (Ed.), *Anthropology for the nineties* (pp. 253–274). New York, NY: The Free Press.

Tsai, E. H. (2000). The influence of acculturation on perception of leisure constraints of Chinese immigrants. *World Leisure, 3*, 33–41.

UNESCO. (2009). The 2009 UNESCO framework for cultural statistics. Retrieved from www.uis.unesco.org/Library/Documents/FCS09_EN.pdf

White, L. (1959). *The evolution of culture: The development of civilization to the fall of Rome*. New York, NY: McGraw-Hill.

World Bank. (2016). GDP per capita. Retrieved from http://data.worldbank.org/indicator/NY.GDP.PCAP.PP.CD?order=wbapi_data_value_2014%20wbapi_data_value%20wbapi_data_value-last&sort=desc

Leisure's Geography

CHAPTER 6

What is leisure's geographical significance?

Leisure is expressed in both space and place, which are basic concepts of geography.

How is leisure expressed in space?

Leisure participation is distributed according to spatial pattern, density, and concentration.

How is leisure expressed in place?

People have a strong emotional attachment to specific leisure places.

What is the future of leisure's geography?

Without wise management many leisure expressions will be lost due to the demise of leisure space and place resources.

Marti Erickson always carries a collapsible chair in her car. When she is having a particularly bad day, she finds a grassy spot, plops down, breathes deeply and soon is soothed by the nature around her. Research over the past decade indicates Marti is not alone (Louv, 2012). Time spent in nature, or nature-based design at home, work, or the hospital is helpful in reducing stress and depression, producing faster healing, and lessening the need for pain medication.

Figure 6.1. While exact numbers are difficult to determine, participation in backyard leisure pursuits is perhaps the most predominant example of the relationship between leisure and geography.

Geography: The study of earth and its life

But the link between leisure and nature is just part of the geography story. Indeed, all leisure expression is based in geography. For example, we know that for suburban Americans, the backyard is the most frequently used space and place for family pastimes. We also know that we feel differently when we're in a large crowd at a football game than when we're walking alone along a beach.

Geography is the scientific study of where things are located on the earth's surface and why (Rubenstein, 2003). Specifically, geographers investigate the way people respond to place and how space is shaped by human behavior (Smale, 1999). The famous German philosopher Immanuel Kant (1724–1804) compared the concern of geography for space with the concern of history for time. Whereas historians identify the dates of important events and explain why human activities follow one another across time, geographers identify the location of important places and explain why human activities are located beside one another in space. That is, historians ask when and why; geographers ask where and why (Rubenstein, 2003).

In this chapter, we explore ways we can understand leisure as a geographical concept. These are organized according to the concepts of space and place. We conclude the chapter by reviewing a particularly relevant geographic leisure concern: environmental impact.

Box 6.1
In Your Own Experience

Where Is Your Best Place?

There are several online quizzes to help you determine where in the U.S. and other countries you should live in order to thrive. Also, some sites will help you select a vacation spot, or a retirement location. Take a couple of these quizzes, and then consider how much of your choices are due to your leisure interests. What other factors about geography did the quizzes use to determine your best spot? To begin, you could try these:

https://internationalliving.com/2015/05/take-the-45-second-quiz-and-find-your-perfect-place-to-live-overseas/

http://www.bestplaces.net/fybp/

http://www.kiplinger.com/tool/real-estate/T006-S001-find-your-best-city/

http://www.quizrocket.com/where-should-i-live-quiz

http://besttripchoices.com/

Leisure as Space

In fact, leisure takes up quite a bit of space. For example, just about every country in the world maintains national parks, with the most being in Australia (685 parks), China (208 parks), and Thailand (138 parks) (International Union for Conservation of Nature, 2015). To understand more about leisure as space, we consider the basic principles of density, concentration, and pattern.

First, the frequency with which something occurs in space is its **density**. This frequency of something in space could be people, houses, cars, softball fields, wilderness areas, or almost anything. Density can be measured in square kilometers, square miles, hectares, acres, and other units of measurement.

Density: The frequency with which something occurs in space

Concentration is the extent of a feature's spread over space. If the objects in an area are close together, they are clustered, or if they are far apart, they are dispersed. It can be difficult to distinguish density and concentration, but they are not the same concepts. For example, in North America, both the density and concentration of major-league baseball teams changed in the second half of the 20th Century. That is, between 1952 and 2000, the number of teams expanded from 16 to 30, thus increasing the density. Also, and at the same time, six of the 16 original 1952 teams by 2000 had moved from a concentration in the northeastern U.S. to the west coast, the southeast, and Canada, thus dispersing their concentration.

Concentration: The extent of a feature's spread over space

The third property of leisure space is pattern. **Pattern** is the geometric arrangement of objects in space. That is, objects such as boat slips at a marina and campsites at a campground can be arranged linearly, in squares, in circles, and so on.

Pattern: Geometric arrangement of objects in space

There are many ways to demonstrate the concepts of density, concentration, and pattern of leisure in space. We'll consider two: crowding and distance.

Figure 6.2. Aerial view of the campground at Kentucky Horse Park, near Lexington, KY. What would you say is the geographical pattern for camping at this state park? Source: Kentucky Horse Park Foundation

Crowding

All of us have probably noticed that parks are becoming more crowded. To return to a U.S. national parks illustration, the number of visits in 1990 was approximately 258 million, compared to over 305 million visits in 2015 (National Park Service, 2016). As the Park Service likes to point out, that's more people than went to every single Disney park, NFL, NBA and MLB game, and NASCAR race combined (National Public Radio, 2016).

Fortunately, this means more people are enjoying these important leisure resources, but unfortunately, **crowding** also means they may be experiencing traffic congestion, jammed parking lots, cramped campgrounds, long lines for services, overworked rangers, more stringent rules, higher fees, conflict among visitors, and degraded facilities (Lime, 1996).

Crowding: A subjective and negative judgment about the number of objects (such as people) in a given space

Of course, determining what is crowded is a value judgment. That is, when the number of visitors to recreation areas (density) increases to a point where visitors and managers perceive its use is interfered with, the result is crowding. Whereas density is a neutral concept, crowding is a negative evaluation of density. For example, visitors to the Great Smokey Mountains National Park in Tennessee and North Carolina are advised how to avoid crowds by visiting during the low season (winter and spring). This advice presumes crowded mountains are undesirable.

Researchers in outdoor recreation study how we determine crowding. For example, they have found perceptions of crowding can result from the personal characteristics of visitors, the characteristics of other visitors encountered, and the nature of the outdoor setting. Let's discuss each of these determinants in turn.

First, several studies have demonstrated that differences in visitor motivations are the source of perceptions of crowding. For example, a study of visitors to the Buffalo National River in Arkansas (Ditton, Fedler, & Graef, 1983) found wide differences in perceived crowding among a sample of river floaters. Those visitors who felt crowded reported significantly higher ratings on the motivation "to get away from other people." Other visitors who did not feel crowded while floating down the river rated the motivation "to be part of a group" higher.

Box 6.2 What Do You Say?

Crowds in U.S. National Parks

On Memorial Day 2015, the Utah Highway Patrol closed the entrance to Arches National Park. The line of cars waiting to get into the park was over a mile long. Within the park, at the Devils Garden trailhead, 300 cars were wedged into 190 spaces, and on the road to Delicate Arch, parked cars lined both sides of the road for half a mile leading up to the parking area.

Also in Utah, Zion National Park—famous for its jaw-dropping, red sandstone cliffs and colorful panoramic views—recently had lines 300 people deep just to get on a shuttle bus that goes from the parking area to the visitors' center.

1. All of these examples represent experiences people do not expect, nor what managers want to provide in national parks. So what are the solutions? Begin by sharing with classmates your visits to national parks and the presence (or not) of crowding.
2. What are some of the negative consequences of crowding in the parks, to the leisure experience, as well as to the parks themselves? Check the Internet for some examples of these.
3. Finally, do an Internet search for solution ideas. What have the various national parks tried to do to reduce the experience of crowding? Are all national parks trying the same things? How successful have the efforts been?

Source: National Park Service, 2016; National Public Radio, 2016; Photo: CBS News

In terms of the characteristics of other visitors encountered, it seems only reasonable to think that tolerance for being with lots of other people in a leisure setting would depend on what these other people were like. For example, studies in the Boundary Waters Canoe Area in Minnesota found paddling canoeists sharply disliked encountering motorboats, were less resentful of encountering motorized canoes, and were relatively tolerant of at least some other paddled canoes (Manning, 1999).

The third factor determining perceptions of crowding is situation specific. From my own interests in camping, I know I have a sliding scale for feeling crowded depending on the type of campground. In a highly developed RV campground, I'm much more tolerant of the presence of other people than I am in a primitive backcountry campground. Certain design aspects of a site, such as trees, rocks, or hedges between sites can also affect one's sense of campground crowding. As well, research has shown the level of disturbance of the leisure area determines the perception of crowding. That is, those trails, campsites, and rivers trashed from overuse are perceived as more crowded (Vaske, Graef, & Dempster, 1982).

Distance

In addition to crowding, distance is another concept of geographic space applicable to leisure. Are we more likely to work out at the gym every day if it is across the street from our house, across town, or across the region? How fantastic does the gym need to be for us to be willing to travel across our region to use it? Distance influences our leisure behavior.

Box 6.3
By The Numbers

Preferred Travel Time to Local Sites

Specialty Shop (18 min.)
Restaurant/Cafe (17 min.)
Beauty Salon (14 min.)
Pub/Bar (14 min.)
Gym/sports Club (12 min.)
Yoga Class (12 min.)

Source: Marchant, 2014

For example, a neighborhood park will likely attract larger numbers of users who live nearby, but participation drops off by these same users as distance to a shopping center or theme park increases. As well, participation in a leisure facility is a combination of the distance from the user's residence and the type of facility. That is, as a site's appeal becomes more specialized, smaller proportions of people are willing to travel farther distances. Geographers call this distance decay. The basic principle of **distance decay** is that different recreational sites have varying abilities to draw participants to them according to distance (Smale, 1999).

Distance decay: Interaction between two locales declines as the distance between them increases.

But, of course, it is not always so simple. In today's world, more rapid connections among places have reduced the distance between them, not literally, of course, but in the effort needed to get there. Geographers call this **space-time compression**. Thanks to advances in transportation and communication, distant places seem less remote and more accessible to us. Thus, distances to recreational sites might be perceived in terms of time or cost rather than by miles or kilometers.

Space-time compression: Processes that accelerate the experience of time and thus reduce the significance of distance

The basic principle of space-time compression suggests that if the distance to a recreation site is perceived to be less (or greater) than its actual physical distance, the perception may have more influence on potential participation in the leisure pursuit than does the actual distance. Even though many recreation sites, such as parks (Table 6.1) are designed according to distance from expected users, the perception of distance is what actually controls leisure behavior.

Table 6.1
Types of Parks According to Distance from Expected Users

Park Type	Definition	Scope of Services	Example
Mini-park	Small – up to 1 acre	To be within a 10-minute walk	Park Ridge Park, Bloomington, Indiana
Neighborhood park	Serves up to 5,000 people in an immediate locale	To serve a single neighborhood	Huber Village Park, Westerville, Ohio
Community/City park	Serves an entire town	To serve multiple neighborhoods	Balboa Park, San Diego, California
Regional park	Serves users from several communities and rural areas. Often governed by coalitions of governments	To serve users from a wide area	Fort De Soto Island Park, Tampa Bay area, Florida
State/Provincial park	Serves an even broader jurisdiction, with historic or natural significance. Governed by state or provincial governments	More remote from population centers	Amherst Shore Provincial Park, Nova Scotia
National park	An area of special scenic, historic, or scientific importance set aside and maintained by a national government	To protect an important resource and also provide enjoyment for visitors	Iguazú National Park, Argentina
Linear park	Area designated for walking, biking, skiing, horseback riding, driving, etc.	To provide for travel-related, often self-propelled leisure	Cape Cod Rail Trail, Massachusetts

One issue that reflects both the concepts of distance decay and space-time compression, is urban sprawl. **Urban sprawl** is an expansion of low-density development outward from a city. In some cases, it results from a desire for larger living space and more private residential amenities. Yet, urban sprawl has been correlated with added energy use, pollution, and traffic congestion. Also, by increasing the physical and environmental "footprints" of metropolitan areas, urban sprawl leads to the destruction of wildlife habitat and to the fragmentation of remaining natural areas. Typified by predominantly auto-dependent development of housing, shopping centers, and fast food chains, urban sprawl is increasing in North America, as well as in Africa, Australia, Europe, and Asia.

Urban sprawl: The uncontrolled expansion of urban areas

Because urban sprawl leads to a weakening of community distinctiveness and cohesiveness, criticism concludes there is a decline of leisure expressions and resources as well. Perhaps because urban sprawl results in fewer pedestrian and bicycle-friendly neighborhoods, social fragmentation is also cited. Neighborhoods do not have compact houses with front porches, a corner store, or a school two blocks away. Public spaces such as parks are replaced with private spaces such as fenced-in yards.

Leisure as Place

In addition to the importance of space, we have a strong sense of place in our leisure. That is, we have feelings for particular places. Graceland in Memphis, Yankee Stadium in New York City, Vieux-Quebec in Quebec City, and Horseshoe Falls at Niagara are all particular places to which many people attach strong personal meaning.

According to eminent geographer Yi-Fu Tuan both space and place are imbued with human emotions. To distinguish, he suggests while space represents freedom to us, place is our security; we long for the one and are attached to the other. To Tuan, our sense of place is not only for monuments, cultural buildings, or spectacular scenic areas, but also for such artifacts as fireplaces and armchairs. For Tuan himself, the most significant place for his emotions is the desert. For example, upon awakening on a camping trip in Death Valley in California, he recalls, "I awoke to lunar beauty," to a "phantasmagoria of shimmering mauves, purples, and bright golds theatrically illuminated" (Tuan, 1977, p. 32).

Box 6.4
In Profile

Yi-Fu Tuan

Yi-Fu Tuan is a Chinese-American geographer famous for pioneering the field of human geography and merging it with philosophy, art, theatre, anthropology, psychology, and religion. This formed what is known as humanist geography. Humanist geography has become the branch of geography that studies how humans inhabit and shape the earth, not just with their bodies, but also with their emotions, minds, and spirits. Tuan's many essays and books published over the past 35 years have been pivotal in moving geography into this new discipline that stresses people's perceptions, creativity, personal beliefs, and experiences in developing attitudes on their environments.

We are not limited only to the visual for our sense of place. The quality of smell is also important. Scholars refer to this as **smellscape**, a concept suggesting, "like visual impressions, smells may be spatially ordered or place related" (Porteous, 1985, p. 359). Smells give character to places, making them distinctive and thus easier to identify and remember (Tuan, 1977). Think of the community gym you knew as a youth. Do you associate this memory with a smell? Is your memory a positive one?

Smellscape: Smells are place related and elicit emotional responses

There is perhaps no better illustration of smellscape than its calculated management at Disney's theme parks. For example, in Epcot, the simulated hang glider ride *Soarin* (the "Around the World" version opened in June 2016) includes the smell of freshly cut roses as you soar over the Taj Mahal, a whiff of the ocean over Fiji, and other artificially produced scents. In the Magic Kingdom, *Frontierland* smells like leather and gun smoke (and roasted turkey legs), and the attraction *Pirates of the Caribbean* smells of musty spices—all this in an effort to enhance visitors' experiences. Indeed, many promoters of tourism fill their marketing with the aromatic framing of places. This is tricky, of course, because just as beauty is in the eye of the beholder, so, too, are aromas in the individual nose.

In addition to sight and smell, our emotional attachment to specific places is based on a kinesthetic sense. For example, the vast number of mountain resorts is testimony to the fact that many of us feel emotionally elevated at moderately high altitudes. When you ask people who love the mountains to explain what is so special there, the reply is likely to be "just something in the air." This is perhaps why we associate certain spiritual practices, such as meditation, with high mountains.

Do we have to physically be in a place in order to become attached to it? Is there a virtual geography? Virtual geography has application in education, emergency management, agriculture, city planning, and tourism, but perhaps a useful example here is the virtual community of *Second Life (SL)*. According to Harrison (2009), "*SL* is an Internet-based graphical interface, three-dimensional computer-mediated communication space in which residents can buy and sell land to create virtual landscapes of recreation, communication, and commerce" (p. 82). *Second Life* was first launched in 2003 and by 2013 had 1 million regular users (Linden Lab, 2013) How do you become a "resident" of SL? Well, you download the software, create an avatar, and immediately begin meeting other residents, socializing, and participating in individual and group activities. In *Second Life*, there are also disability rights groups, which provide virtual support for one another, even if the "resident" does not have a disability in real life.

Figure 6.3. Avatars from *Second Life*. Source: NBC News.com

People participate in *Second Life* because it gives them the opportunity to get away from what is happening in their actual life, as well as to try new things (Plunkett, 2011): "I am a lot more alive in SL than I ever have been in RL (real life)"; "I have fun because I get to do things I have never tried in RL, like skating and sailing"; and "if I could really look out the electronic window of my living room in Boston and see the Alps, hear the cowbells, and smell the (digital) manure in summer, in a way I am very much in Switzerland" (Negroponte, 1995, p. 165).

All this has to do with the concept of place attachment. **Place attachment** suggests that people emotionally bond with specific places; they have a sense of place, rootedness, or "insidedness" (Kyle, Mowen, & Tarrant, 2004). In studying the role of place in leisure, two primary concepts that reflect place attachment are place identity and place dependence. Place identity focuses on the emotional and symbolic meanings recreationists ascribe to recreation settings, and place dependence relates to the functional utility attributed to the setting for enabling leisure experiences (Williams, Patterson, Roggenbuck, & Watson, 1992; Kyle & Chick, 2007). Let's explore both of these.

Place attachment: Emotional bond between a person and a place

Place Identity

What motivates us to have an emotional attachment to a place? One possible explanation is that the place provides an identity for us. **Place identity** claims we are able to convey a sense of who we are from a particular place. As we explored in other chapters, leisure provides opportunities for people to create and develop personal and group identities. And, leisure places have meaning to us because of who they affirm us to be: "I'm a mountain person" or "only a Winnebago for me."

Place identity: A place provides the source of self-identification for a person

Indeed, some leisure scholars argue that because of the process of modernization in society, leisure places have become an increasingly important source of our identity. As Godbey (2007) declared, while we have become nomads, we still need a sense of self that is associated with a place. Leisure places provide for this. Perhaps this is what youth are seeking when they hang out at the mall, or what explains the allure of leisure-based villages for retirees, or why the neighborhood sports bar is "home" for many.

Oldenburg (1989) calls these the "great good places." Accordingly, these great good places represent "third places," a term he uses to describe the many public places that host "regular, voluntary, informal, and happily anticipated gatherings of individuals" (p. 16) beyond the home (the first place) and work and school (the second place). Third places may take many forms, including cafes, coffee shops, bars, beauty shops, community centers, and street-corner hangouts. Oldenburg sees them as providing identity. That is, the third place provides an accessible, socially neutral ground that encourages a playful mood for regulars to engage in their main activity: conversation (Wenner, 1998).

Box 6.5
The Study Says

Time and Place Attachment

One interesting thread woven throughout many writings about place attachment is the importance of time spent at a place. In this study of visitors to the Grand Teton National Park (GTNP), three research questions were answered:

1. Is a person's length of association with a place related to the meanings of that place?
    - People who reported more visits to GTNP and had more years of association with the park were more likely to report a special place there than those with shorter lengths of association.
2. Do people who have a shorter length of association with a place more often refer to either physical setting or activity meanings than people with a longer length of association?
    - People with longer lengths of association more frequently reported social and emotional connections to their special places; yet people with both long and short lengths of association report attachments via the park's scenic beauty and recreation opportunities.
3. Do place meanings change over time, and if so, how?
    - Place dependence tends to develop quickly, while place identity develops over a longer period of time.

Source: Smaldone, Harris, & Sanyal, 2008

Place Dependence

Another concept expressing our emotional attachment to leisure places is place dependence. **Place dependence** relies on two factors: 1) the quality of the place to meet a particular need or function, and 2) the relative quality of other places that are comparable to the current place. Thus, place dependence has been determined to be a more functional aspect of place attachment (Smaldone et al., 2008).

Place dependence: A person's functional association with a place

For example, Bricker and Kerstetter (2000) studied how place dependence varied with levels of specialization among whitewater boaters. They found more specialized whitewater boaters had a stronger dependence on a particular whitewater river. Another study also by Bricker and Kerstetter (2002) concluded whitewater river place meanings included the functions of repose, peace, beauty, wildness, an appreciation of nature, reverence, and a need to protect the river.

Of course there are differences in the functional meaning of a place, and ethnicity is one example. That is, white Americans attach the highest priority to an individually expressive meaning of a place, followed by an instrumental goal-directed meaning, and then a cultural symbolic meaning. For many Native Americans, on the other hand, the priority given to the meaning of a place is just the opposite, with a cultural symbolic meaning first and an individually expressive meaning last (McAvoy, 2002).

Differences such as these help explain why there are conflicts over leisure places. Different users of a recreation resource hold different reasons for loving it. This helps understand, for example, why cross-country skiers and snowmobilers are often at odds when trying to share the same trails. This realization is useful to natural resource managers who can help competing users of a resource negotiate and appreciate others' dependence on a place.

Box 6.6
Web Explore

A Park Under NYC

Dan Barasch and James Ramsey have a crazy plan: To create a park, filled with greenery, underneath New York City. The two are developing the Lowline, an underground greenspace the size of a football field. They're building it in a trolley terminal abandoned in 1948, using technology that harvests sunlight aboveground and directs it down below. Check it out by watching the TED talk:

http://www.ted.com/talks/dan_barasch_a_park_underneath_the_hustle_and_bustle_of_new_york_city?language=en.

Environmental Impact

Growth in all forms of leisure participation has fueled global concern for a special case of leisure's geography—pressure on the health of the environment. In this final section of the chapter, we pursue this more via tourism and outdoor recreation.

Tourism Effects

Perhaps one of the most perilous of environmental impacts is from tourism. Negative impacts from tourism occur when the level of visitor use is greater than the environment's ability to cope with this use. When this happens, the pressure on an area can lead to soil erosion, increased pollution, discharges into the sea, natural habitat loss, increased pressure on endangered species, and heightened vulnerability to forest fires. According to The United Nations (2016), the three main categories of impact are 1) depletion of natural resources, 2) waste, and 3) physical impacts (Table 6.2).

Table 6.2
Examples of Negative Environmental Impact from Tourism

Impact Area	Types of Impact	Illustration
Depletion of Natural Resources	Water resources	An average golf course in a tropical country (such as Thailand) uses as much water as 60,000 villagers.
	Land degradation	One trekking tourist in Nepal can use 4–5 kilograms of wood a day.
	Air pollution	A single transatlantic return flight emits almost half the CO_2 emissions produced by all other sources (lighting, heating, car use, etc.) consumed by an average person yearly.
Waste	Water pollution	Wastewater from tourism sites has damaged flora and fauna, stimulating the growth of algae, and changed the salinity in coastal environments.
	Littering	Some trails in the Peruvian Andes have been nicknamed "toilet paper trail."
	Solid waste	Cruise ships in the Caribbean are estimated to produce more than 70,000 tons of waste each year.
Physical Impacts	Trampling on vegetation	Include breakage and bruising stems, reduced plant vigor, loss of ground cover.
	Trampling on soil	Results include reduction in soil macro porosity, increase in run off, decrease in air and water permeability.
	On marine areas	Anchoring, snorkeling, sport fishing, scuba diving, and cruising cause direct degradation of coral reefs, fish stock, and nesting spots.

Source: United Nations, 2016

Outdoor Recreation Effects

As well, outdoor recreation tends to use more fragile natural resources, thus creating environmental havoc. For example, snow-grooming machines and artificial snow-making cause irreparable damage to soil and vegetation at ski areas. Also, the chlorofluorocarbons (CFCs) often found in the refrigeration systems in indoor skating rinks, the chemicals needed to purify the water in swimming pools, and the emissions and spills from powered toys such as snowmobiles and jet skis also represent environmental health threats. Even the impact of human-produced noise on park wildlife ranging from birds to elk has been a growing focus of scientific study, suggesting that animals modify their behavior as if they were suddenly being threatened by predators (Whittaker, 2011).

Solutions

At the root of the solution for leisure's negative environmental impact are the concepts of conservation and preservation. **Conservation** involves the scientific and rational planning of natural resources for their best use. Conservation implies the renewal of resources as they become damaged. In contrast, the **preservation** of natural resources means they are protected from human influence. Preservation applies mainly to nonrenewable resources. For example, whereas conservation refers to managing deer populations through hunting, preservation is keeping recreationists out of bald eagle habitat completely.

Conservation: Efficient use of natural resources over the long term

Preservation: Protection of natural resources from human damage

Let's illustrate the problem and its conservation and preservation solutions by considering climate. What is climate? Climate refers to the average conditions of temperature, barometric pressure, wind, and precipitation in a locale over a long period of time. It is different from weather, which refers to current conditions. Climate is primarily determined by latitude and altitude, dividing the earth into five basic climatic zones: tropical, dry, temperate, cold, and polar (Koppen Climate Classification), and expressions of leisure are determined accordingly. For example, climate determines not only those pastimes we choose in different seasons of the year, but also where we choose to travel for vacations.

Therefore, of particular concern is climate change. The relationship between climate change and leisure can perhaps best be presented again in terms of tourism. In fact, climate is a principal resource for tourism, as it determines the suitability of locations for a wide range of tourist activities. In order to consider the impact of climate change on the pattern of tourism worldwide and how tourist behavior might itself change as a result of changing climate, we first need to summarize global tourism patterns.

Tourist flows are unevenly distributed between the various regions of the world (World Tourism Organization, 2003). Among the world's 715 million international tourist arrivals, the concentration is heavily focused on three regions: Europe, North and South East Asia, and North America. As the climates of these regions change, partly due to the effects of mass tourism itself, the nature of tourism to these regions will also change. Table 6.3 provides a summary of climate changes and their probable impact on major international travel flows to three of these regions (World Tourism Organization, 2003).

Thus, global climate changes are predicted to cause a shift of attractive climatic conditions for tourism toward higher latitudes and altitudes. As a result, the competitive position of some popular vacation areas is anticipated to decline (e.g., the Mediterranean in summer), whereas other areas (e.g., southern England) are expected to improve (World Tourism Organization, 2008).

How might the challenges for global tourism brought on by climate change be met? Let's consider ideas for both conservation and preservation. For example, such conservation management strategies as dispersed use and carrying capacity may be helpful.

Table 6.2
Climate Changes and Impact on International Tourism

Region	Change in Climate	Implications for Tourism
North America	• Increase in winter and summer temperatures • Slight increase in annual rainfall • Beach erosion and greater storm risk in Florida • Greater storm risk and higher rain fall in Pacific coast • Coastal erosion and storm damage risk on east coast • More tropical diseases	• Florida may become less attractive at peak times • Northeast U.S. and Canadian cities too hot in summer • Increased popularity of Pacific Northwest • Stronger winter ski market due to reduced capacity in Europe • Increase demand on artificial snow-making
Northern Europe	• Increase in winter and summer temperatures • Increase in amount and intensity of winter rainfall • Decrease in summer rainfall • Beach degradation as sea level rises • More tropical diseases • More flash floods	• Increasing leisure travel market • More domestic holidays trips • Decreased incentive for northern European travel to southern Europe
Southern Europe	• Warmer, wetter winters • Much warmer, drier summers • Increased heat index • More arid landscape • Greater sea level rise	• Reduced peak summer visits • More beach degradation • Increased incentive for southern European travel to northern Europe

Figure 6.4. Tourism is an important revenue source for Egypt, yet tourists are also creating environmental degradation. For example, humidity levels inside the Great Pyramid can reach 80% because of the volume of people going in. The condensation causes a build-up of salt on the pyramid's 4,500-year-old stone walls, leading to flaking and cracks. To correct this, government resources recently committed to installing new ventilation systems, which change the air inside every 45 minutes, reducing humidity and carbon-dioxide levels. Also, now only 300 visitors a day are allowed to enter the pyramid. And to prevent further damage from vibration, airliners are being banned from overflying the site.

The idea of dispersed use encourages spreading out the use of a particular area over a wider swath. For example, increasing the amount of parking at lesser used public beaches could disperse beach use. Determining carrying capacity has also been helpful. Standards are determined for the saturation point for the impact of people and participation is limited to this. An example is limiting to 300 visitors per day to the Great Pyramid in Egypt (Figure 6.4).

In terms of preservation, one illustration is the establishment of wilderness designated areas. A wilderness designation can apply to desert, forest, water, and coastal resources. The point is that minimal human intervention is allowed, including motorized equipment, signage, built recreation facilities, and commercial use.

Also, some tourists themselves are deciding that "saving the world is more important than seeing the world" and are increasingly having stay-at-home vacations (Karp, 2008, p. W3). Global Cool (http://www.globalcool.org/) features a campaign in the United Kingdom to fight global warming. In 2008, it received pledges from site visitors to cut out enough air travel to reduce carbon emissions by a combined 2,205 tons (equivalent to 1,770 New York-to-Los Angeles round trips).

Figure 6.5. Backroads is an adventure travel company offering luxury accommodations, fine dining, and special attention to ecotourism. Small groups travel to their destinations via their own efforts—walking, biking, or kayaking. They abide by a "leave no trace" philosophy and directly support wildlife and natural resources of the areas visited. © Patricia D. Setser

One of the best illustrations of the usefulness of such conservation and preservation initiatives to tourism is ecotourism. **Ecotourism** is a form of tourism involving visiting fragile, pristine, and relatively undisturbed natural areas, intended as a low-impact and small scale alternative to mass tourism. Its purpose includes educating the tourist, providing funds for ecological conservation, and benefitting the economic development of local cultures. In addition, an integral part of ecotourism is the promotion of recycling, energy efficiency, and water conservation at tourist sites. The rise in interest in volunteer tourism, where tourists spend some portion of their vacation working on conservation or preservation projects, reflects an ecotourism concern.

Ecotourism: Tourism in threatened, natural environments that supports conservation efforts

Sustainable tourism: Controlling visitation to tourist sites so that impact is neither permanent nor irreversible

Another illustration is sustainable tourism. **Sustainable tourism** implies not consuming natural resources at a higher rate than they can be protected or replaced. This includes the responsible management of environmental, economic, and sociocultural aspects of tourism. This effort is best achieved by balancing the needs of tourists with those of the destination.

What We Understand About Leisure's Geographical Significance

From the perspective of geography, leisure can be understood as having meaning in space and place. As a result of reading this chapter, you should know the following.

1. The distribution of leisure in space differs according to density, concentration, and pattern.
   Distinguish each of these three concepts of geographical space:

   ____

   ____

2. Distance is a concentration and pattern phenomenon that affects participation rates for different types of leisure sites.
   Define distance and give an illustration in leisure:

   ____

   ____

3. Attaching strong sentiment to leisure places comes from our visual, olfactory, kinesthetic, and virtual senses.
   Select a leisure place for which you have a strong sentiment and describe it in terms of your visual, olfactory and kinesthetic attachment:
   ____
   ____

4. Strong leisure place attachments contribute to our self-identity and dependency.
   Define place attachment, incorporating self-identity and dependency into its description:
   ____
   ____

5. Considerable attention must be applied to the conservation and preservation of leisure resources if opportunities are to remain viable.
   Select one of the environmental concerns discussed in the chapter and describe it. How can leisure both harm and help this concern?
   ____
   ____

References

Bricker, K. S., & Kerstetter, D. L. (2000). Level of specialization and place attachment: An exploratory study of whitewater recreationists. *Leisure Sciences, 22*, 233–257.

Bricker, K. S., & Kerstetter, D. L. (2002). An interpretation of special place meanings whitewater recreationists attach to the South Fork of the American River. *Tourism Geographies, 4*, 396–425.

Ditton, R. B., Fedler, A. J., & Graef, A. R. (1983). Factors contributing to perceptions of recreational crowding. *Leisure Sciences, 5*, 273–288.

Godbey, G. (2007). *Leisure in your life: An exploration* (7th ed.). State College, PA: Venture.

Harrison, R. (2009). Excavating *Second Life*: Cyber-archaeologies, heritage and virtual communities. *Journal of Material Culture, 14*, 74–106.

International Union for Conservation of Nature. (2015). Resources. Retrieved from https://www.iucn.org/resources.

Karp, H. (January 18, 2008). The stay-at-home vacation. *The Wall Street Journal.*

Kyle, G., & Chick, G. (2007). The social construction of a sense of place. *Leisure Sciences, 29*, 209–225.

Kyle, G. T., Mowen, A. J., & Tarrant, M. (2004). Linking place preferences with place meaning: An examination of the relationship between place motivation and place attachment. *Journal of Environmental Psychology, 24*, 439–454.

Lime, D. W. (Ed.). (1996). Congestion and crowding in the national park system. *Minnesota Agricultural Experiment Station Miscellaneous Publication 86-1996.* St. Paul, MN: University of Minnesota.

Linden Lab. (June 20, 2013). Infographic: 10 years of *Second Life.* Retrieved from http://www.lindenlab.com/releases/infographic-10-years-of-second-life

Louv, R. (2012). *The nature principle: Human restoration and the end of nature-deficit disorder.* Chapel Hill, NC: Algonquin Books.

Manning, R. E. (1999). Crowding and carrying capacity in outdoor recreation: From normative standards to standards of quality. In E. L. Jackson & T. L. Burton (Eds.), *Leisure studies: Prospects for the Twenty-first century* (pp. 323–334). State College, PA: Venture.

Marchant, R. (2014). Consumers will travel 17 mins to reach a local business. Bright Local. Retrieved from https://www.brightlocal.com/2014/05/01/local-business-travel-times/)

McAvoy, L. (2002). American Indians, place meanings and the old/new West. *Journal of Leisure Research, 34*, 383–396.

National Park Service. (January 27, 2016). National Park Service press release. Retrieved from https://www.nps.gov/aboutus/news/release.htm?id=1775

National Public Radio. (March 7, 2016). Long lines, packed campsites, and busy trails: Our crowded national parks. Retrieved from http://www.npr.org/2016/03/07/466308123/long-lines-packed-campsites-and-busy-trails-our-crowded-national-parks

Negroponte, N. (1995). *Being digital*. New York, NY: Alfred A. Knopf.

Oldenburg, R. (1989). *The great good place: Cafes, coffee shops, community centers, beauty parlors, general stores, bars, hangouts, and how they get you through the day*. New York, NY: Paragon House.

Plunkett, D. (2011). On place attachments in virtual worlds. *World Leisure Journal, 53*(3), 168–178.

Porteous, J. (1985). Smellscape. *Progress in Human Geography, 9*, 356–378.

Rubenstein, J. M. (2003). *The cultural landscape: An introduction to human geography*. Upper Saddle River, NJ: Pearson Education.

Smaldone, D., Harris, C., & Sanyal, N. (2008). The role of time in developing place meanings. *Journal of Leisure Research, 40*(4), 479–504.

Smale, B. J. A. (1999). Spatial analysis of leisure and recreation. In E. L. Jackson & T. L. Burton (Eds.), *Leisure studies: Prospects for the Twenty-first century* (pp. 177–197). State College, PA: Venture.

Tuan, Y.-F. (1977). *Space and place: The perspective of experience*. Minneapolis, MN: University of Minnesota Press.

United Nations Environment Programme. (2016). Impacts of tourism. Retrieved from http://www.unep.org/resourceefficiency/Business/SectoralActivities/Tourism/FactsandFiguresaboutTourism/ImpactsofTourism/tabid/78774/Default.aspx

U.S. Census Bureau. (2012). Table 1252; 1255. *Statistical Abstract of the United States: 2012*. Retrieved from https://www.census.gov/compendia/statab/

Vaske, J. J., Graef, A. R., & Dempster, A. (1982). Social and environmental influences on perceived crowding. In *Proceedings of the Wilderness Psychology Group Conference* (pp. 35–41), Morgantown: West Virginia University.

Wenner, L. A. (1998). In search of the sports bar: Masculinity, alcohol, sports, and the mediation of public space. In G. Rail (Ed.), *Sport and postmodern times* (pp. 210–231). Albany, NY: State University of New York Press.

Whittaker, M. (February 22, 2011). Shhh, and not because the fauna are sleeping. *The New York Times*.

Williams, D. R., Patterson, M. E., Roggenbuck, J. W., & Watson, A. (1992). Beyond the commodity metaphor: Examining emotional and symbolic attachment to place. *Leisure Sciences, 14*, 29–41.

World Tourism Organization. (2003). Climate change and tourism. Proceedings of the 1st International Conference on Climate Change and Tourism, Djerba, Tunisia, 9–11 April 2003.

World Tourism Organization. (2008). *Climate change and tourism: Responding to global challenges*. Madrid, Spain: CEDRO.

CHAPTER 7

Leisure and Technology

Cowritten with Patricia D. Setser

Why is technology important to leisure?

Beginning over 5,000 years ago, technological innovations have reflected humankind's efforts to control their environment for their own benefit, including their leisure benefit.

In what ways has technology changed our lives?

Chiefly it has made us "prosumers," professional knowledge workers who produce and consume media.

In what ways have these changes to our lives affected our leisure?

Examples include social network games, GPS games, virtual reality entertainment, streaming media entertainment, as well as travel mobile apps.

What is the future of technology and leisure?

The future holds both promise and challenge. Such dilemmas as the quality of the cyberhood, Internet and smartphone addiction, and other issues will have to be addressed.

From the invention of the wheel over 5,000 years ago to the perfection of robotics today, there has always been a connection between leisure and technology. Indeed, the history of technology is the story of humankind's efforts to control the material environment for its own benefit (Woodbury, 1972), including for its leisure benefit.

Why else would the average young person today now spend practically every waking minute using a smartphone, computer, television, iPad, iPod, game console, and other technological devices? For example, aided by the convenience and constant access to mobile devices, 92% of teens report going online daily, including 24% who say they go online "almost constantly" (Lenhart, 2015).

And why else did Jacksonville, Florida in 2013 approve a $63 million improvement to EverBank Field, where the Jaguars NFL team plays? Renovations included two end zone video (HD LED) scoreboards 362 feet long, a platform area in the north end zone with two wading pools and interactive activities, a fantasy football lounge, and a game day app that delivers virtual reality instant replay during games.

And why else is it seriously predicted that someday very soon your pizza will be dropped at your doorstep by a drone. In 2016, the food delivery app "Foodpanda" was testing this technology in Singapore. Already Foodpanda has cut delivery times from an average of 60 to 70 minutes down to 30 minutes in Hong Kong (Houck, 2016).

Technology has given people innovative places to play, better equipment and clothing to aid their fun, and new activities to pursue. Thanks to technology, we have greater access to information about leisure options, new horizons in leisure for persons with disabilities, and tourism is an easy and global enterprise. The efficiencies of technology have also been a boon to professionals working in the leisure fields, providing better ways to match participants with programs.

Figure 7.1. Pizza delivery in Singapore.

Box 7.1
In Profile

Athleisure Ware

"Athleisure" is a fashion trend in which clothing designed for workouts and other athletic activities is worn in other settings, such as during work, casual, or social occasions. Outfits include yoga pants as well as tights and leggings. Making this possible is research that has led to the innovation of new fibers specifically for odor reduction, sweat soaking-up, stretchability to conform to the body's shape, breathability to allow air in and out, and protection from dirt. Some clothing designs permit selected parts of the clothing to be more breathable, while other parts can have greater tension. One type of athleisure ware that is sometimes called "technical wear" is clothes that are more suitable for wearing to the office while being comfortable, too.

In this chapter, we discuss the rapidly evolving nature of leisure and technology. We begin with an introductory discussion of technology's definitions and history. This is followed by consideration of the pervasive nature of technology in our lives and then specifically in our leisure. We conclude with conjectures about the future of technology in leisure.

Definitions and History

Inventions and innovations typically progress very logically with each new discovery evolving from the last, and often born out of necessity. We usually refer to these innovations as technology. Technology is not a neutral word; people will assign it different meanings depending on their viewpoint and context. So, to be clear about terms here, we define **technology** as the application of scientific knowledge for practical purposes. That is, we use the products and processes of technology to accomplish various tasks in our daily lives. We use technology to extend our abilities (Ramey, 2013).

Technology: Innovations that apply scientific knowledge for practical purposes

A particular type of technology is information technology. **Information technology** is the study or use of systems (especially computers and telecommunications) for storing, retrieving, and sending information. It includes such applications as television, computers, cell phones, and so forth. By some estimates, (Dutta & Bilbao-Osorio, 2012), leisure uses of information technology tops the list.

Information Technology: Computing and telecommunications inventions

Box 7.2
In Profile

Alvin Toffler

Alvin Toffler (1928–2016) was an American writer and futurist known for his works discussing modern technologies, specifically digital and communications. In his early works, he focused on technology and its impact, which he termed "information overload." In 1970, his first major book about the future, *Future Shock*, became a worldwide bestseller. Toffler coined the term "future shock" to refer to what happens to a society when change happens too fast, resulting in social confusion and normal decision-making processes breaking down. In 1980, he published *The Third Wave*, where he foresaw such technological advances as cloning, personal computers, the Internet, cable television, and mobile communication. In this book, he described the first and second waves as agricultural and industrial revolutions. The "third wave" represents the information, computer-based revolution. Since Toffler's work, several scholars have further suggested that we are currently in a "fourth wave"—the age of communication, experience, and thought.

Based on the storage and processing technologies employed, it is possible to distinguish four distinct phases of IT development (Open Book Project, 2011):

1. **Premechanical**. This earliest of information technology periods (between 3000 B.C. and 1450 A.D.) describes when humans first started communicating using language and picture drawings.
2. **Mechanical**. Here (between 1450 and 1840) is when we begin to see legacies for our current technologies. Many were developed, including the slide rule. Blaise Pascal invented the Pascaline, which was a popular mechanical computer, and Charles Babbage developed the difference engine, which tabulated polynomial equations using the method of finite differences.
3. **Electromechanical**. The time between 1840 and 1940 marks the beginnings of telecommunication. The telegraph was created in the early 1800s, and the telephone by Alexander Graham Bell in 1876. The first radio was developed by Guglielmo Marconi in 1894. The first large-scale automatic digital computer in the United States was the Mark 1 created by Harvard University around 1940.

This computer was 8ft high, 50ft long, 2ft wide, and weighed 5 tons. It was programmed using punch cards.

4. **Digital**. From 1940 to now marks our current phase. The ENIAC was the first high-speed, digital computer capable of being reprogrammed to solve a full range of computing problems. This computer was designed to be used by the U.S. Army for artillery firing tables. It was even bigger than the Mark 1, taking up 680 square feet and weighing 30 tons. It mainly used vacuum tubes to do its calculations.

Figure 7.2. The evolution of technology traces the progression of using tools.

Within the current era of digital computing, there have been four main phases (Open Book Project, 2011):

- The first was the era of vacuum tubes and punch cards like the ENIAC and Mark 1. Rotating magnetic drums were used for internal storage.
- The second generation replaced vacuum tubes with transistors, punch cards were replaced with magnetic tape, and rotating magnetic drums were replaced by magnetic cores for internal storage. Also during this time, high-level programming languages were created, such as FORTRAN and COBOL.
- The third generation replaced transistors with integrated circuits, magnetic tape was used throughout all computers, and magnetic core turned into metal oxide semiconductors. An actual operating system showed up around this time along with the programming language BASIC.
- The fourth and latest generation brought in CPUs (central processing units) that contained memory, logic, and control circuits all on a single chip. The personal computer was developed (Apple II), as was the graphical user interface (GUI).

Figure 7.3. The ENIAC computer circa 1946. In addition to being 50 feet long and weighing 5 tons, it came complete with 20 banks of flashing lights.

Table 7.1 provides a timeline of this history, including the technological phases just presented, Toffler's four waves, and innovations from these eras that you might recognize.

Table 7.1
Timeline of the History of Technology

Years	Technological Phases (Open Book Project)	Toffler's Wave	Innovations
3000 B.C.–1450 A.D.	Premechanical		Petroglyths, Alphabet
1450-1840	Mechanical		Pascaline Mechanical Computer, Difference Engine
1840-1940	Electromechanical		Telegraph, Telephone, Morse Code
1900-1910	Electromechanical	First–Agricultural	Radio signal sent across the Atlantic, Model T
1910-1920	Electromechanical	First–Agricultural	Mechanical pencil, Arc welder
1920-1930	Electromechanical	Second–Industrial	Black and white television, Robot, Traffic signal
1930-1940	Electromechanical	Second–Industrial	Electron microscope, Color television
1940-1950	Digital	Second–Industrial	ENIAC computer, Transister, COBOL, Velcro, Atomic Bomb
1950-1960	Digital	Second–Industrial	Barcode, Integrated circuit, Overhead projectors
1960-1970	Digital	Second and Third Waves	Compact discs, LCD projectors, ERIC National Information Systems
1970-1980	Digital	Third–Information	Microprocessor, Calculators, Apple II, Computer Mouse, WWW
1980-1990	Digital	Third–Information	IBM PC, Windows, Dell computer, Internet, Nintendo, Sony Walkman
1990-2000	Digital	Third–Information	SmartBoards, HDTV, Internet Browsers, 1G, 2G and 2.5 G networks
2000-2010	Digital	Fourth–Communication, etc.	3G networks, Streaming Discovery Education to classroom, IPod, IPad, IPhone, YouTube
2010-present	Digital	Fourth–Communication, etc.	Fiber optics, 4G networks, 3D television, supercomputers, FitBit, IWatch, Nanotechnology, Social Media, Apps

Technology's Pervasiveness in Our Lives

Information technology is now infused into almost every aspect of life. It is driving virtually every profession and creating immense amounts of data to be processed in every aspect of life. For example, while still in its infancy, safety monitoring and assistance technologies for elder care are improving quickly, driven by advances in bio-sensing, sensory networks, robotics, and cloud computing.

For individuals, as information technology has become more available, with smaller "chips" and lower cost, the stage has been set for the "technology of me." For example, wearable technologies enable us to work and play anytime and anywhere. Such wearables as smart watches, activity trackers, and eyeglasses with cameras and GPS systems encourage us to blur the distinctions of when and how we work and enjoy leisure. For example, it used to be that work and leisure balanced on a kind of seesaw in our lives. Now we work; later we play. Currently, driven by our technologies, work and leisure are completely blurred, like ingredients in a blender. Now we work while playing and play while working.

Prosumer: Production by consumers

All of this has led to the emergence of life as prosumers. Derived from the dot-com era in business, a **prosumer** is a person who consumes and produces media. A term originally coined by American futurist Alvin Toffler, the prosumer is a "professional knowledge worker" (Cunningham, 2016) who also happens to be a consumer. That is, we are professional consumers of technologies.

Here are some examples:

- We use accounting skills when we use software such as *Quickbooks*.
- We use search engines on the Internet with sophisticated techniques of placing "meta tags" in the search field in a "Boolean Algebra" way to find information on the web.
- We use photography skills as we manipulate images and jpeg files on the IPhone–cropping, rotating, touch-up, etc.
- We use marketing skills of contact management, lead management, and demographics as we decide who in our contact list is a candidate for texting vs e-mail vs phoning based on that person's demographics.
- We use publishing skills, marketing skills, and graphic arts skills as we use software to publish web pages, publishing software to create brochures and fliers, software to self-publish books and magazines, etc.

Figure 7.4. The prosumer of today is a professional knowledge worker using sophisticated user-friendly software and apps hosted on various electronic devices.

This prosumer concept draws us to an inevitable conclusion: Information technology has invaded every aspect of our lives. This is because since the middle of the last century, we have been on a wave of fusion of technologies that is muddling the lines between the physical and the digital (Schwab, 2016). The speed of current breakthroughs has and is transforming everything at an exponential pace. Because they have direct implications for our leisure, we now highlight social media, GPS, virtual reality, streaming media, and mobile apps as examples.

First, social media has become so powerful in our lives that it has been known to start revolutions! (Think Occupy Wall Street and the Arab Spring in 2011.) While a definition of **social media** is challenging because of the variety of platforms and uses, a broad description includes that it involves computer-mediated tools that allow people to create and share information about themselves. Social media technologies take on many different forms including blogs, forums, photo sharing, social bookmarking, enterprise social networks, and social gaming.

Social media: Forms of electronic communication (such as websites) through which people create online communities to share information, ideas, and personal messages

Social media depends on mobile and web-based technologies through which individuals, communities, and organizations exchange user-generated content. The most popular sites include Facebook, Whatsapp, Instagram, Twitter, and Snapchat (Statistica, 2016a). These technologies have introduced substantial and pervasive changes to communication—so much so that these changes are the focus of the emerging field of "technoself" studies, the interdisciplinary field of research dedicated to understanding human identity within a technological society (Luppicini, 2013).

Box 7.3
Web Explore

Being Alone in Social Media

Many questions have been raised about the role of social media in our lives. Watch this TED Talk for one perspective on the answer:

https://www.ted.com/talks/sherry_turkle_alone_together?language=en

Another illustration of the pervasiveness of technology in our lives is GPS (Global Positioning System). **GPS** is an American global navigation satellite system that provides location and time information anywhere on or near the Earth when there is an unobstructed line of sight. While GPS has positioning capabilities to military, civil, and commercial users around the world, other systems are also provided by Russia, India, and China.

GPS: Radio navigation system that allows land, sea, and airborne users to determine their exact location, velocity, and time 24 hours a day, anywhere in the world

Figure 7.5. As of 2016, 21 GPS satellites and three spare satellites were in orbit at 10,600 miles above the Earth (Rouse, 2016).

While originally a U.S. military project, today GPS has widespread civilian applications for commerce, scientific studies, tracking and surveillance, banking, mobile phone operations, astronomy, and forensics. It is the technology behind driverless cars, robotics, earthquake measurement, disaster relief, and, of course, none of us can go anywhere without the GPS system in our cars or even wrist watches.

Virtual reality is a computer-generated simulation of a three-dimensional environment that can be interacted with by a person using special electronic equipment, such as a helmet with a screen inside or gloves fitted with sensors. Sometimes also referred to as "immersive multimedia" or "computer-simulated reality" it simulates a user's physical presence in a fictional world. The experience can include not only sight, but also touch, hearing, and smell.

Virtual reality: An artificial world of images and other experiences created by a computer that is affected by the actions of a person

Figure 7.6. There are certain health and safety considerations with virtual reality, especially from prolonged use. These include anxiety, eyestrain, and motion sickness.

There are wide-ranging uses of virtual reality, including in architecture, engineering, medicine, and urban design; however, a majority of the advances have been made in the entertainment industries, including games, film, and theme parks. The immersive environment can be similar to the real world (such as when used to train pilots), or it can differ significantly from reality (such as in virtual reality games).

In **streaming media** technologies, content is sent in compressed form over the Internet and displayed by a viewer in real time. This means a user does not have to wait to download an entire file in order to use it; it is sent in a continuous stream of data that is played at the same time it arrives. Internet television is a common form. The technology can also apply to closed captioning, ticker tape, and real-time text. Typical uses of the streaming concept include video conferencing, as well as delivery of long lectures, whole concerts, movies, and television shows.

Streaming media: Video or audio content sent in compressed form over the Internet and played immediately

Finally, mobile applications, or **mobile apps,** are computer software tools developed specifically for small, hand-held wireless mobile devices, such as smartphones and tablets. Sometimes apps are preinstalled into the device but are more commonly distributed through app stores, such as the Apple App Store or Google Play. Some apps are free, while others must be purchased. Originally, mobile apps were offered for general productivity and information retrieval, including email, calendaring, stock market, and weather forecasting. However, public demand drove rapid expansion into other categories.

Mobile apps: Generally small, individual software units with a specific function

For example, The Apple Store (for "I" devices) and Google Play (for android devices) each hosts approximately 1.4 million apps to download on topics ranging from travel, medicine, health and fitness, food and drink, finance, gardening, and gaming. In terms of their design pattern, according to Thon (2014), there are three types of mobile apps. First, utility apps are quick-access tools that get you to the information you need about basic things, such as weather reports, traffic hold-ups, and sports scores. On the other hand, productivity apps are more complex and have fuller features. These are perhaps the most varied type of app that includes anything from social media monitoring and Instagram. Finally, there are the immersive apps, which focus solely on content. These apps are designed to create a unique experience, ranging from video games to music making.

Figure 7.7. Bottom line: "There's an app for that!"

Leisure Applications of Technology

Leisure activities have always changed over time, but the digital age has probably changed them the most in the least amount of time (Ramasubbu, 2015). In some cases, certain traditional forms of leisure activities, such as socializing, travel, and reading, have been modified perhaps beyond recognition—or at least been "updated" by newer technology-induced activities. As well, in many cases, the distinctions between leisure and technology have become difficult to tease out.

Box 7.4
Web Explore

How We Run, Swim, Bike Faster

Check out this TED talk on the role of technology in shattering athletic performance records:

https://www.ted.com/talks/david_epstein_are_athletes_really_getting_faster_better_stronger?language=en.

One example is toys. While you might not at first think of children's toys as leisure technology, their history traces increasing technological developments. The origin of toys is prehistoric; dolls representing infants, animals, and soldiers, as well as representations of tools used by adults have been found at archaeological sites (Powell, 2001). The earliest toys were made from materials found in nature, such as rocks, sticks, and clay. Later, Ancient Egyptian children played with dolls that had wigs and movable limbs made from pottery and wood, and in Ancient Greece and Ancient Rome, children's dolls were made of terra cotta or wax.

As technology changed and civilizations progressed, toys also changed. The toys you grew up with, for example, were likely made from plastic, cloth, and synthetic materials, and were often powered by batteries. Today there are computerized toys, including dolls that can recognize and identify things, including the voice of the owner. Hot Wheels cars can now zoom across iPad screens, Laser tag can be played with an iPhone in a gun with the display showing live video of whatever is ahead of the barrel, and Barbie has become a video camera (the lens is in her necklace and an LCD video screen is on the back of her shirt) (Clifford, 2012). And, what kid (or adult?) wouldn't love to build his or her own 4-foot tall robot (the Meccanoid) that's capable of mimicking its owner and responding to instructions? Fair warning: in the kit there are about 1,200 parts, including a brain, LED eyes, and eight motors.

Box 7.5
The Study Says

Disney's Human-Computer Interaction Research

Disney Research is an international network of research labs, with the mission to push the scientific and technological forefront of innovation at The Walt Disney Company. Combining academia and industry, the labs carry out both basic and application-driven research. Study topics include computer graphics, robotics, wireless communications, data mining, machine learning, and human-computer interaction.

For example, here is a sample of projects in the area of human-computer interaction as of 2016:

- **Safe robotic arm.** When designing a robot for human safety during direct physical interaction, one approach is to size the robot's actuators to be physically incapable of exerting damaging impulses, even during a controller failure.
- **AIREAL.** This project enables users to feel virtual objects without requiring the user to wear or touch a physical device. Using 3D printing, this technology uses a vortex – a ring of air that can impart a significant force the user can feel at large distances.
- **Electric Flora.** This is an interactive, human-powered energy harvesting system that converts a person's movement into light. Relying on a person's interactions with a polyester covered floor, hanging acrylic rods with embedded LEDs, and garments, the user's movements are electromechanically converted to electricity.

Source: Disney.com, 2012

To more fully tell the story of what leisure has become, let's now extend the discussion of the technologies that have impacted our lives from the previous section of the chapter to leisure examples. That is, what are some of the uses of social media, GPS, virtual reality, streaming media, and mobile apps that illustrate changes in leisure interests and expressions?

To begin, one unique application is the merging of social media and gaming. Not too long ago, social media and the video game industry remained largely separate; however, the line between those two popular industries seems to be getting more indistinct by the day (Minguez, 2014). A social network game is a type of online game that is played through social contacts. For example, in 2016, popular games included FarmVille, Zuma Blitz, Words with Friends, Mafia Wars, and World of Warcraft. Zynga Poker, a Texas Hold' Em style poker game, is probably the most popular social network game today, which suggests that social casinos are one of the strongest branches of the industry.

Overall, social network games are among the most popular computer games played in the world, with some hosting tens of millions of players. For example, in 2015, the social online games market in the U.S. was worth $1.97 billion, and sources predict this figure to surpass $2.4 billion by 2020 (Statistica, 2015). Eighty-four percent of these revenues are attributed to app-based social gaming. Asia is the largest market, however, with sources estimating that revenues reached $2.27 billion in 2015, increasing to nearly $2.5 billion in 2017 (Statistica, 2015). With the number of monthly active users having already surpassed 500 billion and growing, Asia has a strong chance of becoming the hub of this pastime.

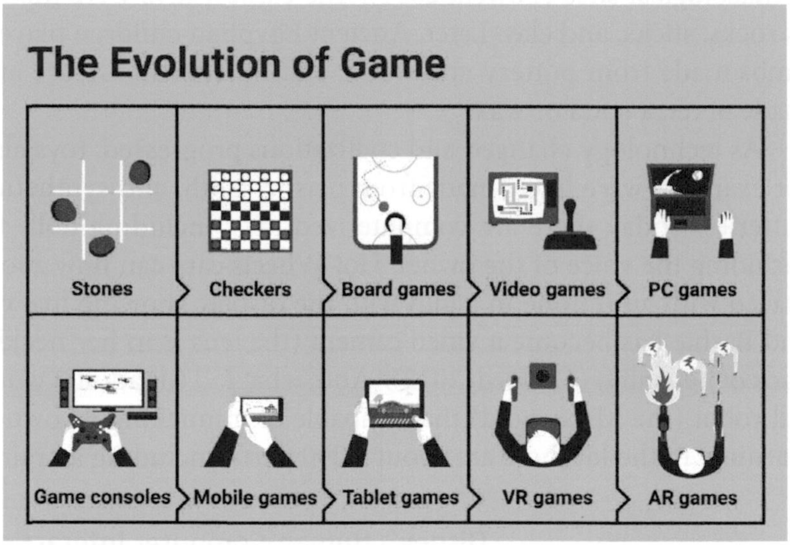

Figure 7.8. The evolution of games spans about 2161 years, with the advent of computer-based games (video games through augmented reality (AR) games) occupying only the last 2% of this time.

As for GPS, there are many illustrations of its use for leisure. Foremost, GPS has eliminated some of the hazards associated with typical recreational activities by providing a capacity to determine a precise location. As well, GPS has broadened the scope of outdoor activities by simplifying some of the traditional problems, such as being able to stay on the correct trail or returning to the best fishing spot.

An example of this is a website based in Malaysia dedicated to GPS for mountain bikers. Riders post waypoint files marking their favorite rides allowing other riders to try out the trails (GPS.gov, 2014). Golfers use GPS to measure precise distances within the course and improve their game. Other applications include downhill skiing, cross-country running, and boating. GPS technology has also generated entirely new sports and outdoor pastimes. One example of this is geocaching, a kind of treasure hunt. Estimating that there are about 15 million geocachers in the world, hunting for over 83 million caches (The Geocaching Blog, 2015), participants use navigational techniques through GPS to hide and seek containers.

However, as I write this, perhaps the most popular treasure hunt using GPS is Pokémon Go. This activity is a free, location-based reality game developed by Niantic for smartphone mobile devices. It was initially released in selected countries in July 2016. Using the mobile device's GPS system, players locate, capture, battle, and train virtual creatures (the Pokémon) who appear on the screen as if they were actually in the same real-world location of the player. So far (August 2016) it has been downloaded by more than 130 million people worldwide (Smith, 2016). The game was released to mixed reviews, however, with both praise for the game's concept of being active in the real world and concerns for its contribution to accidents and becoming a public nuisance.

Figure 7.9. Playing Pokémon Go while driving has led to multiple governments passing laws against it.

Now, on to virtual reality (VR) applications in leisure. For starters, home-use VR goggles are becoming more available and less expensive. For example, Sony has announced that its PlayStation VR headset is scheduled to launch in October of 2016. Also, while it is little more than a piece of folded cardboard with some lenses in it, Google Cardboard will soon be available for all smartphones. Other examples of VR in leisure include more smells while gaming, more "immersion" in horror films, and yes, VR pornography.

Figure 7.10. Virtual reality tools are becoming more available for personal home use.

And, of course, there are the rapidly increasing uses of virtual reality in amusement park attractions. Disney World guests have been able to play virtual reality games such as Aladdin's Magic Carpet Ride since 1998. More recently, the parks have been using VR to create a new Avatar Land for Animal Kingdom in Orlando, a new Iron Man Experience for Hong Kong Disneyland, and new Star Wars attractions for multiple parks (Gaudiosi, 2015).

Meanwhile, between 2015 and 2016, 19 either new or VR-extended attractions opened at parks worldwide. For example, Six Flags amusement parks (joining up with Samsung Electronics) in 2016 began to debut virtual reality roller coasters in nine parks. Some of the Six Flags' most popular coasters are being equipped to allow riders to wear VR headsets to feel the "heart-pumping adrenaline of steep drops, inverted loops and powerful twists and turns as gyros, accelerometers, and proximity sensors synchronize all of the action in an incredibly realistic 360-degree virtual reality world" (Six Flags, 2016).

Figure 7.11. A virtual reality roller coaster. Source: Six Flags Entertainment Corporation

As if it weren't already bad enough ...

> On the six new 'Revolution' virtual reality coasters, riders are transported to a futuristic battle to save planet earth from an alien invasion. Riders are the co-pilots in their own fighter jets as they strap in for air-to-air combat. Taking in the view around them, riders will see other aircraft in an underground secret bunker. As the aircraft moves to a landing pad, it begins to launch its thruster engines, lifting the craft straight up through the roof. During the ascent, riders can test fire their weapons using the world's first-ever interactive gameplay technology on a roller coaster. As riders clear the roof, they realize they are on top of a skyscraper and about to launch off the edge of the building diving straight down on the first drop of the ride. The aircraft races through the city until reaching the edge of the skyline where riders see the mother ship hovering above. The mother ship is heavily protected by drones and the mission is to get past the drones, fire on the mother ship, and destroy it. (Six Flags, 2016)

Also pervasive in our lives is streaming media—on demand, anytime, on any device. How has this changed leisure expression? Streaming media—bringing music and film to you in real time—may seem advanced compared to the kind of technology people had a few years ago, but it is relatively in its infancy (Woodford, 2016). For streaming these entertainments to your own devices, the information has to be compressed dramatically so that it comes quickly.

One application for streaming media is The Digital Concert Hall. This is an active website that offers live concerts of the Berlin Philharmonic Orchestra on your computer, television, tablet, or smartphone (https://www.digitalconcerthall.com/en/home). Similarly, live broadcasts from New York City of the Metropolitan Opera are in movie theatres everywhere, as well as in live streaming videos on their website.

Finally, while we've already mentioned applications of mobile apps elsewhere, just a note of example here will finish this discussion. Let's highlight the area of recreational travel. There are multitudes of examples, including specific hotel apps to help you find a room and track your reward points, as well as third-party hotel apps such as TripAdvisor.com and Booking.com. If you are driving, you might need GasBuddy to help you find the cheapest gas, Roadtrippers for sightseeing, and iExit to find a rest area or a Starbucks. For camping, you should probably download MyNature Animal Tracks to help you identify what you've been following on the trail, Star Walk Stargazing, Ultrasonic bug spray, and AllTrails to help you find the best places to hike. There are many more, but you get the idea.

The Future of Leisure and Technology

Some scientists and futurists have recently declared that we stand on the brink of another technological revolution that will alter the way we live even more. "In its scale, scope, and complexity, the transformation will be unlike anything humankind has experienced before" (Schwab, 2016, p.1). This is because the speed of current technological breakthroughs has no historical precedent—changing every aspect of life in every country. And in the future, this will be multiplied by new technology breakthroughs in fields such as artificial intelligence, robotics, autonomous vehicles, 3-D printing, nanotechnology, biotechnology, and quantum computing (Schwab, 2016).

This future will change everything—our sense of privacy, our ideas of ownership, our consumption patterns, the time we devote to work and leisure, how we develop our careers, meet people, and nurture relationships. We are becoming "quantified" selves (Schwab, 2016). For example, we increasingly judge how healthy we are by the numbers produced on our handhelds. As well, staying law abiding is becoming murkier. Exactly who owns the Internet? What laws from what countries/states/cities do we follow, given that the Internet is not based on geographical borders? It's the wild west out there!

Like all revolutions, this coming one could result in consequences that are both good and bad for our lives. Some see a future as one where technology improves the quality of life for everyone, while others envision one where technological advancements yield greater inequalities; those who keep up with innovation will thrive, while others are disillusioned and fearful.

Many technological advancements will continue to be focused on leisure, particularly entertainment. In terms of specific leisure activities, some have clearly improved due to technology. For example, while in the past you had to visit a library to read a variety of books, now an entire library can be carried in a small box and read on a glowing screen, without you ever leaving home. Pursuing certain hobbies has also become easier with the Internet; 83% of online Americans use the Internet to pursue their hobbies (Ramasubbu, 2015).

Box 7.6
What Do
You Say?

Drone Moves in with Grandma

Globally, the number of people 80 years old and over is expected to more than double by 2050 (United Nations, 2015). Accordingly, the number of frail adults is also growing rapidly, raising concerns about how they are going to be able to continue to take care of themselves. Naira Hovakimyan, University of Illinois roboticist has an idea: drones. She's working on designing small autonomous drones to perform simple household chores, such as retrieving a medicine bottle.

Mabu, the personal health care companion from Catalia Health, will help people take their medications, interact with them, and connect with their pharmacist when needed (Sahi, 2015).

But beyond her research is the intention of one day being able to employ drones for the entire range of tasks of taking care of the frail elderly. Even today, artificial-intelligence-derived robotics that will be commercially available in the next decade include intelligent walkers, smart pendants that track falls and wandering behaviors, room and home sensors that monitor health status, balancing aids, and even virtual and robotic companions to combat loneliness.

1. Perhaps the most profound question about this is whether drones or virtual assistants can help forestall the effects of aging, including dementia and isolation? What do you think?
2. Do you believe that a friendship with a drone will do as much for the frail elderly as a friendship with an actual person? Might the drone friend be more helpful than the real person? Why or why not?

Source: Markoff, 2015

There have also been some serious negative consequences for leisure as a result of technological change. As an example, what used to be outdoor play time for children is increasingly being replaced by sedentary device-based gaming time. Yet "exergaming" can raise children's activity levels to meet guidelines for moderate intensity activity (Ramasubbu, 2015).

Figure 7.12. Scientists (and parents) have asked questions about the pros and cons of video gaming. For example, one study suggested overuse could lead to a higher risk for Alzheimer's (West et al., 2015)

The issue of goodness with technological leisure is not so simple and definitively good or bad, of course. The situation is more of a complex dilemma. To highlight the future for leisure, let's conclude the chapter by discussing the pros and cons of two specific consequences of technology: the cyberhood and smartphone addiction.

Virtual communities, or online communities, are an important location for leisure activity. In

Cyberhood: Virtual neighborhoods formed on the Internet

the **cyberhood**, we are able to make connections based on leisure interests and lifestyles. Commonly, people in these communities relate to each other via social networking sites, chat rooms, and forums, as well as video games and blogs.

Figure 7.13. The cyberhood is a virtual neighborhood. Is it a good one?

These are sensation-based places, rather than physical locations for leisure. For participants, it has been claimed that cyberhoods renew a lost sense of community and at the same time empower individuals. Specifically, these virtual worlds are similar to third places. (See Chapter 5 for a review of this anthropological concept.) That is, the cyberhood provides spaces for social interaction and relationships beyond the home and workplace. And, like the neighborhood bar, these social relationships, while not usually providing deep emotional support, typically function as sources of informal sociability.

Although they can promote an array of positive qualities, such as relationships without regard to race, religion, gender, or geography, they can also lead to multiple problems. These can include financial, safety, social, and psychological loss. For example, one specific problem is identity formation with the ambiguous real-virtual life mix. This may be because we have just one identity in the real world, but online communities allow us to create as many different "electronic" personae as we please. This can lead to identity deceptions (i.e., claiming to be someone you are not). Anonymity in the cyberhood increases unethical behavior and susceptibility to being victimized.

According to Barlow (2004), as a neighborhood, there is a lot missing in the cyberhood. To his thinking, foremost, is *prana*. Prana is the Hindu term for both breath and spirit. Barlow uses the term to mean that even though the cyberhood offers connection, it does not offer experience. When we're in a chat room, for example, we cannot really sense the others—their smell, tone of voice, the breeze from their bodies—the qualities that Barlow claims make an experience. There is something else missing in the cyberhood, claims Barlow: diversity. Those with lower incomes, less education, and who are over the age of 75 often find themselves on the other side of the digital divide. As also argued by Bryce (2001), the freedom of choice quality of leisure is missing in the cyberhood as it is limited by the ability to acquire and maintain the technology—a privileged position of access.

Another dilemma to consider about the future of technology and leisure is addiction. This is a very slippery topic, with many scholars trying to tease out what leisure addiction is or is not. Studies have suggested there is, for example, shopping addiction (Illinois Institute for Addiction Recovery, 2016), exercise addiction (Landolfi, 2013), TV addiction (Kubey & Csikszentmihalyi, 2004), and gambling addiction (Welte et al., 2015). How is leisure addiction defined then?

According to Goodman (1990), a psychiatrist, in addiction there is a physical and psychological dependence on something. In terms of an addiction to a leisure activity, this means the addict feels that life is horribly dull when the activity is removed from his/her life and is physically affected by this loss. Stebbins (2010) considers the application of addiction to leisure activities to reflect a positive dependence rather than a negative one. What, then, is the difference between leisure addiction and serious leisure, a concept promoted by Stebbins and discussed in Chapter 2? Is it possible that serious leisure may become addictive? Could a dependency on a particular activity result in such serious leisure benefits as self-development, feelings of accomplishment, enhancement of self-image, enhanced social interaction, and a sense of belongingness?

As applied to technological leisure, a malady labeled "Internet addiction disorder (IAD)" provides an example of overuse and dependency of the Internet (Byun, 2009). IAD has received coverage in the press but continues to be debated and researched in the psychiatric field. Such activities as playing lots of computer games or watching large numbers of Internet videos, such as on *YouTube*, are perhaps troubling only to the extent that these activities interfere with a person's regular life. Or is it more concerning than this? In a 2010 book by Nicholas Carr (*The Shallows: What the Internet is Doing to Our Brains*), this is all explained as a rewiring of our brains due to the hypnotic pull of our smartphones, tablets, and televisions.

Box 7.7
By The Numbers

Teens* and Social Media

75%	Have or have access to a smartphone
85%	African American teens have access to a smartphone
71%	White and Hispanic teens have access to a smartphone
71%	Use Facebook
52%	Use Instagram
41%	Use Snapchat
71%	Use more than one social media site

*American teens aged 13–17

Source: Lenhart, 2015

What about smartphone addiction? You have heard people say they're addicted to their phones, but is this truly an addiction? In 2016, there were 2.08 billion smartphone users worldwide (Statistica, 2016b), and over 50% of Smartphone users grab their phones immediately upon waking up in the morning (Sukhraj, 2015). And, according to one poll, a third of users check their phones during movies (Pak, 2015). How about you? Do you get twitchy trying to keep yourself from constantly checking Facebook, e-mail, or text messages?

Smartphone addiction has been widely researched in recent years, and the effects of various demographic, personality-linked, psychological, and emotional variables, have been found. For example, a study by Zhitomirsky-Geffet and Blau (2016) compared these factors for three generations of smartphone users (Generations X, Y, and Z). The main finding of the study was that a significantly higher level of addictive behavior was found for Generation Y compared to the other two generations, with the strongest predictive factors being social environment pressure to use a smartphone and emotional gain. For Generation Z positive emotional gain was more predictive.

Box 7.8
In Your Own Experience

Are You Addicted to Your Smartphone?

Do you agree or disagree with the following statements?

1. The first thing I reach for after waking in the morning is my cell phone.
2. I would turn around and go back home on the way to work or school if I had left my cell phone at home.
3. I often use my cell phone when I am bored.
4. I become agitated or irritable when my cell phone is out of sight.
5. I have gone into a panic when I thought I had lost my cell phone.
6. I have argued with my spouse, friends, or family about my cell phone use.
7. I use my cell phone while driving my car.
8. I need to reduce my cell phone use, but am afraid I can't do it.

If you agreed with 7 or 8 of the statements, you need an immediate intervention.
If you agreed with 5 or 6 of the statements, you need to be on guard.
If you agreed with 4 or fewer of the statements, you probably aren't into technology much at all.

Source: Adapted from Yahoo Tech, 2015

To conclude this discussion of the future, it would be useful to be reminded that neither technology nor the changes that come with it is an inexorable force over which people have no control. There has never been a time of greater promise, or one of greater potential peril (Schwab, 2016). In terms of leisure, futurists are predicting some pretty fantastical things (such as being able to purchase high-quality emotions online). How do we want to smartly incorporate them into our lives?

What We Understand About Leisure and Technology

The use of technology in leisure is as old as leisure itself, yet the current revolution of particularly information technologies has assisted, invented, and changed contemporary leisure in significant ways. From studying this chapter, you should know the following:

1. Beginning over 5,000 years ago, technological innovations have reflected humankind's efforts to control their environment for their own benefit, including their leisure benefit.
   Name at least two ways that you use technology daily to control your environment. What technology have you used recently in the pursuit of leisure?

   ____

   ____

2. Chiefly information technology has made us prosumers, professional knowledge workers who produce and consume media.
   What is a prosumer? How are you a prosumer? What application software or Apps have you used recently as a prosumer?

   ____

   ____

3. Examples of the impact of technology on leisure include social network games, GPS games, virtual reality entertainment, streaming media entertainment, as well as travel mobile apps.
   Give an example from your leisure interests for each of these:

   ____

   ____

4. The future holds both promise and challenge. Such dilemmas as the quality of the cyberhood, internet and smartphone addiction, and other issues will have to be addressed.
   What are the pros and cons of these dilemmas? In each case, please specify if you think the con crosses the line "legally" and why.

   ____

   ____

References

Barlow, J. P. (2004). Cyberhood vs. neighborhood. In M. Petracca & M. Sorapure (Eds.), *Common culture: Reading and writing about American popular culture* (pp. 211–236). Upper Saddle River, NJ: Prentice Hall.

Bryce, J. (2001). The technological transformation of leisure. *Social Science Computer Review, 19*(7), 7–16.

Byun, S., Ruffini, C., Mills, J. E., Douglas, A. C., Niang, M., Stepchenkova, S., ... Blanton, M. (2009). Internet addiction: Metasynthesis of 1996–2006 quantitative research. *Cyberpsychology and Behavior, 12*(2), 203–207.

Clifford, S. (February 26, 2012). Barbie, Monopoly, and Hot Wheels for iPad generation. *The New York Times*, p. A1.

Cunningham, P. (April 6, 2016). The human side of IT resource implementation. Toffler Associates. Retrieved from http://blog.tofflerassociates.com/vanishing-point/the-human-side-of-it-resource-implementation. Retrieved 8/16/16

Disney.com (2012). Human-computer interaction. Retrieved from https://www.disneyresearch.com/research-areas/human-computer-interaction/

Dutta, S., & Bilbao-Osorio, B. (2012). The global information technology report 2012: Living in a hyperconnected world. World Economic Forum and INSEAD. Retrieved from weforum.org/docs/Global_IT_Report_2012.pdf

Gaudiosi, J. (August 13, 2015). How Disney uses virtual reality to build new park rides. *Fortune*. Retrieved from http://fortune.com/2015/08/13/disney-imagineering-vr/

Geocaching Blog. (December 29, 2015). Retrieved from https://www.geocaching.com/blog/2015/12/geocaching-in-2015-a-year-in-review/

Goodman, A. (1990) Addiction: Definition and implications. *British Journal of Addiction, 85*, 1403–1408.

GPS.gov. (2014). Recreation. Retrieved from http://www.gps.gov/applications/recreation/

Houch, B. (Mary 22, 2016). Food delivery via drone will soon be a reality. Eater. Retrieved from http://www.eater.com/2016/3/22/11284144/food-delivery-drones-foodpanda-singapore

Illinois Institute for Addition Recovery. (2016). Shopping addiction recovery. Retrieved from http://www.addictionrecov.org/Addictions/index.aspx?AID=34

Kubey, R., & Csikszentmihalyi, M. (2004). Television addiction is not mere metaphor. In M. Petracca & M. Sorapure (Eds.), *Common culture: Reading and writing about American popular culture* (pp. 251–272). Upper Saddle River, NJ: Prentice Hall.

Landolfi, E. (2013). Exercise addiction. *Sports Medicine, 43*(2), 111–119.

Lenhart, A. (April 9, 2015). Teens, social media and technology overview. Pew Research Center. Retrieved from http://www.pewinternet.org/2015/04/09/teens-social-media-technology-2015/

Luppicini, R. (2013). The emerging field of technoself studies. In R. Luppicini (Ed.), *Handbook of research on technoself: Identity in a technological society* (pp. 1–25). Hershey, PA: Information Science.

Markoff, J. (December 5, 2015). As aging population grows, so do robotic health aids. *The New York Times*. Retrieved from http://www.nytimes.com/2015/12/08/science/as-aging-population-grows-so-do-robotic-health-aides.html?_r=0

Minguez, K. (November 7, 2014). The merging of social media and gaming. *Social Media Today*. Retrieved from http://www.socialmediatoday.com/content/merging-social-media-and-gaming

Open Book Project. (2011). History of information technology. Retrieved from http://openbookproject.net/courses/intro2ict/history/history.html

Pak, S. (February 17, 2015). Are you a cell phone addict? Survey reveals Americans' smartphone use during sleep, sex, selfie taking. *Yibada*. Retrieved from http://en.yibada.com/articles/13928/20150217/cell-phone-addict-survey-reveals-americans-smartphone-use-during-sleep-sex.htm

Powell, B. B. (2001). *Classical myth* (3rd ed.) Upper Saddle River, NJ: Prentice Hall.

Ramasubbu, S. (September, 2, 2015). Digital age happiness, relaxation and leisure. *The Huffington Post*. Retrieved from http://www.huffingtonpost.com/suren-ramasubbu/digital-age-happiness-rel_b_8066758.html

Ramey, K. (December 12, 2013). What is technology: Meaning of technology and its use. Retrieved from http://www.useoftechnology.com/what-is-technology/

Rouse, M. (2016). Global positioning system (GPS). Retrieved from http://searchmobilecomputing.techtarget.com/definition/Global-Positioning-System

Sahi, M. (2015). New jobs for robots in personal health care. Tractica. Retrieved from https://www.tractica.com/automation-robotics/new-jobs-for-robots-in-personal-healthcare/

Schwab, K. (January 14, 2016). The fourth Industrial Revolution: What it means, how to respond. *World Economic Forum*. Retrieved from https://www.weforum.org/agenda/2016/01/the-fourth-industrial-revolution-what-it-means-and-how-to-respond/

Six Flags Entertainment Corporation. (2016). Six Flags and Samsung partner to launch first virtual reality roller coasters in North America. Retrieved from https://www.sixflags.com/america/attractions/vr/news-release

Smith, C. (August 11, 2016). Hot game: Amazing Polemon Go statistics. Digital stat articles. Retrieved from http://expandedramblings.com/index.php/pokemon-go-statistics/

Statistica. (2015). Statistics and facts about social gaming worldwide. Retrieved from http://www.statista.com/topics/2965/social-gaming/

Statistica. (2016a). Leading global social networks 2016. Retrieved from http://www.statista.com/statistics/272014/global-social-networks-ranked-by-number-of-users/

Statistica. (2016b). Number of Smartphone users worldwide from 2014 to 2019 in millions. Retrieved from http://www.statista.com/statistics/330695/number-of-smartphone-users-worldwide/

Stebbins, R. A. (July 2010). Addiction to leisure activities: Is it possible? *Leisure Reflections No. 24. LSA Newsletter Number 86*, pp. 19–22.

Sukhraj, R. (November 2, 2015). 25 mobile marketing statistics to help you plan for 2016. Impact Branding and Design. Retrieved from https://www.impactbnd.com/blog/mobile-marketing-statistics-for-2016

Thon. (2014). The three types of mobile apps. Motionkick. Retrieved from http://motionkick.com/the-3-types-of-mobile-apps/

United Nations. (2015). World population aging report. Retrieved from http://www.un.org/en/development/desa/population/publications/pdf/ageing/WPA2015_Report.pdf

Welte, J. W., Barnes, G. M., Tidwell, M. C. O., Hoffman, J. H., & Wieczorek, W. F. (2015). Gambling and problem gambling in the United States: Changes between 1999 and 2013. *Journal of Gambling Studies, 31*: 695–715.

West, G. L., Drisdelle, B. L., Konishi, K., Jackson, J., Jolicoeur, P., & Bohbot, V. D. (May 2015). Habitual action video game playing is associated with caudate nucleus-dependent navigational strategies. *Proceedings of the Royal Society*. Retrieved from https://www.sciencedaily.com/releases/2015/05/150519210303.htm

Woodbury, R. S. (1972). *Studies in the history of machine tools*. Cambridge, MA: MIT Press

Woodford, C. (March 15, 2016). Streaming media: Explain that stuff. Retrieved from http://www.explainthatstuff.com/streamingmedia.html

YahooTech. (2015). Are you addicted to your smartphone? Retrieved from https://www.yahoo.com/tech/are-you-addicted-to-your-smartphone-read-these-12-110817737379.html

Zhitomirsky-Geffet, M., & Blau, M. (November 2016). Cross-generational analysis of predictive factors of addictive behavior in smartphone usage. *Computers in Human Behavior, 64*, 682–293.

CHAPTER 8

Popular Culture

What is popular culture?

Popular culture refers to the everyday pastimes of the majority of people in a society. It is leisure for the masses.

What are examples of popular culture?

In contemporary societies, popular culture examples are typically media based forms of entertainment including television, spectator sports, popular music, films, and amusement parks.

Why is understanding popular culture important?

Mediated entertainment as a form of leisure is perhaps the most obvious reflection of a society's character.

What did you do yesterday? Did you drink a Coke? Did you watch television, go to a movie, listen to music, fist-pump someone, check your fantasy football scores, or shop for a bomber jacket? You most likely did at least one of these activities, perhaps all of them. In fact, you probably do at least one of these activities every day. If so, you are not unusual at all, because these are the sorts of things most people in modern societies do with most of their free time. These are examples of popular culture.

Popular culture encompasses the most immediate, pervasive, and contemporary leisure expressions in our lives. It offers a common ground for a visible level of culture in a society. It is the "culture of the people" (Delaney, 2012). Not so much defined by its content, but rather by its typicality, it could be music, literature, drama, food, fashion, slang, or sport spectating. Other terms for popular culture include *common culture, pop culture, mass culture, and mass leisure.*

We begin this chapter by clarifying why it is important to study popular culture. Then we extend this to a discussion of the characteristics of popular culture along with specific examples. Finally, the chapter's conclusion debates the role of popular culture's core: mediated entertainment.

Popular culture: Heavily influenced by mass media, the collection of ideas, images, and other phenomena that permeate the everyday lives of members of a society

Figure 8.1. Eating at McDonald's is an example of popular culture in many societies around the world. This restaurant is located in Beijing, China.

The Importance of Popular Culture

Why focus on popular culture? What can we learn by studying the motivations of flash mobs, the language of hip-hop, the images of Katy Perry, or the plots in *The Simpsons*? Understanding these forms of popular culture is important because they reflect a society's commonly held standards and beliefs about beauty, success, love, equality, and justice. We also see reflected in popular culture important social contradictions—the tension between races, genders, and generations. As Lipsitz (1990) suggested, "perhaps the most important facts about people have always been encoded within the ordinary and commonplace" (p. 5).

Box 8.1
Web Explore

Popular Culture and Politics

Might the political consciousness of today's generation be taking shape in and around popular culture? What similarities are there between our popular culture and political preferences? How are political leaders utilizing metaphors from popular culture? To explore some possible answers to these questions, begin by checking out these websites:

http://web.mit.edu/comm-forum/forums/politics_pop_culture.html

http://www.cnn.com/2015/12/30/politics/politics-and-pop-culture-2015/

http://global.oup.com/us/companion.websites/9780199374229/stud/ch1/pcp/

Debate your conclusions with classmates.

Another argument for studying popular culture is the important influence it exerts on us (Petracca & Sorapure, 2004). Today, for many societies, popular culture is driven by media. Media contains the primary fund of ideas that inform our daily lives, sometimes exerting a more compelling influence than family, friends, school, or work. When we play sports, for example, we mimic the gestures and movements of the professional athletes we see on TV. We learn to dance from music videos. Popular culture delivers messages that we internalize and act on later. This means we should examine it in order to assess, and perhaps also resist, its influences.

Characterizing Popular Culture

How do we know what pastimes to put on the popular culture list? Why is eating at McDonald's on the list and dining at Commander's Palace not? Why is NFL Football on the list and Pop Warner football not? In characterizing popular culture, we refer to it as popular, inclusionary, commercial, trendy, and specific to age groups. Let's discuss each of these characteristics of popular culture more fully.

Beginning with its popularity, these everyday forms of leisure are what most of us engage in most often. It is the way the masses primarily use free time. Television watching is popular culture, for example, because it is a fundamental leisure expression of an entire society. To further make the distinction about popularity, we can compare popular culture with both folk culture and high culture.

High culture: Typical pastimes of the social elite of a society

High culture refers to the typical pastimes of a society's elite, such as intellectuals or the upper socioeconomic classes of people. High culture is not mass produced nor meant for mass consumption. Examples of high culture might include listening to classical music by composers such as Beethoven, viewing art in a museum by impressionist painter Manet, attending a performance of a play by Shakespeare, and reading the literature of Sartre. In some societies, high culture can also be very popular. For example, classical ballet is one of Russia's more popular pastimes.

Folk culture: Local or regional traditional pastimes

Folk culture, on the other hand, refers to local pastimes that are shared through direct, oral communication by a specific community or ethnic group. Folk culture is typically noncommercial, reflecting a simple and often rural lifestyle. Examples of American folk culture include quilting, Creole cuisine, bluegrass music, clogging, the Hawaiian hula, and the cakewalk. Sometimes folk culture is appropriated and marketed and becomes popular culture. When this happens, the folk items gradually lose their original form and meaning. Wearing blue jeans is certainly an illustration of this.

Figure 8.2. Bluegrass music is a form of American roots music and a related genre of country music. Influenced by the music of Appalachia, it has mixed roots in Irish, Scottish, Welsh, and English traditional music, and was also later influenced by the music of African-Americans through incorporation of jazz elements.

A second characteristic of popular culture is that it is inclusionary; it allows large heterogeneous masses of people to identify collectively. Thus it serves the societal role of uniting the ideals of acceptable forms of activity. Consuming popular culture enhances our prestige in our peer group. Imagine if you'd never heard of The Beatles! Popular culture appeals to us because it provides opportunities for communal bonding.

As you already realize, another characteristic of popular culture is that it is commercial. It is leisure that is marketed and sold as a product. For example, in the U.S., over $60 billion is spent annually on pets (NBC

News, 2015), $191 billion on fast food (Statistica, 2013), and $219 billion on amusement and theme park admissions (IAAPA, 2016). And, by the way, in 2015, Katy Perry was the top grossing female musician by earning $135 million that year (Billboard, 2015). Yes, popular culture is for sale.

You're probably wondering who the top grossing female musician is in the year you are reading this. Is it still Katy Perry, or someone else? Most likely you're going to guess it is someone else, because this, too, is a characteristic of popular culture. It is trendy. What exactly is popular culture does not last long (The Rolling Stones are an exception!). Although television, film, popular music, and spectator sport are categories of popular culture that are generally enduring, particular shows or titles or musicians or athletes are not. Katy Perry took the place of Lady Gaga, who took the place of Beyonce, who took the place of Britney, who supposedly took the place of Madonna, who took the place of Gidget, and so on. What is popular culture responds to what is actually contemporary in people's lives. This means things once popular are inevitably not popular later.

Table 8.1
Generations and Popular Culture

Generation	Year of Birth (approx.)	Notable Events	Popular Culture
Greatest	1910–1927	WWII, stock market collapse, Great Depression	Big Band music, baseball and Babe Ruth, films by Clark Gable and Ginger Rogers, radio entertainment
Silent	1928–1945	WWII, Korean War, early civil rights movement, "Ikers"	Birth of rock 'n roll, jazz and swing music, film *Gone with the Wind*
Baby Boomers	1946–1964	Vietnam war, environmental movement, counterculture, space exploration, Civil rights and women's movements, assassination of JFK	Rock 'n roll, the Beatles, Elvis, Woodstock, cannabis and LSD, sexual revolution, widespread television
Generation X (or Baby Busters)	1965–1980	Cold war, fall of Berlin Wall	MTV, home computer, video games, hip hop, grunge music, cable TV, rise of mass media
Millennials (or Generation Y or Echo Boomers)	1981–1994	Technology revolution, War on Terror, Iraq War, 9/11 attack, gay rights, Great recession, cell phones	Transformers, Tickle Me Elmo, Spice Girls, Eminem, reality television
Generation Z (or Net or New Silent)	1995–2010	The Internet, Dot com bubble, digital globalization	Starbucks, Harry Potter, Beyonce, Lady Gaga, YouTube, mobile Internet entertainment, American Idol-style television

This also leads us to the final characteristic of popular culture: It is specific to age groups. For example, let's consider the cinema. A couple of years ago, two very popular movies were *The King's Speech* and *True Grit*. What sort of audience powered their popularity? It was baby boomer audiences who were 50 years of age and older. These are the same people for whom the film *Twilight*, which also came out that year, sounded vaguely threatening (Barnes & Cieply, 2011).

Thus, popular culture is typically specific to age groups. However, that popular culture that is common among all age groups at a particular point in time is usually dependent on the tastes of youth. That is, a culture's best-selling music, movies, foods, etc., are largely determined by youth culture. This means young people can be a powerful force in precipitating change in society.

Examples

There are sundry examples of popular culture worthy of highlighting. Beginning with spectator sport, we'll also mention popular music and movies. Then we will pay particular attention to television—undoubtedly the standard-bearer of popular culture.

In many societies, it's no secret that spectator sports are more important than ever to both individuals and communities. But it is perhaps in the demonstration of the commercial characteristic of spectator sport that we find our best illustration. For example, increases in broadcast revenue over the past decades have provided the Olympic movement with a sizeable financial base. By the time of the London summer games in 2012, the International Olympic Committee (IOC) was worth $47.5 billion, second only to Apple at $70.6 billion and just ahead of Google at $47.4 billion (Morely, 2012). As well, the television network NBC will pay $4.38 billion to broadcast in the United States four Olympic Games between 2014 and 2020 (Sandomir, 2011). Further, the mass commercial appeal of sport is something that is clearly not lost on the companies that spent $5 million for one 30-second advertising slot in the 2016 Super Bowl, which may have been worth it, as an estimated 114 million fans watched (USA Today, 2016).

Figure 8.3. Popular culture typifies the interests of the youth of an era. What generation does this statue in Key West, Florida, represent? © Patricia D. Setser

Ironically, the sports of the Olympics are themselves not popular culture examples in all countries. For example, many of the individual Olympic events are niche spectator sports in the U.S., but do represent the most popular spectator sports in some other parts of the world. This demonstrates the inclusionary characteristic of popular culture.

Next, let's consider the example of music. Because of its popularity, music has been a tremendously important barometer of the character of a culture throughout history. Thinking back over the 20th century in the United States, for example, every decade has a melody or rhythm that characterizes it.

The century started off blue with Robert Johnson selling his soul to the devil at the crossroads. Then came the jazz age epitomized by Louis Armstrong and Duke Ellington. By mid-century, things started to rock: The beginning brought a confused hodge-podge of Buddy Holly's hillbilly style, Little Richard's frenzy, and Elvis Presley's blend of country and African American rhythms. Later, the boy and girl groups, such as The Coasters and The Shirelles, relayed the trials and joys of young love. By the mid-1960s, Bob Dylan and Joan Baez combined folk lyrics with the beat and instrumentation of rock to produce folk music, while Led Zeppelin and Frank Zappa pinned their anti-establishment tone to hard rock. Then on to the Beatles invasion, Aretha Franklin, Bob Marley, and Stevie Wonder. (Are you singing along?) Eventually the memorable sounds of R.E.M., U2, and Prince drowned out the thumping sounds of disco in the 80s. So powerful have been all of these musical legacies they can still be heard on the radio today.

But, how will we remember the end of that century and the beginning of this one? Added to blues, jazz, country, rock, folk, and disco music is **hip-hop**. Hip-hop music is part of an entire subculture (which also includes dance movements, slang, clothing, and films), that began in the Bronx in New York City in the early 1970s. Founded by young African Americans and Latinos who just wanted to get a party going, the music quickly gained in popularity and widespread acceptance. The current smash-hit Broadway musical *Hamilton* has brought hip-hop into the consciousness of the main

Hip-hop: A type of music typically consisting of a rhythmic style of speaking called rap often over backing beats performed on a turntable by a DJ

stream music audience, and today, visionaries foresee hip-hop-inspired housewares, furniture, linens, and food (Watson, 2012).

As the first decade of the new century progressed, hip-hop has transformed from an edgy rhythmic rap to a more melodic sound that contains elements of jazz, classical, pop, and reggae. In fact, this is the main point about popular music as an example of popular culture—American popular music, as well as that of any other culture, is not just of one form. It is at heart **pluralistic.**

Pluralistic: Ethnically, religiously, racially, and socially diverse

Box 8.2 What Do You Say?

Hip-Hop's Meaning

The origin of hip-hop music embodies the complex character of some of the most downtrodden urban communities in the East Coast of the U.S. It originated as apolitical party music, but because it arose during a time of economic downturn and political conservatism, it garnered a high level of social significance. Viewed as a sociopolitical innovation, it became one of the few social spaces where disenfranchised minority youth could assume a public voice for expressing their angst (Rebollo-Gill & Moras, 2012). As a result, hip-hop artists sometimes adopt a hostile stance toward commerce, government, and media, seeking to draw attention to racial injustice and social neglect. Yet, for some, the hip-hop problem is instead the vulgarity of the language and the violence in the content. Described as "the unabashed glorification of crime and the unrelenting objectification of women" (Rebollo-Gill & Moras, 2012, p. 118), hip-hop is often criticized as highlighting the moral depravity of the artists or the wantonness of the culture.

1. What do you think has been the significance of hip-hop in your culture? Has it been an engine for social change or a reflection of social misconduct?
2. Two early star icons of hip-hop were Queen Latifah and Tupac Shakur. Do some investigation about their early lives. (For example, Queen Latifah's autobiography is *Ladies First*, published in 2000, and a biography of Tupac Shakur is *Tupac Shakur Legacy* published in 2006.) Are there any clues from their lives for answering the question of the meaning of the hip-hop movement?
3. Also study the early lyrics of Queen Latifah and Tupac Shakur in terms of their positions about women. Do you think they agree with the criticisms of misogyny in hip-hop?

Although different music forms appeal to different social and ethnic groups, foremost it is always an interwoven reflection of the whole culture. Rock, jazz, blues, country, and hip-hop do not remain pure forms as they become popular; they become amalgamations of all ethnic strands and social group values. In directly interpreting the emotional language of a culture, popular music picks up influences as it goes, much like a snowball rolling downhill.

What is your most anticipated popular culture event for the coming year? Many of us when asked this would respond with the name of a movie. Even though movies have experienced declines in theater attendance in many societies since the 1950s (Lang & Rainey, 2016), with the advent of other visual media alternatives, watching movies remains a useful popular culture example as it reflects, defines, and redefines society.

Figure 8.4. A "flash mob" is a large public gathering at which people perform a seemingly random act of music, dance, or theater, and then disperse; typically organized by means of the Internet or social media. Flash Mob at Palais Royal Square, Paris, 2012.

Movies are categorized in terms of **genre**—action, drama, comedy, disaster, crime, horror, documentary, and so forth, and as such, use different plot, characterization, imagery, and symbolism conventions to relate to audiences. Psychologically, for example, viewers of the drama film genre can identify with the characters and project their own feelings into the plot, giving them a deep emotional tension and ultimately a release. From a sociological perspective, movies of every genre instruct and reflect social norms and depict urgent social problems. Such action films as the **blockbuster** can also have significant financial importance. For example, worldwide the highest grossing films of all time are *Avatar* (2009), *Titanic* (1997), and *Star Wars: The Force Awakens* (2015), each grossing over $2 billion (Box Office Mojo, 2016).

Genre: A kind or type, usually applied to films, books, and plays

Blockbuster: Lavishly produced film, having wide popular appeal and financial success

Box 8.3
In Profile

Slasher Films

In 2016, remakes of popular slasher films were released. Based on the originals [*The Texas Chainsaw Massacre* (1974), *Halloween* (1978), *Friday the 13th* (1980), and *I Know What You Did Last Summer* (1997)] fans were very much looking forward to being scared out of their wits. A sub-genre of the horror film, these slasher films typically involve a psychopathic killer who stalks and vividly murders a series of teen victims who are usually in an isolated setting doing something they shouldn't. Slasher films typically open with the murder of a young woman and end with a lone woman survivor who manages to subdue the killer—but not permanently.

What do these films tell us about the nature of the culture that loves them? One interpretation is that these films are an assault on all that society is supposed to cherish: youth, home, and school. The individual, the family, and the institution are dismembered in gruesome ways. For example, *The Texas Chainsaw Massacre* has been analyzed as a critique of capitalism, since it shows the horror of people quite literally living off other people. Another analysis suggests that in slasher films the attractive young women who are threatened by the maniac embody sexual pleasure, which must be annihilated. Film analysts also suggest the audiences' expectation of nonclosure by the end of the film reflects the impermanent nature of the culture (Modleski, 1986).

Social fears can perhaps be traced across the entire history of horror films. For example, in the 1950s, mutant monsters rose from our fear of the nuclear bogeyman, and Zombies in the 60s with Vietnam and Zombies again in the 2000s as a reflection of viral pandemic fears (Griffiths, 2015).

Film production is now a worldwide enterprise with some critics arguing the film industries in Asia and Europe have produced the majority of socially and artistically worthwhile works. This has also meant movie audiences have become more diverse and film as a popular culture example is universal. Thanks to multiple media options for viewing, all cultures, ages, socioeconomic classes, genders, ethnicities, and educational levels enjoy movies. Yet the movie viewer in the U.S. is still more likely to be young, female, affluent, educated, and urban.

In addition to spectator sport, popular music, and film, there are many more examples of popular culture, including comics and serialized novels, radio, and popular print (e.g., magazines), but our final illustration is television because it is at the hub of popular culture, providing a particularly fascinating reflection of culture. Not only does it hold a central place in our use of free time, but it also has become a primary means of communicating and validating what is popular (Fiske, 2010). Television tells us what music to dance to, what movies to see, what to wear, and what to eat.

Indeed, the amount of time people spend watching television is astounding. According to a Nielsen Media Research report (2016), in the average American household, the television is on for eight hours and 15 minutes in every 24-hour period, with the average daily amount of viewing time per individual a little over five hours.

Box 8.4
By the Numbers

TV Watching in America

5:11 hours	Average time spent watching television (all members of household)
9	Years the average person will have spent watching television if he/she lives to 75
2.24	Number of TVs in average household
67	Percentage of Americans who regularly watch television while eating dinner
1,480	Number of minutes per week the average child watches television

Source: A.C. Nielsen Co., 2016

Who watches television? Almost everyone, of course, but studies indicate women watch more than men, the average age of viewers is 50, and African Americans watch more than other ethnic groups. More educated people tend to watch less, as do divorced and widowed people, while viewing for all adults living with children is slightly higher (Kubey & Csikszentmihalyi, 2004). Most people do not watch television exclusively; typical accompanying activities include talking on the telephone, texting and other electronic device handling, eating meals, getting dressed, doing chores, caring for children, and studying.

Television's hold on us has been of keen interest to scientists, and for decades, research has demonstrated heavy television viewing may lead to serious health consequences. For example, to determine if watching television is harmful, researchers have undertaken a wide variety of studies, including laboratory experiments monitoring brain waves (using an electroencephalograph, or EEG), skin resistance, and heart rate of people while they watch. From the EEG studies, as you might expect, people show less mental stimulation while watching TV (Kubey & Csikszentmihalyi, 2004).

Other studies have focused on the effects of the experience of television watching. For example, Kubey and Csikszentmihalyi (2013) sampled people's feelings while they were engaged in various activities, including television watching. Foremost, and in agreement with the EEG studies, they found television viewing to be a passive, relaxing, low-concentration activity. Consequently, in contrasting this with other activities (Table 8.2), television watching was found to be less challenging, less social, and less active.

Table 8.2
Rank Ordering of the Experience Qualities for TV Viewing and Other Activities (1 = strongest to 5 = weakest)

Experience Qualities	TV Viewing	Public Leisure (i.e. Dining Out)	Working Outside the Home
Concentration	3	2	1
Challenge	5	2	1
Skill	5	2	1
Cheerful	3	1	4
Relaxed	1	2	5
Sociable	4	1	3
Alert	4	1	2
Strong	4	1	2
Active	4	2	1

Source: Kubey & Csikszentmihalyi, 2013

Because television watching is so easy to do, results from the same study also showed loneliness and negative feelings often drive the motivation to watch TV. Heavy viewers wish to escape something or avoid negative feelings. In addition, television seems to become less rewarding the longer it is watched. That is, although it is relaxing, as we increase the amount of time spent watching TV, our satisfaction and enjoyment in the experience tend to drop off. Ironically, this means even though people often choose to watch TV to escape bad feelings, they can feel worse as a result. Long TV hours are also linked to higher material aspirations and anxiety (Frey, Benesch, & Stutzer, 2007).

In fact, some scholars liken television watching to substance addiction. According to Rutgers University psychologist Robert Kubey, millions of people are so hooked on television that they fit the criteria for substance abuse as defined in the official psychiatric manual (in *Sourcebook for Teaching Science*, 2012). According to Kubey, heavy viewers exhibit five dependency symptoms—two more than necessary to arrive at a clinical diagnosis of substance addiction: 1) using TV as a sedative, 2) indiscriminate viewing, 3) feeling loss of control while viewing, 4) feeling angry with oneself for watching too much, 5) inability to stop watching, and 6) feeling miserable when kept from watching.

Box 8.5
In Your Own Experience

Are You Addicted to TV?

There are many self-assessment quizzes that help you assess your dependency on television. Try this one: http://www.quibblo.com/quiz/8YsVzeY/Are-You-Addicted-To-Television.

Based on your results, would you say you do or do not have a television addiction? Why?

What is it about TV, then, that has such a hold on us? In part, the attraction seems to spring from our biological orienting response. First described by Ivan Pavlov in 1927, the **orienting response** is our instinctive visual or auditory reaction to any sudden or new stimulus (Kubey & Csikszentmihalyi, 2004). It is part of our evolutionary heritage, a built-in sensitivity to movement from potential threats.

Orienting response: Instinctive visual or auditory reaction to novel stimulus

Typical orienting responses include dilation of the blood vessels to the brain, slowing of the heart, and constriction of blood vessels to major muscle groups. The brain focuses its attention on gathering more information while the rest of the body quiets. This is why it is very difficult not to watch television when it is on. The stylistic features of television, such as cuts, edits, zooms, pans, and sudden noises activate the orienting response, thereby keeping our attention on the screen.

Figure 8.5. When the orienting response is overworked, we watch more television than we want.

Producers of television programming have found these features help increase viewers' attention, but increasing the rate of cuts and edits eventually overloads the brain. For example, music videos and commercials that use rapid intercutting of unrelated scenes are designed more to hold our attention than to convey information. Thus, the orienting response becomes overworked.

Another answer to how television is able to have such a strong hold on us comes from the leisure quality of pleasure (see Chapter 2). British cultural studies scientist John Corner (1999) maintains we watch television simply because it is a source of personal pleasure. Specifically, it provides four types of pleasure: knowledge, comedy, fantasy, and distraction. For example, knowledge could be derived from history and nature programs; comedy from sit-coms; fantasy from soap operas and reality shows; and distraction from the pattern of repetition of the viewing week.

In other words, this suggests the pleasure of television is in the act of viewing itself. This is labeled **scopophilia**—being the onlooker to unfolding events. As noticed early by psychologist Sigmund Freud (1915), watching other people is considered a way to objectify them, both in order to gain control and out of curiosity. Although the concept of scopophilia is applicable to films, photographs, and other visual popular culture forms as well, it is a particularly powerful pleasure in television viewing because of how much time we spend at this pastime.

Scopophilia: From the Greek "love of looking"; deriving pleasure from watching other people

Commenting on the trend of reality television in particular, Mark Andrejevic, in the book *Reality TV: The Work of Being Watched* (2003), explained scopophilia democratizes celebrity. In doing this, reality television paves the way for what he refers to as the coming interactive economy—relinquishing control of the media to consumers and viewers. That is, being watched is doing economic work.

The Role of Entertainment

What do spectator sports, popular music, films, and television suggest is the character of the society that loves them? We have explored many things popular culture reveals about culture, but in contemporary societies, perhaps the overarching reflection is that we crave entertainment.

Entertainment: Amusements provided by someone or something else that divert and hold attention

Mediated entertainment: Entertainment provided via media

Entertainment comes from a variety of sources, but its goal is to have someone else or something else amuse us. In the case of many societies, entertainment as the basis for popular culture is delivered primarily through the media. Even theme parks are forms of **mediated entertainment**. This hasn't always been the case, however.

For example, the roots of "amusement parks" go back to the Middle Ages, with pleasure gardens and fairs located on the outskirts of major European cities. These gardens featured live performances, fireworks, dancing, games, and freak show attractions. One of these, Bakken, north of Copenhagen, Denmark, which opened in 1583, continues to operate today. Amusement parks entered their golden era with the 1893 World's Columbian Exposition in Chicago, which introduced the Ferris wheel and the midway. Under full swing by the 1930s, the center of this growing worldwide industry was Coney Island in New York City, where the world's most well-known roller coaster—*The Cyclone*—opened in 1927.

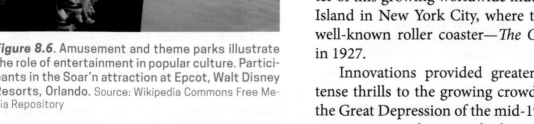

Figure 8.6. Amusement and theme parks illustrate the role of entertainment in popular culture. Participants in the Soar'n attraction at Epcot, Walt Disney Resorts, Orlando. Source: Wikipedia Commons Free Media Repository

Innovations provided greater and more intense thrills to the growing crowds, but following the Great Depression of the mid-1930s, the world's amusement park census had gone from 1,500 to about 400. With the advent of television in the 1950s, the industry was again in distress as people stayed home for entertainment. What was needed was a new concept.

That new concept was Disneyland. When Disneyland opened in 1955, many people were skeptical that an amusement park without any of the traditional attractions would succeed. Instead of a midway, Disneyland offered five distinct themed areas, providing "guests" with the fantasy of travel to different lands and times. But as you know, Disneyland was an immediate success, and the theme park era was born. No longer did patrons want a group of rides in a field by a lake, they wanted an entire perfect world to take them out of the real world for a day. The thrills of theme parks are often obscured from the outside by landscaping, reinforcing the feeling of escape. They are kept clean and the staff play along by way of costumes and mannerisms depicting the theme.

> Disneyland will be based upon and dedicated to the ideals, the dreams and the hard facts that have created America. And, it will be uniquely equipped to dramatize these dreams and facts and send them forth as a source of courage and inspiration to all the world. (Walt Disney, quoted in Mosley, 1985, p. 221)

Today there are six Disney theme park resorts around the world, including the Shanghai Disney Resort, which opened in June 2016. In 2014, the Disney parks hosted approximately 148 million guests, making them the world's most visited theme park company (TEA, 2014). Yet, there are many more theme parks that are thriving, too: Sea World (ocean life), Knott's Berry Farm (the old west), Universal Studios (films), Sesame Place (children's TV program), and Holiday World (Christmas).

Box 8.6
Web Explore

What's the Future of Disney in China?

All things Disney are a brand—an iconic American brand. Sensitive to this in a country with its own strong cultural sentiment, Disney has created its latest resort in Shanghai, China to be full of Chinese elements. From the outset, Disney has catered to Chinese officials who had to approve the park's roster of rides. It can boast the world's largest castle, the longest parade, and a vast central garden aimed at older visitors. Disney has left out stalwarts such as Space Mountain, the Jungle Cruise, and It's a Small World, and instead offers Mandarin Lion King. The Wandering Moon Teahouse at the resort's signature hotel has rooms designed to represent different areas of the country, honoring the "restless, creative spirit" of Chinese poets (Barboza & Barnes, 2016).

Will all this be enough? I am writing this one day before its opening, and the Shanghai Disney Resort is already fielding claims of American cultural imperialism. By the time you are reading this, the resort will have opened. How well is it doing? Is it running the risk of the initial reception that happened at the Disney park in Paris? Do some Internet investigation of both parks to answer this. You might begin by reading an article published in the *New York Times* that asked the same question: http://www.nytimes.com/2016/06/15/business/international/china-disney.html.

Yet there are complaints about what the Disney theme parks reveal about the culture. First, Rojek (1993, pp. 129–130) has written that Disney theme parks present a moralistic and idealized version of the "American Way." Here's how he described it: the moral order of the parks is based on a nostalgic picture of American society—the barbershop quartet; the streets of a small town; shiny-faced youth dressed in red, white, and blue; and the ever-smiling characters from Disney films. Throughout is a narrative of the moral and economic superiority of the American way of life.

For example, in Adventureland (an area within the Magic Kingdom Park), the armchair traveler goes to far-off and mysterious destinations such as the Caribbean. When they encounter "ferocious" wild animals and "barbaric" pirates, the dangers are always defeated by the "superiority of white, middle-class power" (p. 128). Next stop is Frontierland (also in the Magic Kingdom), which "symbolizes the triumph of white, male culture over nature" (p. 128). Essentially, Rojek's criticism is that the Disney theme parks overstep their entertainment role. They are underpinned by powerful political and social values; they distort history and present American society as free of conflict.

Another criticism comes from Bryman (1995). His critique is directed at the nature of control. Control, says Bryman, is in evidence in a variety of ways. It operates at the level of how the visitor is handled while in the parks to the way in which the parks relate to their surrounding environment. For example, there is control over the imagination of visitors. One way this is done is through selecting out undesirable elements in stories told in the attractions.

Also, Bryman cites how visitors' movements are controlled, both overtly and covertly, by the park's physical layout and by its built-in narratives. For example, the distinction between a ride and its queue has been eroded. Also, all staff are trained to behave in the Disney way, including control over language (customers are guests), and rules about physical appearance (the Disney look). Not everyone finds the "Disney way" offensive, however, as the newly created Disney Institute is in the consulting business of helping other companies be more like Disney (Barnes, 2012). Clients have included Haagen-Dazs, United Airlines, the Super Bowl, and the country of South Africa.

The Disney example of theme parks does beg the big question: Is a mediated, entertainment-based popular culture a good thing? Like Rojek and Bryman, others, including Neil Postman, say no. In the book *Amusing Ourselves to Death* (1986), Postman argued our popular culture, particularly television, does not merely reflect our culture, but rather has become our culture. Generations reared on mediated entertainment, he asserts, view the world, and ideas, differently.

Figure 8.7. Harry Potter Theme Park, which opened in 2010, in the Universal Orlando Resort, Florida, routinely turns away visitors because of capacity crowds.

That is, we come to expect life to be presented in small, disconnected, and amusing chunks. As a result, we can no longer think critically or behave rationally. Postman feels, therefore, our ability to live a meaningful life, both individually and communally, is compromised by a medium that "must suppress the content of ideas in order to accommodate the requirements of visual interest" (p. 92). The result of such ignorance is a culture addicted to "fluff."

David Bianculli (2000) also wrote about mediated entertainment. In contrast to Postman's view, Bianculli believes that especially television serves critically important educational and social functions. He asserts TV is actually opening the American mind because it provides positive role models, good storytelling, and likable characters.

Similarly, Steven Johnson (2006) defends mediated entertainment by claiming it is actually making us smarter. In the mid-1980s, Johnson claims, roughly starting with the television show *Hillstreet Blues*, programming of all sorts became more complicated and nonlinear. Since then, viewers have been required to remember bits of information, fill in gaps in plots, and make learned guesses to understand what is going on. Although highly controversial and unproven, Johnson even makes the claim that as a result of television, IQ scores have increased steadily over the past few decades. Just compare the sort of brain that was happy watching *Dragnet* in the 1960s, he points out, to the brain that watches *CSI: Crime Scene Investigation* today.

Box 8.7
The Study Says

The Simpsons

The Simpsons is an American animated television sitcom created by Matt Groening for the Fox Broadcasting Company. It is a satirical parody of a middle-class lifestyle epitomized by its stereotypical family, which consists of Homer, Marge, Bart, Lisa, and Maggie. The show is set in the fictional town of Springfield, and has become "an industry trendsetter, cultural template, and a viewing experience verging on the religious for its most fanatical followers" (Waters, 1990, p. 58).

A content analysis study of this popular television show, which premiered in 1989 and is still being produced, provides insight into how the American culture can be seen. Week after week, the show offers scathing critiques of America's faults and flaws. According to the study, among other things, *The Simpsons* operates from a leftist political position as it mercilessly exposes the hypocrisy and ineptitude of pop psychology, corporate greed, commercialism, consumerism, and modern child-rearing, as well as the potential dangers of fundamental religion, homophobia, racism, and sexism. The study's analysis concluded, however, that the program has not yet given a clear interpretation of feminism, as it presents women with a great deal of ideological confusion and contradiction.

Source: Henry, 2007

What is your position on the goodness of contemporary popular culture? The point is that we must all learn to discern for ourselves what we will consume and why. Television, movies, spectator sport, popular music, and theme parks can make or break us as a culture. It is up to us to decide what entertainment forms make "good" culture.

What We Understand About Popular Culture

Popular culture, or mass leisure, is an important reflection of society. Because of its omnipresent expression of the society itself, it also can shape and instruct society. From studying this chapter, you should know the following:

1. Popular culture is characterized as popular, inclusionary, commercial, trendy, and youth-directed.
   Select two of these popular culture characteristics and describe them, using examples from your own favorites:

   ____

   ____

2. Television is by far the pastime we participate in most frequently, and thus a central example of popular culture.
   In what ways is television such a pervasive example of popular culture?

   ____

   ____

3. Yet, research suggests even though television viewing is freely chosen and provides relaxation and escape, it is the least enjoyable and invigorating of all pastimes.
   Based on the chapter discussion, present at least two reasons why this may be so:

   ____

   ____

4. Other examples of popular culture include spectator sports, popular music, films, and theme parks. **Select one of these examples, and explain why it is a popular culture form in terms of the five popular culture characteristics:**

____

____

5. Since most popular culture in modern societies is media-based entertainment, its positive or negative role in shaping and reflecting the values and character of society is worthy of debate. **Explain this statement by discussing one of the arguments presented in the chapter:**

____

____

References

Andrejevic, M. (2003). *Reality TV: The work of being watched.* Lanham, MD: Roman & Littlefield.

Barboza, D., & Barnes, B. (June 14, 2016). How China won the keys to Disney's magic kingdom. *The New York Times.* Retrieved from http://www.nytimes.com/2016/06/15/business/international/china-disney.html

Barnes, B. (April 22, 2012). In business consulting, Disney's small world is growing. *The New York Times.*

Barnes, B., & Cieply, M. (February 26, 2011). Older audience makes its presence known at the movies. *The New York Times.* Retrieved from http://www.nytimes.com/2011/02/26/business/media/26moviegoers.html

Bianculli, D. (2000). *Teleliteracy: Taking television seriously.* Syracuse, NY: Syracuse University Press.

Billboard. (November 4, 2015). Katy Perry named Forbes' top-earning female musician. Retrieved from http://www.billboard.com/articles/news/6753044/katy-perry-forbes-top-earning-female-musician

Box Office Mojo. (2016). Worldwide grosses. Retrieved from http://www.boxofficemojo.com/

Bryman, A. (1995). *Disney and his worlds.* London, UK: Routledge.

Corner, J. (1999). *Critical ideas in television studies.* Oxford, UK: Clarendon.

Delaney, T. (July/August 2012). Pop culture: An overview. *Philosophy Now.* Retrieved from http://philosophynow.org/issues/64/Pop_Culture_An_Overview

Fiske, J. (2010). *Television culture.* New York, NY: Routledge.

Freud, S. (1915). Triebe und Triebschicksale. *Sigmund Freud Gesammelte Werke. (Instincts and their vicissitudes: Sigmund Freud collected works).* Frankfurt am Main: Fisher Taschenbuch Verlag.

Frey, B. S., Benesch, C., & Stutzer, A. (2007). Does watching TV make us happy? *Journal of Economic Psychology, 28*(3), 283–313.

Griffiths, M. D. (2015). Why do we like watching scary films? *Psychology Today.* Retrieved from https://www.psychologytoday.com/blog/in-excess/201510/why-do-we-watching-scary-films

Henry, M. (2007). "Don't ask me, I'm just a girl": Feminism, female identity, and *The Simpsons. The Journal of Popular Culture, 40*(2), 272–303.

International Association of Amusement Parks and Attractions (IAAPAA). (2016). Amusement park and attraction industry statistics. Retrieved from http://www.iaapa.org/resources/by-park-type/amusement-parks-and-attractions/industry-statistics

Johnson, S. (2006). *Everything bad is good for you: How today's popular culture is actually making us smarter.* New York, NY: Riverhead Books.

Kelly, J. R. (1982). *Leisure.* Englewood Cliffs, NJ: Prentice Hall.

Kubey, R., & Csikszentmihalyi , M. (2013). *Television and the quality of life: How viewing shapes everyday experience* (2nd ed.). Hillsdale, NJ: Lawrence Erlbaum.

Kubey, R., & Csikszentmihalyi, M. (2004). Television addiction is no mere metaphor. In M. Petracca & M. Sorapure (Eds.), *Common culture: Reading and writing about American popular culture* (pp. 251–272). Upper Saddle River, NJ: Prentice Hall.

Lang, B., & Rainey, J. (2016). Box office meltdown: Hollywood races to win back summer crowds. *Variety*. Retrieved from http://variety.com/2016/film/features/box-office-decline-summer-blockbusters-the-bfg-1201822322/

Lipsitz, G. (1990). *Time passages: Collective memory and American popular culture.* Minneapolis, MN: University of Minnesota Press.

Modleski, T. (1986). The terror of pleasure: The contemporary horror film and postmodern theory. In T. Modleski (Ed.), *Studies in entertainment: Critical approaches to mass culture* (pp. 76–89). Bloomington, IN: Indiana University Press.

Morley, G. (July 25, 2012). Is the Olympics worth more than Google? *CNN*. Retrieved from http://edition.cnn.com/2012/07/25/sport/olympics-london-2012-google-apple/index.html

Mosley, L. (1985). *The real Walt Disney*. London, UK: Futura.

NBC News. (July 12, 2015). Americans will spend more than $60 billion on their pets this year. Retrieved from http://www.nbcnews.com/business/consumer/americans-will-spend-more-60-billion-their-pets-year-n390181

Nielsen Media Research. (2016). *Reports*. Retrieved from http://www.soundscan.com

Petracca, M., & Sorapure, M. (Eds.). (2004). *Common culture: Reading and writing about American popular culture.* Upper Saddle River, NJ: Prentice Hall.

Postman, N. (1986). *Amusing ourselves to death.* New York, NY: Viking.

Rebollo-Gill, G., & Moras, A. (2012). Black women and black men in hip hop music: Misogyny, violence and the negotiation of (white-owned) space. *The Journal of Popular Culture, 45*(1), 118–132.

Rojek, C. (1993). Disney culture. *Leisure Studies*, 12, 121–135.

Sandomir, R. (June 7, 2011). NBC wins U.S. television rights to four more Olympics. *The New York Times*. Retrieved from http://www.nytimes.com/2011/06/08/sports/nbc-wins-tv-rights-to-next-four-olympics.html?_r=0

Sourcebook for Teaching Science. (2012). Television and health. Retrieved from http://www.csun.edu/science/health/docs/tv&health.html

Statistica. (2013). Statistics and facts about the fast food industry. Retrieved from http://www.statista.com/topics/863/fast-food/

Themed Entertainment Association (TEA). (2014). Global attractions attendance report. Retrieved from http://www.teaconnect.org/images/files/TEA_103_49736_150603.pdf

USA Today. (February 7, 2016). Super Bowl ad costs soar … but so does buzz. Retrieved from http://www.usatoday.com/story/money/2016/02/07/super-bowl-ad-costs-soar----but-so-does-buzz/79903058/

Waters, J. (April 23, 1990). Family feuds. *Newsweek*, 58–62.

Watson, J. (February 24, 2012). Hip-hop: Billion-dollar biz. *Forbes*. Retrieved from http://abcnews.go.com/Business/story?id=89840&page=1

CHAPTER 9

Taboo Recreation

Is leisure always wholesome?

No. Even though leisure is vitally important to the positive well-being of individuals and societies, it can also produce harmful outcomes.

When is leisure harmful?

If leisure is a condition of personal attitudes, preferences, and values, labeling certain leisure pursuits as harmful is useless. On the other hand, if leisure is a matter of making good choices, labeling certain pastimes as unworthy, and perhaps taboo, is possible.

What is taboo recreation?

Pastimes that are forbidden by law, custom, or belief are taboo. Examples are vandalism, gambling, risky health behaviors, and violence in sport.

Why does taboo recreation happen?

There are many explanations. The theories we explore in this chapter are anomie, differential association, and retreatism.

Leisure is, in simple fact, one of the most positive and wholesome aspects of contemporary life. Leisure can help relieve tensions, maintain physical fitness, enhance mental equilibrium, unite communities, yield a productive workforce, and help us return to health when ill or injured. However, leisure also has a dark side. Leisure can also cause conflict, injure us physically and mentally, reduce workforce productivity, and take a financial toll when paying for solutions to problems it creates.

The focus of this chapter is the adverse outcomes of engaging in pastimes that society considers deviant. We begin with a general discussion of the basic meanings and characteristics of leisure and deviance, and then suggest several examples: vandalism, gambling, risky health behaviors, and violence in sport. We conclude with some explanations for deviance in leisure.

Figure 9.1. Cage fighting, or mixed martial arts, is a full-contact combat sport that allows the use of both striking and grappling techniques, both standing and on the ground. The roots of modern mixed martial arts can be traced back to the ancient Olympics.

Leisure and Deviance

Some pastimes are labeled as taboo recreation. Is cage fighting taboo recreation? Is ultra-marathon running taboo recreation? Both can cause serious injury and even death, but are they both examples of deviance in leisure? What about going shopping? Some consider the U.S. shopping phenomenon known as Black Friday to fall under the deviant leisure rubric. The distinction lies in society's perspective.

For example, in the United States, certain forms of gambling are legal and allowed in certain locations, while others are not. Buying sexual pleasure is considered a problem in several countries of the world, but not in others. Vandalism can be considered fun for participants, but it costs property owners billions of dollars each year. Binge drinking is increasingly popular for college students, but campus administrators spend significant amounts of energy trying to curb it. Thus, in all groups of people, there are strong social prohibitions against certain actions, but the same taboos are not universal.

What is considered taboo can change within the same group. For example, since the 1970s, body tattoos have become a mainstream part of American fashion, common among both sexes, to all economic classes, and age groups from the later teen years to middle age. For many younger Americans, the meaning of the tattoo has shifted from a form of deviance to an acceptable form of self-expression (Roberts, 2012).

Therefore, pursuits such as gambling, buying sexual pleasure, vandalism, binge drinking, and tattooing are considered taboo only when the values and beliefs of a society deem them so. The word **taboo** comes from the Polynesian word "tapu," which usually refers to a prohibition of supernatural force. We use the term here to signify behaviors restricted by social custom or belief, which often become prohibited by laws.

Taboo: Restriction of a behavior based on social tradition

Box 9.1
Web Explore

The Goddess Pele

According to Polynesian tradition, *tapu* refers to something holy or sacred, a "spiritual restriction." A contemporary example of this comes from the Kilaeua National Park in Hawaii. Over the years, the volcano in the park erupts, sending molten hot lava through the landscape as it makes its way to the sea. A particularly spectacular view of this is at http://www.youtube.com/watch?v=ndB-2WRwyK1w

Pele is the goddess of fire, whose home is believed to be Halema'uma'u crater in the Kilauea volcano. Sometimes locals and tourists will place small shrines in the park to Pele. It is believed that the molten hot lava will not destroy Pele's tribute. To see what happens otherwise, check this out: http://www.youtube.com/watch?NR=1&feature=endscreen&v=-zp6ePkQWy0

Another way of describing the taboo nature of some leisure pursuits is through the concepts of ideational and sensate mentality. For example, **ideational mentality** suggests that laws and beliefs against such activities as substance use and gambling are primarily morally derived (Heise, 1988). That is, people have an "idea" that something is bad. Even though they do not wish to participate in it themselves, they feel the need to prohibit others from being involved because they believe such a restriction is for the public good. On the other hand, **sensate mentality** is an explanation that focuses on the more tangible and physical aspects of laws, such as antisocial acts of crimes with victims (Heise, 1988). Accordingly, when we consider substance use and gambling as deviant leisure it is because our own senses tell us through our own experiences that they are harmful.

Ideational mentality: Something is bad based on our own ideas

Sensate mentality: Something is bad based on our own experience

Nevertheless, the root concept of taboo recreation is deviance—any behavior that violates a group's norms. In some cases, the group's norms are codified into laws. For example, in most cultures, robbery, theft, rape, murder, and assault are considered acts of deviance that are against the law. This is referred to as **formal deviance**. In other cases, the group's norms do not have legal authority over people's behavior; here the deviant behaviors and consequences are more casual, such as in **informal deviance**. Picking your nose or shouting loudly indoors might be examples of informal deviance.

Formal deviance: Behavior that violates formal cultural norms, such as laws

Informal deviance: Behavior that violates informal cultural customs

The incidence of both formal and informal deviance in leisure is not only documented in police records and social work files but in research as well. For example, in one study (Agnew, 1990), a sample of teens indicated the reasons for their participation in 14 illegal activities. These included pleasure, thrill seeking, social pressure, and boredom—all qualities associated with leisure. Further, Aguilar (1987) provided rationale for considering deviant behavior a game: "In vandalism activities, the object of the game is to complete the task without getting caught" (p. 5). And in a study by Liebregts et al. (2015), it was concluded that frequent use of cannabis by young adults mostly occurred during leisure time as a way to enhance other leisure activities (such as socializing and video gaming).

The connection for deviance and leisure is extended by some studies that refer to the idea of playful deviance. As typically applied to the behaviors of attendees of Mardi Gras in New Orleans and college students on a spring break trip, playful deviance is defined as unseemly ways of performing for others (Rojek, 2000). Usually including raucous dancing, drinking alcoholic beverages, and public nudity, playful deviance is considered fun because it is concentrated in leisure spaces that are structured for such (a warm beach and Bourbon Street), and in front of others who encourage it.

Further, the concept of prole leisure also helps to flush out our understanding of deviance in leisure. Rather than being considered deviant, prole leisure is a label for those pastimes typical of the "proletariat" or working classes of people. Prole leisure expressions include motorcycling, professional wrestling, demolition derbies, bar hopping, roller derby, street racing, paintball, mudding, and cage fighting. While some might argue leisure in modern society is becoming more prole and thus more debased, the idea that leisure expression is better or worse according to its attachment to social class, makes this concept appear elitist.

Figure 9.2. in addition to playful deviance (i.e., Mardi Gras), other forms of taboo recreation include invasive leisure (self-loathing, i.e., solvent abuse), mephitic leisure (self-absorbed desire for gratification at the expense of others, i.e., serial killing), and wild leisure (i.e., rioting and looting) (Rojek, 2000).

Yet even with all these clarifications, what is deviant in leisure is still ambiguous. Going for a jog builds fitness levels, but so might hooking hubcaps. Joining a Scout troop provides outlets for socialization and improved self-esteem, but so could hanging out with a street gang. In truth, everyone is involved at least occasionally in deviant behavior. We've all run on the swimming pool deck in spite of signs instructing us not to. This is because the rules governing social life are inherently equivocal and thus open to different interpretations: Why is running on a swimming pool deck bad and running at the beach not? Indeed, deviant leisure is nothing but the activity that exploits this ambivalence (Rojek, 1999). Can we conclude, then, that leisure is only leisure when it is healthy, moral, optimistically productive, and legal, or is leisure more an honest personal expression that should be free of societal norms? This question is at the crux of a dilemma. Let's discuss both sides.

Aristotle wrote in *Politics* that the cultivated ability to use leisure properly is the basis of a person's and a society's worth. Making good and healthy free-time choices is leisure, not simply doing anything one pleases. Aristotle's leisure is a matter of social responsibility—making the right choices among life's many alternatives, and also doing them well (Sylvester, 1991). Thus, according to this perspective, deviant actions and events that are harmful and destructive are not leisure at all.

This is the side of the argument that serves as the premise of professionals who work in leisure service agencies. Helping people achieve responsible free-time choices is why the YMCA, Girl Scouts, municipal parks and recreation departments, camps, and other organizations exist. Professionals in leisure services consider leisure to be a force of good that allows us the space and time to develop our healthy selves.

Contrary to this, an alternative view maintains leisure is derived from personal feelings. Thus, leisure is in the heart and mind of the individual and has nothing to do with outside factors, such as what other people think. In this perspective, leisure is considered a private choice based on intrinsically motivated freedom and is thus not a matter of morality. Let's continue this debate by exploring some examples.

Examples of Taboo Recreation

Indeed, as pointed out by Rojek (1999), "an obvious and indisputable fact about leisure in modern society is that many of the most popular activities are illegal" (p. 82). Although there are hordes of examples to illustrate this, vandalism, gambling, risky health behaviors, and sport violence offer a breadth of "taboo" leisure activity illustrations. Sometimes these activities cause no harm at all; sometimes they are harmful to only those who participate; and sometimes such taboo pastimes are harmful to others who do not participate and to the society as a whole.

Vandalism

Defined as damaging or defacing private or public property, vandalism takes many forms: covering walls with graffiti, breaking streetlights, salting lawns, knocking over grave markers, egg throwing, tire slashing, draping toilet paper in trees, keying, tearing out pages of library books, throwing shoes over power lines, and even creating crop circles. In many cultures, vandalism is often considered one of the least serious crimes, but in Singapore, a person who commits an act of vandalism may be liable for a fine, a term in prison, and a corporal punishment of between three and eight strokes of the cane.

Regardless of legal sanctions, vandalism is usually expensive to correct, and for many private property owners and community public agencies, the cost is rising each year. Indeed, vandalism costs more than $15 billion a year, and estimates from a variety of cities across the U.S. suggest that graffiti cleanup alone costs taxpayers about $1-$3 per person each year (U.S. Department of Justice, 2010).

According to the National Crime Prevention Council (2008), some vandals work in groups, and most vandals are young people who vandalize out of boredom, anger, revenge, defiance, celebration, and in association with peer pressure. These motives vary, actually, according to the category of vandalism.

For example, *slovenly vandalism* is an expression of bad manners and carelessness, such as littering. Although the least destructive, it is so pervasive that this form is the most expensive to solve. *No-other-way-to-do-it* vandalism results from such actions as sitting on a fence because there is no bench, or leaning a bicycle against a tree because there is no bike rack. In addition, *conflict vandalism* occurs from doing what is most logical and natural, regardless of the intent of a facility's design, such as paths that result from people choosing the most direct route through an open space. *Malicious vandalism* usually results from people feeling mistreated and wanting to get back at society, or a particular agency or person, such as by defacing a park sign. This form of vandalism can feel quite threatening and frightening to the victim. *Cybervandalism* is vandalism on the Internet—the most common of which is website defacement. The primary motivation seems to be the desire to prove that the feat can be accomplished. Once inside the website, vandals leave their mark so there is no denying their presence. Vandalism on web maps has been called *cartographic vandalism* (Ballatore, 2014).

Figure 9.3. Graffiti or outdoor pop art? © Qatar Culture Club, 2011

Many vandals declare that for them vandalism is a form of leisure, and ironically, places of leisure, such as parks and playgrounds, suffer the most. Indeed, the most common forms of vandalism are the ones that can be considered the most recreational. For example, *thrill vandalism* arises from the goading or daring of friends, or from a desire for excitement, and *self-expression vandalism*, such as graffiti, is usually an attempt to be noticed. Indeed, it is self-expression vandalism that is perhaps at the heart of the taboo dilemma. Is graffiti, for example, pop art or is it vandalism?

Gambling

Next, we consider gambling as an illustration of taboo recreation. Gambling is the wagering of money or something of material value on an event with an uncertain outcome, with the expectation of winning additional money or material goods. It is one of humankind's oldest activities, as evidenced by writings and equipment found in tombs in ancient China, Egypt, and Rome. For example, a version of keno, an ancient Chinese lottery game, is played today in casinos around the world, and organized sanctioned sport betting dates back to the late 18th century.

How can gambling provide many of the qualities of leisure but also be harmful? Often throughout history, religious and civic laws have sought to prohibit gambling. But, in the 19th century there began a gradual, albeit irregular, shift in the official attitude toward gambling, from considering it a sin to considering it a human weakness and, finally, to seeing it as a mostly harmless and even entertaining activity, which is also useful in making money for sponsors. Additionally, the Internet has made many forms of gambling accessible today on an unheard-of scale, and by the beginning of the 21st century, approximately four out of five people in Western societies gamble at least occasionally (Glimne, 2016).

Box 9.2
In Profile

Las Vegas

Las Vegas is the most populous city in the state of Nevada. It bills itself as "The Entertainment Capital of the World," and is an internationally renowned resort city for gambling. Over 368 million people visit each year, often joining the more than 19,000 conventions held annually, and staying in 17 of the 20 biggest U.S. hotels. Established in 1905, the city's tolerance for various forms of adult entertainment also earned it the title of "Sin City," and this image has made Las Vegas a popular setting for films and television programs. However, a 1910 law made it illegal to gamble in Las Vegas, until the Nevada Legislature later approved a legalized gambling bill in 1931. Since then the town is well known for some pretty interesting facts. For example, when Paul Anka first performed in Vegas he was too young to be allowed in the casino. Howard Hughes stayed at the Desert Inn for so long that he was asked to leave, so he bought it. And, over 60,000 pounds of shrimp are consumed in Las Vegas every day, almost as much as in the whole rest of the United States (Las Vegas Convention and Visitors Bureau, 2016).

With the pastime of gambling, it is perhaps easiest to understand the application of the term *taboo*. Some gambling is legal—indeed government sponsored. Other gambling events are illegal. The distinction is quite hazy. When many state, provincial, and national laws continue to prosecute people for engaging in it, yet increasingly sponsor lotteries and receive tax receipts from casinos, racing tracks, and so forth, there seems to be a contradiction.

In the United States today, gambling in some form is promoted in 48 states, employs over 700,000 people, pays total wages of $14 billion annually, and each year earns $240 billion in gross gaming revenue—contributing $7.59 billion in direct gaming taxes (Statistica, 2016). Overall, the most popular form of gambling is playing the lottery, with nearly half of Americans claiming they play at least once a year. Betting on horse racing is a leading form of gambling in English-speaking countries throughout the world, and in France. Poker has exploded in popularity, principally through the high visibility of poker tournament broadcasts on television and the proliferation of Internet venues. Online betting (mostly casino and sport) accounts for $41.4 billion in revenues each year (Statistica, 2016).

In the U.S., on-site casino gambling accounts for one-third of all gambling (Statistica, 2016). At casinos, slot machines account for about 63% of the action, and in Delaware and Nevada (the only states with legal land-based sport betting), 43% of the total wagers are for NFL football (American Gaming Association, 2013). The demographic profile of casino visitors is similar to that of the general U.S. population in terms of income and level of education, except that men are more likely to have visited a casino than women, and the average casino visitor is slightly older than the population in general. Also, casino visitors are more likely to be active in their free time—going to movies, concerts, sporting events, museums, and amusement parks more often than the general public.

Another word for gambling is "gaming," and as a game, gambling rewards the player with the excitement of competition. Psychologists believe the real attraction of gambling lies in the thrill of uncertainty, the daring involved in taking chances, and the challenge of testing one's skill. For example, in a study examining gambling motives among college students (Neighbors et al., 2002), primary reasons were to win money, for fun, for social reasons, for excitement, and just to have something to do.

Unfortunately, some people gamble despite a desire to stop. This is referred to as problem gambling and is what characterizes the activity as taboo. Problem gambling often is considered in terms of the harm experienced by the gambler, as well as to others. For example, people with gambling problems tend to have lost significant amounts of money, need to bet more money more frequently, are restless or irritable when attempting to stop, use gambling as a way to escape and withdraw from family and jobs, are preoccupied with thoughts of gambling, and continue to gamble in spite of mounting negative consequences. In extreme cases, problem gambling can result in financial ruin, legal problems, loss of career and family, or even suicide (National Council on Problem Gambling, 2012).

Figure 9.4. Las Vegas contains 53,000 slot machines. According to studies (c.f. Collier, 2008) gambling addicts are more likely to play electronic gaming machines such as the slots.

Do some types of gambling have characteristics that may exacerbate gambling problems? While this is still poorly understood, anecdotal reports indicate that one risk factor may be a fast speed of play: The faster the wager to response time with a game, the more likely players may be to develop problems with that particular game (National Council on Problem Gambling, 2012).

Risky Health Behaviors

As you already know, leisure is an important factor in achieving good health. For example, when we participate in physical recreational activities, we improve not only our physical health, but our intellectual, social, and emotional health as well. But what about recreational activity choices leading to illness, accidents, or even death? Risky health behaviors such as tobacco use, alcohol and drug misuse, unhealthy dietary behaviors, physical inactivity, and unprotected sex are a major source of preventable health problems. To illustrate this aspect of taboo recreation, let's discuss substance abuse, particularly binge drinking.

Box 9.3
By The Numbers

Top 5 Teen Risky Behaviors

1. Not wearing a bicycle helmet
2. Riding in/driving a car after drinking alcohol
3. Texting while driving
4. Not using a condom during sex
5. Body piercing and tattooing

Source: Centers for Disease Control and Prevention, 2016a

Substances, such as narcotics, alcohol, tobacco, and marijuana are a major part of leisure expression in many contemporary societies. Alcohol, for example, in modest amounts, provides a means of relaxation from hectic pressures, offering both physical and psychological benefits. Drugs and alcohol are often used because they themselves provide many leisure qualities. Cocktails are served at parties; beer is sold at baseball games; and pills are popped at concerts. Interestingly, a euphemism for using drugs is "taking a trip"—meaning to enjoy a change of pace, just as we do when we go on vacation.

However, alcohol, drugs, and other substances provide only short trips, and overuse to make the trip longer and the party more fun can lead to insurmountable personal and social problems. This is **substance abuse**—perhaps the most prevalent type of taboo recreation. Experience-altering drugs are present in every region of the world, and every society has alcoholics. It began, in fact, with the invention of agriculture, which was not only motivated by a need for a constant food supply, but also by the discovery of the use of cultivated grains for beer (Lazare, 1989).

Substance abuse: Overindulging in and depending on a drug, alcohol, or other chemical, to the detriment of physical and mental health

How prevalent is recreational substance abuse? Witness the more than 2 million members in 170 countries of Alcoholics Anonymous (AA), an organization that helps people with alcohol-related problems (AA, 2016). Between 149 million and 271 million people worldwide used an illicit drug at least once in 2009, according to a review of studies attempting to estimate the extent of the behavior (Degenhardt, 2012). That translates to 1 in 20 people aged 15 to 64.

The relationship between dysfunctional substance use and leisure is a reciprocal one. Although substance use often begins as a leisure expression, if use increases to the point of harm, the individual's leisure becomes secondary to the substance. Let's consider binge drinking as an illustration of this.

Who binges? About 92% of U.S. adults who drink excessively report binge drinking in the past 30 days, and although college students commonly binge drink, 70% of binge drinking episodes involve adults aged 26 years and older (Centers for Disease Control, 2016b). The National Institute on Alcohol Abuse and Alcoholism (2012) defines binge drinking as a pattern of drinking that brings a person's blood alcohol concentration (BAC) to 0.08 g/dL. or above. This typically happens when men consume 5 or more drinks, and when women consume 4 or more drinks, in about 2 hours.

Figure 9.5. More than half of the alcohol consumed by adults in the U.S. is in the form of binge drinks (CDC, 2016b).

According to researchers who studied undergraduate students at a liberal arts college in the U.S. (Fowler, 2012), students who reported binge drinking ironically also reported being happier than their non-binge drinking peers. Specifically, the study showed that happiness in the case of binge drinking in college was directly related to status—with wealthy, white, male, heterosexual, and/or Greek-affiliated students being happier than "lower status" students. That is, for the lower status students, those who binge drink reported levels of social satisfaction that are comparable to their high status counterparts. Binge drinking is therefore a symbolic proxy for higher social status in college (Fowler, 2012).

On the other hand, while binge-drinking college students may be happier, they are also at greater risk of harm. Binge drinking is associated with many health problems, including unintentional injuries (e.g., car accidents, falls, drowning), intentional injuries (sexual assault, domestic violence), alcohol poisoning, high blood pressure, stroke, liver disease, sexual dysfunction, and neurological damage. The National Institute on Alcohol Abuse and Alcoholism (2012) estimates that each year for college students 1,700 deaths, 696,000 assaults, and 400,000 incidents of unprotected sex can be attributed to binge drinking. Furthermore, approximately 25% of college students reported academic consequences.

Box 9.4
The Study Says

College Drinking Games and The Guys

Drinking games (DGs) involve heavy alcohol consumption, and although such games have been characterized as a male-dominated activity, studies have not specifically examined how conformity to masculine norms are associated with playing drinking games. Thus, the purpose of this study was to investigate the associations between masculine norms and frequency of DGs participation in a sample of white and Asian American college men from a public university who completed self-report questionnaires. Results indicated that increased levels of conformity to the masculine norms of "being a playboy" and "heterosexual presentation" were significantly associated with more frequent drinking games participation for white but not for Asian American college men.

Source: Zamboanga, Iwamoto, Pesigan, & Tomaso, 2015

Violence in Sport

Sport violence can be described as behavior that causes harm, occurs outside of the rules, and is unrelated to the competitive objectives of the game (Terry & Jackson, 1985, p. 2). In sport, in general, two forms of aggression have been identified. First, instrumental aggression is nonemotional and oriented toward the task required. Otherwise, **reactive aggression** has an underlying emotional component, with harm as its goal. We consider violence in sport as a taboo recreation example as typically an outcome of reactive aggression. And when you consider it, can you think of any other human endeavor that allows us to run the gamut of emotion between thrill and anger, joy and despair? Sports are the ultimate roller-coaster ride of emotions.

Reactive aggression: An emotional response with harm as its goal; violence in sport can be an outcome

Figure 9.6. According to a Canadian study (Rockerbie, 2016), fans prefer ice hockey games without fights. But the study also concludes that fighting is a part of the fabric of the sport and it would take something drastic to change it.

Emanating from players, coaches, parents, fans, and the media, an increase in both the frequency and seriousness of acts of violence in sport has been well documented (Jewell, 2011). It is most prevalent in team-contact sports, such as ice hockey, American football, Australian football, basketball, and rugby, but can also be cited in such sports as NASCAR.

Why is there violence in sport? Some have argued that among U.S. fans, the most popular sport is football, explicitly because of the inherent violence in the game (Leahy, 2011). In fact, studies have found that violence and aggressive play in sports may serve to enhance the entertainment value of a sporting event because it adds drama.

Yet, in capitalizing specifically on the entertainment value of violence, today's professional wrestling is more a circus, with dramatic staging and soap-opera stories about the athletes. Since the violence is an intended part of the sport, an entertainment purpose may not be a useful explanation for sport violence. Such blood sports as bull fights, dog fighting, and cockfighting, while valued by some for their entertainment value, may not be useful explanations of sport violence either, as the violence is explicitly provided in these sports. And, even though billed as entertainment, in many countries, blood sports are banned and the consequences for being involved can be severe, demonstrating public outrage over their brutality.

Thus, while explaining violence in sport as entertainment might be appropriate in some fan settings, what else might explain it? Otherwise cited is that athletes themselves sometimes resort to violence in hopes of intimidating opponents, and thus receiving a competitive edge. Perhaps peer pressure or peer competition also influences violent athletes. For example, aggressive players tend to be idolized by fans (and even parents for child athletes), which may further inspire aggressive acts in the sport.

Perhaps more intriguing from a taboo recreation perspective is why do sport fans sometimes behave violently? With greater frequency, we read about rioting and violence by crowds at sporting events. Fires have been started in the stands, fans have crossed barricades to attack fans for the other team, athletes have been attacked in parking lots after the game, and referees have been assaulted on the field.

Box 9.5
What Do You Say?

Cheering Speech

When you go to a game, the governing body can control drunken behavior. It can control someone standing up and blocking the view of others; it can control signage if it blocks the view of others; but it cannot control the views expressed, even loud ones, by the fans (Wasserman, 2006).

In the U.S., is a fan's protest—known in sport law circles as "fan speech" or "cheering speech"—a form of expression protected by the First Amendment? In other words, do fans have the right to bellow at referees and players all game long, as long as they do not run on the court or field, or physically harm them? What about good 'ole belligerence?

In fact, one fan gained notice in the 1990s for this. He was a fixture at Washington Bullets basketball games, where he sat behind the opposing team's bench and shouted at players, sometimes through a megaphone. He was careful about his language. He was not asked to leave, yet when the Bullets moved to a new arena, the team relocated this season ticket holder behind the basket (Pennington, 2012).

1. What's your position on fan rights?
2. At what point should a referee draw the line and eject a fan from a game where excessive "cheering speech" is being used?
3. At what point does "cheering speech" violate the rights of other fans?

There are numerous estimates as to why sport spectator violence occurs, many having to do with the conditions of the sport event environment itself. For example, alcohol consumption is usually associated with eruptions of fan violence. Also, the media is believed to encourage "hooliganism" at sporting events by way of sensationalizing its occurrence. A recent fireball explosion during the Daytona 500 boosted television ratings and led to national headlines.

Certain sport types seem to be more conducive to spectator disruptions. For example, contact sports such as American football, ice hockey, rugby, boxing, mixed martial arts, wrestling, and water polo involve certain levels of physical violence by the players but include penalties for excessive and dangerous use of force (Snow, 2010). Fans seem to demand a certain level of violence for these sports, even though excessive aggression reduces a team's chance of winning. Jewell et al. (2011) have proposed that this is perhaps because fans experience a sense of catharsis from viewing blows and wrecks, that watching others be aggressive helps people vicariously release their own pent-up negative emotions.

Explanations of Taboo Recreation

Why do people participate in leisure pursuits considered to be harmful, immoral, wrong, abnormal, or a crime? What explains the popularity of vandalism, gambling, risky health behaviors, and violence in sport? Explanations for taboo recreation have been sought in order to reduce its incidence, but, as with deviant behavior in general, available explanations do not fully explain the phenomenon. As a result, there are many theoretical positions. We'll consider three that are perhaps the most applicable to leisure: anomie, differential association, and retreatism.

Anomie

Anomie: Lack of the usual social or ethical standards in an individual or group

The first explanation for taboo recreation is the concept of anomie. **Anomie** is a state of isolation that occurs when once-viable social norms no longer work for people (Merton, 1968). Anomie is when there is a mismatch between individual circumstances and larger social mores—it is the lack of a social ethic.

Anomie is a nurtured condition, and Simmel (1971) blames the changes and disruptions of life in modern society in general as creating ripe conditions for the development of anomie. The point is not that modern stress causes deviant forms of leisure, but rather it does provide an environment in which taboo pastime choices are fostered (Moore, 1982).

Boredom may provide an example of an environment conducive to anomie and thus the creation of deviant leisure choices. Boredom is a human emotion that occurs when one's life experience is not meaningful enough. Boredom usually results from too little stimulation, motivation, and interest. Although we typically consider leisure as an antidote to boredom, boredom commonly occurs for those who regularly perform pre-set exercise routines, is one of the main outcomes of extensive television watching, and is often a reason participants drop out of sports.

Box 9.6
In Your Own Experience

Leisure Boredom

Instructions: Do you relate more to the statements in column A or column B?

Column A	Column B
For me, leisure time just drags on and on.	During my leisure time, I become highly involved in what I do.
During my leisure time, I feel like I'm just "spinning my wheels."	If I could retire now with a comfortable income, I would have plenty of things to do.
In my leisure, I usually don't like what I'm doing, but I don't know what else to do.	Leisure experiences are an important part of my quality of life.
I waste too much of my leisure time sleeping.	I like to try new leisure activities that I have never tried before.
I do not have many leisure skills.	During my leisure time, I almost always have something to do.

If you chose Column A, you may be experiencing what Iso-Ahola and Weisinger (1990) refer to as leisure boredom.

For example, the questions in Box 9.6 are what helped Iso-Ahola and Weisinger (1990) to propose that boredom is actually a typical consequence of our pastimes. They called this **leisure boredom**. Leisure boredom is the perception that leisure is a meaningless routine that does not satisfy the need for optimal arousal. Many consider leisure boredom a special case of anomie that can lead to destructive choices in many aspects of life. For example, in a study of school drop-outs, while adjusting for the effects of age, gender, and race, leisure boredom was a significant predictor of dropping out of school (Wegner et al., 2007).

Leisure boredom: When people feel they cannot escape a meaningless leisure routine

Differential Association

In addition to anomie, other explanations for taboo recreation are plausible. This includes the theory of differential association. **Differential association** simply claims that delinquent behavior, including taboo recreation, is learned through interaction with others. If a person's social group is delinquent, deviant forms of leisure may be learned from it. Such social groups as peers on sport teams, housemates at college, classmates at school, and friends in the neighborhood affect young people in particular.

Differential association: Delinquent behavior learned from others

In addition to possibly explaining risky health behaviors, another obvious example of the differential association explanation is gangs. There is no single, generally accepted definition of a "gang." The term *street gang* is often used interchangeably with *youth gang*. However, the term street gang suggests street socialization, which is a key feature of adolescent gangs (Vigil, 2002).

According to the Federal Bureau of Investigation, in the United States there are at least 30,000 violent street gangs, motorcycle gangs, and prison gangs with about 800,000 members (cited in COPS, 2012), and internationally gangs have been documented in both developed and developing countries in North and South America, Europe, Asia, and Africa. Youth gangs are located in urban, suburban, small-town, and rural areas, and are often organized along ethnic, racial, and gender lines. Their activities include robbery, vandalism, drug sales, aggravated assault, rape, and in some cases, murder.

Figure 9.7. Zombie walks have become somewhat common in towns and cities, especially in North America, often becoming annual traditions, though some are also spontaneous "flash-mob" style performance art. Columbus, Ohio, 2012.

Because gangs may offer opportunities for power, recognition, excitement, and independence (Manson, 1990), they create pleasurable associations that can lead to antisocial acts. Lo (2000) highlighted four dimensions of differential association that controls this: the influence of groups on deviant behavior varies depending on how frequently they assemble, the amount of time they spend together, the level of priority the friendship is to group members, and the intensity of the friendship group.

Retreatism

Retreatism: Differences from the dominant social norms as a matter of personal expression

Finally, a third explanation for taboo recreation may be the idea of **retreatism**. Retreatism is a lifestyle that pulls away from dominant social norms as a matter of personal expression (Rojek, 1999). Dropping out, taking drugs, sexual experimentation, and engaging in other pastimes (such as zombie walks) that are antithetical to the conventional order of life may be considered an expression of self, in which a lifestyle centered around an alternative personal identity is created. Merton (1968) provided the classic description of retreatism as those who have "relinquished culturally prescribed goals, and their behavior does not accord with institution norms" (p. 207).

Box 9.7
The Study Says

Zombie Walking

A zombie walk (also known as a zombie mob, zombie march, zombie horde, zombie lurch, zombie shamble, zombie shuffle, or zombie monsta-mash) is an organized public gathering of people who dress up in zombie costumes. Usually taking place in an urban center, the participants make their way around the city streets and through shopping malls to a public space (or a series of taverns in the case of a zombie pub crawl) in a somewhat orderly fashion. The first zombie walk purportedly took place in 2001 in Sacramento, California, but since then they have experienced great popularity and take place worldwide. Due to their naturally chaotic nature, some zombie walks have been host to criticism, as well as new research to try to understand their appeal. For example, one study suggests these secular "festivals of the dead" are intended to fill a space left vacant by a de-spiritualization of death. The walks are a way to "reintroduce death into society, as well as to confirm what life is" (p. 66). The study focused on the annual zombie walk in Toronto, Canada, which draws up to 5,000 participants, and concluded them to be a ritual of working out the meaning of death, the meaning of birth, and what it means to be alive.

Source: Peake, 2010

What We Understand About Taboo Recreation

Leisure holds tremendous potential for people's well-being, but at times leisure can also have negative outcomes. As a result of studying this chapter, you should understand the following:

1. Taboo recreations are those pastimes typically forbidden by law, custom, or belief.
   Describe the implications of the use of the word "taboo" to label these activities:

   ____

   ____

2. Several concepts offer fuller descriptions of taboo recreation, including ideational mentality, sensate mentality, deviance, and prole leisure.
   Select one of these concepts and define it, and also provide an example from your own experience:

   ____

   ____

3. Examples of taboo recreation include vandalism, gambling, risky health behaviors, and violence in sport.
   Applying information from the chapter, explain the "taboo" nature of one of these examples from your own experience:

   ____

   ____

4. Determining good leisure from bad leisure is both complex and a dilemma. If leisure is a matter of personal preferences, distinctions of worth for specific pastimes are useless.
Explain this dilemma in terms of one of the examples of taboo recreation presented in the chapter:

____

____

5. Explanations for why people choose taboo forms of recreation include anomie, differential association, and retreatism.
Select one of these explanations, define it, and give an example that supports your definition:

____

____

References

Agnew, R. (1990). The origins of delinquent events: An examination of offender accounts. *Journal of Research in Crime and Delinquency, 27*, 267–294.

Aguilar, T. E. (1987). *A leisure perspective of delinquent behavior.* Paper presented at the Fifth Canadian Congress of Leisure Research, Halifax, Nova Scotia.

Alcoholics Anonymous (AA). (April 2016). Estimated worldwide AA individual and group membership. Retrieved from http://www.aa.org/assets/en_US/smf-132_en.pdf

American Gaming Association. (May 6, 2013). 2013 report shows commercial casino industry's highest growth rates since recession. Retrieved from https://www.americangaming.org/newsroom/press-releases/2013-report-shows-commercial-casino-industry%E2%80%99s-highest-growth-rates

Ballatore, A. (2014). Defacing the map: Cartographic vandalism in the digital commons. *The Cartographic Journal 51*(3), 214–224.

Centers for Disease Control and Prevention (CDC). (2016a). Teens' (Ages 12–19) risk behaviors. Retrieved from http://www.cdc.gov/parents/teens/risk_behaviors.html

Centers for Disease Control and Prevention (CDC). (2016b). Fact sheets: Binge drinking. Retrieved from http://www.cdc.gov/alcohol/fact-sheets/binge-drinking.htm

Collier, R. (July 1, 2008). Do slot machines play mind games with gamblers? *Canadian Medical Association Journal, 179*(1), 23–24.

Decker, S. (2012). *Strategies to address gang crime: A guidebook for local law.* COPS (Community Oriented Policing Services). Retrieved from http://www.cops.usdoj.gov/Default.asp?Item=1593

Degenhardt, L. (January 7, 2012). News release. *The Lancet.* Retrieved from www.ncbi.nlm.nih.gov/pubmed/22225671

Fowler, D. (August 20, 2012). Binge drinking college students are happier than their non-binge drinking peers. Annual meeting of the American Sociological Association, Denver, CO.

Glimne, D. (2016). Gambling. *Encyclopedia Britannica.* Retrieved from https://www.britannica.com/topic/gambling

Heise, D. R. (1988). Delusions and the construction of reality. In T. F. Oltmanns & B. A. Maher (Eds.), *Delusional beliefs (Wiley Series on Personality Processes)* (pp. 45–69). New York, NY: John Wiley & Sons.

Iso-Ahola, S. E., & Weisinger, E. (1990). Perceptions of boredom in leisure: Conceptualization, reliability and validity of the leisure boredom scale. *Journal of Leisure Research, 22*(1), 1–17.

Jewell, R. T. (Ed.). (2011). *Violence and aggression in sporting contests.* New York, NY: Springer.

Jewell, R. T., Coates, D., & Moti, A. (2011). A brief history of violence and aggression in spectator sports. In R. T. Jewell (Ed.), *Violence and aggression in sporting contests* (pp. 11–28). New York, NY: Springer.

Las Vegas Convention and Visitors Bureau. (2016). *Las Vegas facts.* Retrieved from http://www.lasvegas.com/planning-tools/vegas-basics/fun-facts/

Lazare, D. (1989). Drugs 'r' us. *Drugs, Society, and Behavior, 91/92*, pp. 26–39.
Leahy, S. (January 25, 2011) Poll: NFL beats baseball again as America's most popular sport. *USA Today.* Retrieved from http://www.content.usatoday.com
Liebregts, N., van der Pol, P., van Laar, M., de Graaf, R., van den Brink, W., & Korf, D. J. (February 2015). The role of leisure and delinquency in frequent cannabis use and dependence trajectories among young adults. *The International Journal of Drug Policy, 26*(2), 143–152.
Lo, C. D. (2000). The impact of first drinking and differential association on collegiate drinking. *Sociological Focus*, 33, 265–280.
Manson, G. W. (1990). *Why join a gang?* Burnaby, British Columbia: Burnaby Parks and Recreation Department.
Merton, R. K. (1968). *Social theory and social structure.* Glencoe, IL: Free Press.
Moore, T. J. (1982). A study of leisure choices of young offenders and young non-offenders and the impact of social structure and anomie on these choices. Unpublished Master's thesis, Acadia University, Wolfville, Nova Scotia.
National Council on Problem Gambling. (2012). FAQs on problem gamblers. Retrieved from http://www.ncpgambling.org/i4a/pages/Index.cfm?pageID=3315#gamblingtypes
National Crime Prevention Council. (2008). *The scoop on vandalism* (brochure). Retrieved from http://www.ncpc.org/publications/brochures/teens-1/vandalism.pdf
National Institute on Alcohol Abuse and Alcoholism. (2012). Moderate and binge drinking. Retrieved from http://www.niaaa.nih.gov/alcohol-health/overview-alcohol-consumption/moderate-binge-drinking
Neighbors, C., Lostutter, T. W., Cronce, J. M., & Larimer, M. E. (2002). Exploring college student gambling motivation. *Journal of Gambling Studies, 18*(4), 361–370.
Peake, B. (2010). He is dead, and he is continuing to die: A feminist psycho-semiotic reflection on men's embodiment of metaphor in the Toronto Zombie Walk. *Journal of Contemporary Anthropology, 1*(1), 49–71.
Pennington, B. (March 29, 2012). Examining fans' rights to jeer at games. *The New York Times*. Retrieved from http://www.nytimes.com/2012/03/29/sports/examining-fans-rights-to-jeer-at-games.html?_r=0
Qatar Culture Club. (2011). Graffiti an art or deviant act? Retrieved from http://qatarcultureclub.blogspot.com/2011/11/graffiti-art-or-deviant-act.html
Roberts, D. J. (2012). Secret ink: Tattoo's place in contemporary American culture. *Journal of American Culture 35*(2):153–165. Retrieved from https://www.researchgate.net/publication/228080110_Secret_Ink_Tattoo's_Place_in_Contemporary_American_Culture
Rockerbie, D. (October 2016). Fighting as a profit maximizing strategy in the National Hockey League: More evidence. *Applied Economics, 48*(4), 292–299.
Rojek, C. (1999). Deviant leisure: The dark side of free-time activity. In E. L. Jackson & T. L. Burton (Eds.), *Leisure studies: Prospects for the Twenty-first century* (pp. 81–96). State College, PA: Venture.
Rojek, C. (2000). *Leisure and culture.* New York, NY: St. Martin's Press.
Simmel, G. (1971). *On individuality and social forms.* Chicago, IL: Chicago University Press.
Snow, N. (March 23, 2010). Violence and aggression in sports: An in-depth look (Part one). Bleacher report. Retrieved from http://bleacherreport.com/articles/367924-violence-and-aggression-in-sports-an-in-depth-look-part-one
Stastica. (2016). Statistics and facts about the gambling industry in the U.S. Retrieved from http://www.statista.com/topics/1368/gambling/
Sylvester, C. (1991). Recovering a good idea for the sake of goodness: An interpretive critique of subjective leisure. In T. L. Goodale & P. A. Witt (Eds.), *Recreation and leisure: Issues in an era of change* (pp. 83–96). State College, PA: Venture.

Terry, P. C., & Jackson, J. J. (1985). The determinants and control of violence in sport. *Quest, 37*(1) 27–37.
U.S. Department of Justice. (2010). Youth in action. National Youth Network. Office of Justice Programs. Retrieved from www.ncjrs.gov/pdffiles/94600.pdf
Vigil, J. D. (2002). *A rainbow of gangs: Street cultures in the mega-city*, Austin, TX: University of Texas Press.
Wasserman, H. (2006). Fans, free expression, and the wide world of sports. *University of Pittsburgh Law Review, 525.*
Wegner, L., Flisher, A. J., Chikoubvu, P., Lombard, C., & King, G. (2007). Leisure boredom and high school dropouts in Cape Town, South Africa. *Journal of Adolescence, 31*(3), 421–431.
Zamboanga, B. L., Iwamoto, D. K., Pesigan, I. J. A., & Tomaso, C. C. (October 2015). A "player's" game? Masculinity and drinking games participation among White and Asian American male college freshmen. *Psychology of Men and Masculinity, 16*(4), 468–473.

PART 3

Leisure as Instrument: Systems Context

Leisure is a powerful tool that both helps and harms the social order.

In this final section, we turn our attention to the functional side of leisure—its ability to be an instrument for accomplishing other things beyond itself.

Chapter 10

Demonstrates how an instrumental web of leisure, work, and money dictates our lives.

Chapter 11

Considers both the freedom and tyranny of time on our leisure.

Chapter 12

Focuses on leisure as a means of both achieving and resisting equity.

Chapter 13

Concludes our explorations by overviewing today's leisure services systems.

CHAPTER 10

For and Against Productivity

Why do we work?

Today, the productivity brought about by working is necessary for human survival, yet it may or may not allow us to live well.

What is leisure's relationship to work?

There are conflicting answers to this. Some argue work is a less desirable human condition and leisure is needed to overcome it, while others claim work is more uniquely satisfying in life. And some declare work and leisure are equally desirable life situations.

If leisure's relationship to work is capricious, does leisure have economic value nonetheless?

Leisure is an economic balancing tool. It mirrors a nation's level of economic development and its economic system. Leisure also drives an economy by fostering consumerism.

Like work, is leisure good for an economy?

Leisure makes good economic sense. It benefits employment, taxes, investments, and profits. But leisure can also result in undesirable costs, such as from injuries and lost productivity.

At a very early age we begin to play. But most of us also understand from an early age that work is a constant in life. As we grow up, we begin to sense there can be a conflict about what is more worthwhile; should we focus on work or on play? On the one hand, we are advised that if we want to get to the top of our chosen careers, we have to put in long work hours. On the other hand, we are admonished that working too hard ruins our physical and psychological health—that we need more leisure in our lives. Are there economic ramifications either way? In this chapter we consider leisure's relationship with work and economics. We begin with the idea of balancing work and leisure, and then discuss the economic consequences of this balance.

Figure 10.1. School's out! Well, almost. A growing number of youth are attending summer school. In fact, in the U.S. the percentage attending summer school recently set record highs: 45.6% for 16- to 19-year-olds and 26.3% for 20- to 24-year-olds. Some economists blame the reduced number of summer jobs available for youth (Bureau of Labor Statistics, 2015).

Balancing Leisure and Work

What is work? Why do people work? Why do some people work harder than is required? Is there a work problem in society? Work, most simply, can be defined as the expenditure of effort. It is the use of energy (human, animal, mechanical, electrical, solar, etc.) to produce something. For example, in the U.S., the level of productivity of workers has more than doubled in the past 60 years. In other words, we can now produce their 1948 standard of living (measured as marketed goods and services) in less than half the time it took that year (Schor, 1992).

Why Work?

Answering the question of why people work is complex. One source of the answer is based in the Latin expression **homo faber** ("Man the Maker"). Homo faber is considered the biological name for humans, suggesting work is what makes us human. Humans create, build, change, and control the world with tools. Work is for making possibilities—things that did not exist before.

Homo faber: Human as worker

Homo ludens: Human as player

Yet, there is also the idea of **homo ludens**, connoting that play also makes us human. First labeled by Dutch historian Johan Huizinga in 1938, play is primary to and a necessary (though not sufficient) condition of the creating of culture. Huizinga writes, "All peoples play, and play remarkably alike." Therefore, leisure is also for making possibilities.

The relationship of work and leisure has a long and noble tradition. As we've already explored in Chapter 1, for example, to the ancient Romans leisure was seen as a means to oversee the work of a large empire. There were wars, taxes, barbarians, and millions of citizens to manage, so mass spectacles were used to placate it all. Later, the powerful influence of early Christianity in medieval Europe elevated work to godliness and leisure to an obstruction. Across several more centuries, industrialization solidified the idea of a work ethic, a transition that continued to separate work and leisure in everyday life. Driven by voracious machines, work came to be associated with the values of speed and efficiency, and thus productivity (Robinson & Godbey, 1997), devaluing leisure because it was viewed as nonproductive.

Indeed, in spite of some predictions, work is probably here to stay. In the U.S., the average full-time salaried employee is now putting in nearly 10 hours a day (Saad, 2014), while the average work week for all types of U.S. workers (including part-time, seasonal, etc.) is 34 hours (Snyder & Jones, 2015). This places the U.S. 16th in workweek hours worldwide. As well, 83% of employed Americans aged 25 and older say they do some type of work-related activities when on vacation (Bank of America, 2016).

Box 10.1
By The Numbers

Country Rank of Average Work Week

1. Mexico (43 hours)
2. Costa Rica (43 hours)
3. Korea (41 hours)
4. Greece (39 hours)
5. Chile (38 hours)
6. Russia (38 hours)
7. Latvia (37 hours)
8. Poland (37 hours)
9. Iceland (36 hours)
10. Estonia (36 hours)

Source: Snyder & Jones, 2015

Whether people work because they have to or because they want to, work provides many rewards. One obvious reward is that workers exchange their time, energy, and talent for money to buy things. Yet, anyone who has ever worked, even for the necessity of earning money, knows work provides other rewards, too. Work activities are often challenging, filled with opportunities for self-development and sociability. Work can provide a sense of contributing, and help us develop new skills. In fact, work often offers people their central identity. When we meet someone new, we typically introduce ourselves by what we do for work. "I am a lawyer," or "I am a student." Even those retired from work are tempted to claim their identity through their former work, especially if they worked in a high-status occupation.

So work offers many rewards, but does all work provide these rewards, and is work satisfying to all workers? Clearly not. For example, according to a 2015 survey by Gallup, only 57% are satisfied with the amount of vacation time they receive, 33% are satisfied with the amount of money they earn, 54% are satisfied with their immediate supervisor, and 45% are satisfied with the recognition received for work accomplishments. And, according to a 2012 survey by *Parade* magazine and *Yahoo/Finance* of 26,000 Americans, almost 60% would choose a different career if they could. Despite this, almost 80% of the surveyed workers plan on postponing retirement until they turn 71 years of age. According to the United States Bureau of Labor Statistics (2016), the current voluntary turnover rate for all industries is only 2%, compared to 2.5% 10 years ago.

Figure 10.2. Pike Place Fish Market, Seattle, Washington. Job descriptions here include throwing customer-ordered fish and rigging a string to the tail of a big fish that is jerked when a customer gets close to inspect it. What if all work was more fun?

Often, workers characterize their work as boring, stressful, unrewarding, and uninteresting—opposite the qualities of leisure. Why is there dissatisfaction in work? Causes include excessive workloads, concerns about management's ability to lead the company, anxieties about future incomes and retirements, lack of challenges, stifled creativity, frustration over the nature of the work, and insufficient levels of recognition. The tangible symptoms of work dissatisfaction show up as tardiness, apathy, and complaining. The intangible symptoms are worse and include depression, anxiety, and impulsivity.

Work For Leisure or Leisure For Work?

Leisure and work are often directly compared. For example, leisure is considered a solution for the dissatisfactions of work. Yet, just as often, other people love their jobs so much it seems like play to them. Some people don't feel they deserve leisure if they don't have a job. While studies suggest we are just as likely to develop good friends from our place of work as from our leisure activities, other studies claim work is more likely than leisure to create the dissatisfaction of stress (Reid, 1995). These are complex and contradictory views, so let's explore work and leisure comparisons a bit more.

There are basically three ways of comparing work and leisure. One view is pro-leisure; it maintains work is a less desirable human condition and leisure is needed to control or even overcome its problematic effects. This perspective suggests that a leisure-filled life is more natural. Another, and opposite, view is more pro-work, holding that work is the expected state of humans and leisure's role is in support of work. It should serve only to help us be more productive. Finally, perhaps neither a pro-leisure nor pro-work perspective is true, but rather the relationship is simply neutral. That is, it maintains all is well with both work and leisure, and healthy people need the rewards and satisfactions from both. Life is only meaningful when both are in balance. Let's check these three view points out more thoroughly.

1. ***We'll begin with the pro-leisure view:***

Leisure is the paramount human condition, and its relationship to work is in helping overcome work's inhumane consequences. One such consequence is workaholism. **Workaholism** has been described as an addiction to work—the pursuit of the work persona. It is working long hours in order to gain approval and success. Workaholism is considered a serious problem in many (but not all) contemporary societies.

Workaholism: Colloquially, compulsiveness about working

While there is no generally accepted medical definition, Griffiths (2011) has summarized clinical and anecdotal literature to suggest that in workaholism work becomes the single most important activity in the person's life and dominates thinking, feelings, and behavior. For instance, even if the person is not actually working, he/she will still be preoccupied with thinking about it.

A strong work ethic can certainly have its benefits; hard workers are considered to be desirable in a job because they work with vigor, tenacity, and enthusiasm. Yet working hard is not the same thing as workaholism. A hard worker will be at his or her desk dreaming of a holiday on a beach; a workaholic will be on the beach fretting about work in the office (Brennan, 2008).

Workaholism interferes with life and not only negatively affects social health, but there are physical and mental health consequences as well. For example, too little sleep and too much stress, often associated with workaholism, can lead to elevated blood pressure, headaches, chest pain, digestive difficulties, fatigue, anxiety, and irritability (Kubota et al., 2010). The prescription for workaholism is leisure: To return to health, the worker needs to incorporate more leisure into life. Common advice is to develop meaningful hobbies, get more outdoor exercise, and do enjoyable pursuits with friends and family.

Box 10.2
The Study Says

New Concerns for Workaholics

A study determined that workaholism commonly co-occurs in people with attention deficit hyperactive disorder (ADHD), obsessive-compulsive disorder (OCD), and depression. The study correlated these conditions with the responses of 16,000 people, aged 16 to 75. Workaholics were defined by high responses to these criteria:

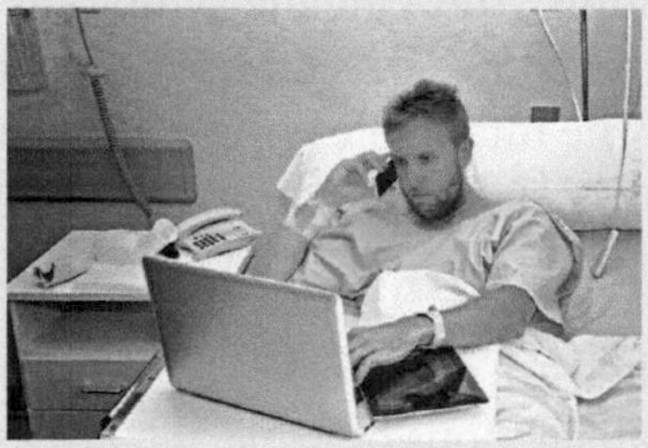

1. You think of how you can free up more time to work.
2. You spend much more time working than initially intended.
3. You work in order to reduce feelings of guilt, anxiety, helplessness, or depression.
4. You have been told by others to cut down on work without listening to them.
5. You become stressed if you are prohibited from working.
6. You work so much that it has negatively influenced your health.
7. You deprioritize hobbies, leisure activities, and/or exercise because of your work.

Source: Andreassen, Griffiths, Sinha, Hetland, & Pallesen, 2016

Yet, what is particularly interesting is that the compulsive nature of workaholism can be applied to leisure as well! That is, we can engage in pastimes too in a work-like way. Many people today overcommit themselves to recreational activities to the point where leisure takes on the characteristics of work. Their weekends are booked with social obligations, shopping, gardening, youth sport schedules, and planned outings. No free time is left for spontaneity. Workaholism applied to leisure is called **play-aversion** (Dickens, 1991). Symptoms include placing a high value on always being busy in leisure, playing hard, over scheduling activities, and feeling anxious when nothing is scheduled.

Play-aversion: Applying the behaviors and standards of work to leisure

2. On the other hand, according to the pro-work perspective:

Work is not at fault; work is ennobling. Even the most unpaid, unimportant, and unpleasant work is better than no work. Work builds something new; we feel elevated. We improve ourselves through work. In contrast, leisure is considered by this view as outside ordinary life, something that remains separate from the rest of life. Because of this, leisure is simply able to help us work better.

An illustration of the pro-work view is the concept of **central life interest**. Originally identified by sociologists in 1956, the idea usually cites work as playing the major role in people's lives. When our work is a central life interest (also labeled high work centrality), we identify with our work role and see work as the most important aspect of life. Work as central life interest is a relatively stable attitude that is not sensitive to conditions of a particular work setting (Hirschfeld & Field, 2000). However, work as a central life interest tends to be stronger for older workers than for younger workers (Bal & Kooij, 2011).

Central life interest: The primary focus of one's life and identity

How about you? Suppose you won an obscene amount of money in the lottery. Would you still work if you never needed to work again? If you answer yes, work is a central life interest for you. Actually, this is a fairly common interview question that assesses people's commitment to work, and according to polls taken across the years, most people would continue to work even when they don't have to for money.

Figure 10.3. Is there truth in the phrase "Work Hard, Play Hard"? According to a study by Aarssen and Crimi (2016), there really is a go-getter personality type that desires success in both work and play.

Box 10.3
What Do
You Say?

90% Unemployment

The man from the Department of Creative Technology (DOCT) had left, leaving Eve Smith in a somewhat skeptical frame of mind. Was it possible?

Eve owns a shoe factory. One thousand workers are directly involved in the production of shoes at an average annual pay of $40,000 each or a yearly payroll of $40 million. They produce 1 million pairs of shoes per year, with $80 million in sales. The difference between total sales and payroll ($40 million) covers other expenses and profit.

The man from DOCT suggested she install a computer-controlled robotic system that would enable Eve to lay off 90% of her workforce, that is, 900 workers. Output of shoes would remain the same: one million pairs per year. Eve would turn over the salary previously paid to the 900 workers to the DOCT. It, in turn, would keep 10% and put 90% into a Guaranteed Income Fund (GIF). The 900 laid-off workers would be paid 90% of their previous salary from the GIF, either indefinitely or until they secured other employment. In Eve's profit picture, nothing would change. She would have as many shoes to sell, and also fewer labor and production problems. Nine hundred workers, human beings, would be freed from the necessity of wasting their time making a living. They would be able to develop their capabilities, skills, and talents, or if desired, work voluntarily for the betterment of society.

Just then, Eve heard a faint ringing, as of a far-away bell. Then it became more insistent. She opened her eyes, realizing that she had dozed off. Had it all been a dream?

1. Is this truly a dream or can you see some real possibility in it? Why or why not?
2. If you were given the opportunity to receive 90% of your salary and not work at a job, would you take it? What about 75% or 50% of your salary?
3. Is it possible for leisure to be a central life interest? Read J.B. Nash's classic book *Spectatoris* (1932) and form your own opinion.

(Based on Neulinger, 1989, pp. 22–24; used with permission from the American Alliance for Health, Physical Education, Recreation and Dance)

Yet, there is also a shift underway. Enjoying ample and meaningful leisure is beginning to replace the centrality of work for some people. However, as summarized by Veal (2012), many scholars argue that leisure as a central life interest is not viable because leisure is not capable of replacing work in providing not only productivity, but also the major source of meaning in people's lives. As well, leisure and work are not the only sources of meaning in life: there is also care for family, and religious and community involvement, although all of these can involve leisure activity.

3. *Finally, the neutral view:*

This perspective about the relationship between work and leisure maintains that work and leisure are not at battle with each other—both are desirable for their respective benefits. Meaning and satisfaction exist in both, and both are required for realizing life to its fullest. The secret, for this view, is balance. How can this be achieved? People have implemented numerous ways to get a more leisurely work schedule, including **downshifting**, which affords more freedom to choose when and how much to work. Like changing to a lower gear on a bicycle, downshifting reduces work life to a lower speed or intensity. It usually involves creating a simpler lifestyle, including living with less money by working fewer hours.

Downshifting: Change a financially rewarding but stressful career or lifestyle for a less pressured and less highly paid but more fulfilling one

In searching for balance between work and leisure, downshifters may do any or all of the following:

- Reduce their work hours to have more time and less stress
- Reduce their income, often as a result of reducing work hours

- Reduce their spending and consumption levels, often to compensate for reduced income
- Reduce their job responsibilities or change careers to reduce stress and work in an environment that matches their personal values

Box 10.4
Web Explore

Work-Life Balance

For some inspiration in creating a more balanced relationship between work and leisure, watch this TED talk: http://www.ted.com/talks/nigel_marsh_how_to_make_work_life_balance_work.

Downshifting affords more balance between work and leisure by adjusting the hours of the day or days of the week. What about freeing time for more leisure that is an adjustment to the entire lifetime schedule? Most of us live on a lifetime schedule that follows a straight line. That is, life begins with play, is followed by a period of education, then a long term at work, and finally returns to a life of play again through retirement (Figure 10.4.1). Such an approach organizes life by strictly adhering to a single direction as preordained by society's custom. Is there another way?

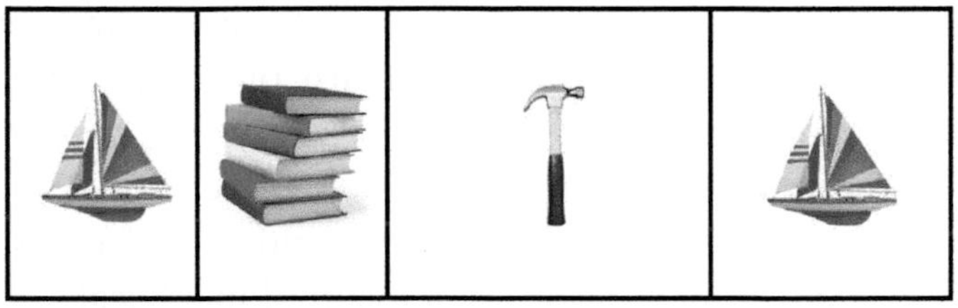

Figure 10.4.1. A linear life plan. © Patricia D. Setser, 2016

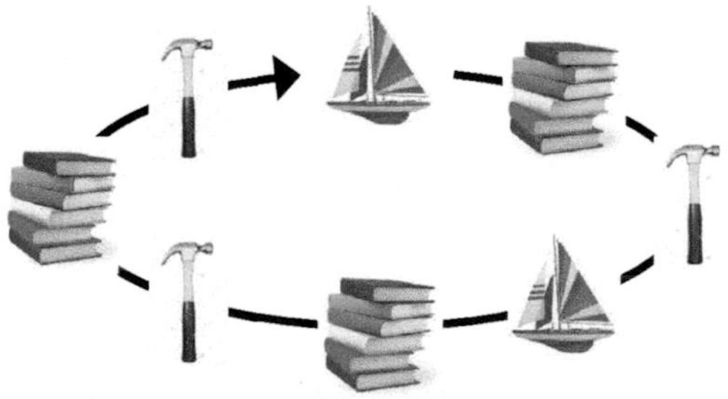

Figure 10.4.2. An alternating life plan redistributes schooling, work, and leisure throughout life. © Patricia D. Setser, 2016

As also shown in Figure 10.4.2, an alternating life plan would redistribute some years of schooling from youth and some free time from retirement into the middle years of life. Work wouldn't need to be the dominant theme in middle age, nor leisure in old age. Advantages of an alternating plan are a more even distribution of income over the life span with more people having the opportunity to realize personal goals, such as a college degree and child rearing. Foremost, it would also mean a more evenly distributed expression of leisure interests.

Economic Consequences

The complicated web that is the leisure/work relationship has implications for not only societal and individual quality of life, but also there are economic ramifications. We may already recognize how work is at the heart of economics, but we also need to afford leisure the same conclusion. Through work, both private and public leisure goods and services are being produced, which means leisure is central to consumption and investment in an economy. In fact, questions of how to distribute leisure goods and services have become central to concern for economic growth and economic decline.

Box 10.5
In Your Own Experience

Convincing Yourself

To convince yourself of leisure's economic significance, try these little experiments:

1. The next time you are driving along a highway containing billboards, count the number of advertisements in a 10-mile stretch that have something to do with leisure, parks, recreation, sports, tourism, cultural arts, etc. Calculate a percentage.
2. How much did you spend last weekend for leisure? As best you can remember write down the money spent the previous Friday through Sunday for a good time. Include pizzas, movies, gasoline, admission tickets, and everything to do with your leisure expressions.
3. Open your closet. Count the number of items there that have some relationship to leisure. Your tennis racket? Running shoes? Jewelry? Party clothes?

Essentially, economics, work, and leisure form an elaborate, yet functional, tri-part relationship—one that has implications for development, capitalism, and consumerism—resulting in both economic benefit and harm. We'll take up each of these consequences one at a time.

Leisure as Economic Development

Standard of living: The degree of prosperity in an economy, measured by income levels, quality of housing and food, medical care, educational opportunities, etc.

Gross domestic product (GDP): Total market value of the goods and services produced in an economy

An economy must grow if its people want a higher **standard of living**. As an economy grows, it is able to satisfy more and more of its people's needs and wants, and thus increase their standard of living. One way economists measure an economy's rate of growth is by studying its **gross domestic product (GDP)** over time. For example, the GDP of the world in 2016 was $73 trillion (USD), which in spite of a major global fiscal setback between 2008 and 2012, is gradually increasing (International Monetary Fund, 2016).

How is all this related to leisure? Basically, economies develop when they increase the wealth of their inhabitants, and the quality of leisure time, resources, and expressions is a part of this growth. It works this way. Beginning with developing economies, free time and recreation resources are much more limited because the wealth of inhabitants is low. For example, in Sierra Leone, which ranks 156th in GDP in the world (International Monetary Fund, 2016), two thirds of the population is engaged in subsistence agriculture, unemployment is close to 80%, and poverty and corruption are endemic.

In developing countries such as Sierra Leone, leisure is typically only possible for those who because of their economic status, do not need to be directly involved in producing food or shelter. Often such a leisure class is supported by a working class system. As an economy develops, industrialization reaches a successful level of output so that people have command over consumption. People's basic needs for food, shelter, and clothing are satisfied, and they can focus on leisure opportunities. In mature economies, where people have even more wealth, leisure itself becomes an industry.

Tourism is a good example of this. Tourism is an aggregate of many different businesses: attractions, transportation, lodging, restaurants, entertainment, and advertising. In Malaysia, for example, a majority of those with jobs in the service sector of the economy work in the tourist industries. In fact, in 1991, through the "Wawasan 2020" (Vision 2020) plan, Malaysia designated that tourism would be part of its economic development tool kit for becoming a world-class self-sufficient economy by 2020, thus leisure is being used there as an economic development strategy.

But what is the wealth from economic development for? Leisure configures centrally in the answer to this question, as well, and there are several illustrations. For example, to economist John Maynard Keynes wealth is explicitly for leisure. Keynes is credited, along with Adam Smith and a few others, with founding modern economics. Keynes provided the foundation for macroeconomics, the study of economies on the whole, including interest rates, employment, budgets and many other factors. Keynes revolutionized economics and its forecasts, and when he made the predictions in his 1930 essay, "Economic Possibilities for our Grandchildren," people listened. In the essay, Keynes posits that by 2030, developed economies will be wealthy enough that leisure, rather than work, will characterize national lifestyles.

Figure 10.5. Malaysia's tourism sector is now the sixth largest contributor to the national economy, attracting 27.44 million tourists and contributing a total of RM161 billion (14.9%) of Gross Domestic Product (GDP) in 2014 (Mohsen, 2015).

Keynes used a realistic estimate for growth—2% per year—and pointed out that with that growth the "capital equipment" in the world would increase seven and a half times. The thesis was simple. As technological progress made possible an increase in the output of goods per hour worked, people would have to work less and less to satisfy their needs, until in the end they would have to work hardly at all. While Keynes was correct in his estimate of increasing world wealth, he missed the mark with his prediction of leisure. With fewer than 14 years before Keynes' 100-year forecast is up, today economists wonder why we don't have the life of leisure Keynes envisioned.

Another early economist, Thorstein Veblen, argued a different answer for the purpose of wealth—that leisure is the status symbol of wealth. Veblen was a late 19th century scholar who concluded that as a nonproductive consumption of time, leisure is an aristocratic possession. To Veblen, leisure was a decadent economic exploitation because it was characterized by idleness and conspicuous consumption—that people spent lavishly on visible goods to prove they were prosperous. Veblen's writings reflected his own time, for in the late 19th century the pastimes of the wealthy few in Europe and North America contrasted starkly with the poverty of the rest.

Thorstein Veblen | Adam Smith | John Maynard Keynes | Karl Marx | Juliette Schor

Figure 10.6. Economists who have written about leisure's role in an economy.

Many have wondered whether today's economically developed societies still reflect Veblen's thesis. Does leisure still designate wealth? Through our leisure consumption we often do make a clear statement about our place in society, or at least our intended place. Our "toys" are our social ID. Interestingly, some more recent research updates Veblen's conclusions. According to a study by three contemporary economists (Charles, Hurst, & Roussanov, 2007), the less money your peer group has, the more bling you buy—and vice-versa. That is, conspicuous consumption for leisure occurs within the context of wealth. The study found that wealthy people living in locales with other wealthy people spent less on conspicuous leisure goods and services, while wealthy people living near poorer people spent more. The researchers concluded that people comparatively richer than their surroundings want to show off their wealth through leisure.

Does Leisure Drive Capitalism?

Not only does the level of economic development affect the expression of leisure, but also the economic system itself impacts leisure. An **economic system** is a particular set of social institutions that manage production, distribution and consumption of goods and services in a society. It is the systematic way in which economics are carried out.

Economic system: The organized way a society allocates its resources and apportions goods and services

Although today no economic system is considered a "pure" version of its basic principles, contemporary economic systems include barter, capitalism, market, socialism, and gift. Some world economies are considered "mixed" in that they combine two or more basic systems. Most mixed economies can be described as market economies with strong governmental regulatory oversight. Countries in the European Union, the United States, and Canada are examples of mixed economies because both private enterprise and government regulation are integral to their system. Yet, these countries have different mixtures, for example, with the United States being closer to capitalism and France with a larger dose of socialism in its mixture.

Different economic systems relate to leisure differently. We'll illustrate this point with the economic system of capitalism. Is capitalism good for leisure? **Capitalism** is based on the principle of private ownership of the means of production and distribution of goods and services. It promotes a free market regulated by supply and demand, with the goal of making profits for private individuals and companies.

Capitalism: The economic system of privately possessing capital

The central idea of the capitalistic free-enterprise system dates back to the Middle Ages in Western Europe with the early forms of merchant capitalism practiced especially in the Netherlands. The idea was "the advancement of private persons will be the advantage of the public" (Joseph Lee, quoted in Goodale & Godbey, 1988, p. 74). Scottish economist Adam Smith later expanded on this idea in his book *An Inquiry into the Nature and Causes of the Wealth of Nations* (1937). According to Smith, the basic premises of economic order under capitalism were (a) self-interest is a prime motivation, (b) individual striving and work will lead to a common good, and (c) no regulation of the economy is best.

How does leisure fare under a capitalist economic system? An early comment about this was made in the 1880s by Karl Marx—the father of socialism—when he criticized the suppression of leisure under capitalism. Because capitalism's idea of free enterprise is based on the labor of individuals, leisure was considered an obstruction. "In capitalist society ... leisure time for a privileged class is produced by converting the whole lifetime of the masses into labor time" (cited in Cunningham, 1980, p. 515).

Even to Adam Smith the relationship was antagonistic: The more leisure, the less progress; the more progress, the less leisure (1937). Similarly, in more contemporary writings, the relationship between leisure and capitalism remains contrary. Based on the question of whether leisure meets individual or societal needs, Torkildsen (2005) maintains that under capitalism leisure is not an individual right, but rather something to be given as a reward or withheld as a punishment.

Contemporary economist Juliet Schor (1992) argues capitalism tends to expand work to the detriment of leisure. Personal economic need and desire often requires workers to hold down more than one job or seek overtime above the 40-hour workweek standard. Schor's (2010) advice for more leisure is: Work and spend less, create and connect more.

Box 10.6
In Profile

Veblen, Smith, Marx, and Schor

Do economists consider the relationship between leisure and economics similarly? Separated by many years, is there still a contemporary thread in the ideas of Adam Smith, Karl Marx, Thorstein Veblen, and Juliet Schor?

	Adam Smith	Karl Marx	Thorstein Veblen	Juliet Schor
Time Period	Late 1700s	Mid-1800s	Late 1800s	Early 21st century
Biography	Moral philosopher at University of Glasgow. Generally considered the founder of capitalism.	From Prussia (now Germany). Working with Friedrich Engels, is known as socialism's most zealous intellectual.	From Wisconsin. Professor at University of Chicago. Coined the expression "conspicuous consumption."	Professor of sociology at Boston College. Focuses on trends in work, leisure, consumerism, environmental and economic justice.
Economic premise	Individual self-interest with no regulation provides for a common good.	Exchanges of equal value for equal value, where value is determined by amount of work put into whatever is produced.	Economic behavior is driven by human instincts of emulation, predation, and curiosity. His ideas are the basis of modern advertising.	Economics based on consumerist mentality (spending for social meaning) harm people and communities.
Consequence for leisure	Leisure is an obstruction to progress.	Leisure is harmed when not equally available. To gain more leisure, the lower classes must overthrow the upper classes.	Leisure is the outward expression of the upper classes. To gain more leisure, the lower classes must climb up to the upper classes.	Keeping up with the Joneses requires working more, which means less leisure time and energy.

Other economic systems also have a roller-coaster relationship with leisure.For example, those within a socialist economic system have been able to acquire free time but are often unsuccessful in producing the goods and services people want for leisure. This might all mean that when leisure is defined as buying something, a capitalist economic system is effective. Let's take this idea up in the next section.

Consumerism

A fundamental part of any economic system is **consumption**. In most economies, it is the largest spending category. It includes purchases of nondurable goods, such as bowling shoes, and durable goods, such as a bowling ball. We also consume services, such as bowling leagues. You can actually tell a lot about an individual's (and a society's) economic situation by observing their consumption patterns. Do they drive a Hummer or an old VW bus? What do they eat? What do they wear? Although you sometimes come across people who live well below or above their means, consumption and income tend to be closely tied.

Consumption: All purchases of goods and services for personal use

We all participate in an economy through consumption, yet not all of us participate in consumerism. **Consumerism** is buying things that are unnecessary in an exaggerated way. Consumerism is most likely found in capitalist societies where it is typically stimulated by media. Unlike consumption,

Consumerism: A social and economic order that encourages the purchase of goods and services in ever greater amounts; preoccupation with and an inclination toward the buying of consumer goods.

consumerism has emotional, social, and psychological origins, as well as economic, that encourage people to buy things they can and cannot buy to evade social discrimination.

Leisure is a primary source of both consumption and consumerism. Indeed, expenditures for leisure are at the center of some economies. People buy fishing licenses, amusement park admissions, gasoline for power boats, golf clubs, pets, iPod downloads, flower seeds, and jogging shoes. For example, expenditures for just sports footwear in the U.S. is about $21 billion annually (Statistica, 2015).

Economists also report expenditures for leisure goods have been increasing at a faster rate than other types of merchandise. For example, in the late 1800s in the U.S., less than 2% of household expenditures were devoted to recreation goods, as compared to 2008 when leisure claimed over 9% of all personal consumption. What about more recently?

Economists have labeled the 2008–2012 economic recession the "Great Recession," marking it as an economic decline that affected the entire world economy. It caused higher detriment in some countries than others and was characterized by a variety of systemic imbalances sparked by the financial crisis of 2007–2008. In the U.S., for example, persistent higher unemployment resulted, along with mediocre consumer confidence, continuing flat home values, high foreclosures, escalating federal debt, and rising petroleum and food prices.

In times of recession, is leisure considered a luxury good and therefore consumers reduce their expenditures? To answer, let's consider world tourism. According to the World Tourism Organization (2012), international tourism receipts in 2011 exceeded $1 trillion (USD) for the first time ever, up from $928 billion in 2010. In real terms, this means receipts grew by 3.8%, based on a 4.6% increase in international tourists. By regions, the Americas (+5.7%) recorded the largest increase in receipts, followed by Europe (+5.2%), and Asian and the Pacific (+4.3%).

However, not all leisure sectors demonstrated this much resilience to the recession. For example, between 2009 and 2011, U.S. consumers increased their expenditures on entertainment by 2.7% (an average of $2,572 per household), which is less than the 3.3% increase in consumer spending overall (Bureau of Labor Statistics, 2012).

And now, is the recession over? In terms of leisure, it seems to be. Travel and tourism, for example, generated US $7.6 trillion (10% of global GDP) and 277 million jobs (1 in 11 jobs) for the global economy in 2014. Recent years have seen tourism growing at a faster rate than both the wider economies of the world, and other significant sectors such as automotive, financial services, and health care (World Travel and Tourism Council, 2015). In checking Table 10.1 below it is also evident that leisure expenditures of various types are a strong factor in driving the U.S. economy.

Table 10.1
Comparison of Leisure Versus Other Expenditures in the U.S. (First Quarter, 2016)

Personal Consumption Category	Expenditures (in billions of dollars)
Housing and Utilities	$2,255
Health Care	$2,111
Food and beverages in restaurants, bars, etc.	$900
Recreation Services	$497
Motor Vehicles	$441
Recreational goods and vehicles	$385
Furnishings and Durable Household Equipment	$394
Gasoline and Other Energy Goods	$257

Source: Bureau of Economic Analysis, 2016

Figure 10.7. Shopping for leisure goods, or shopping as leisure?

This means leisure remains a growth industry. That is, buying leisure goods and services is good for the economy, but the web entangling leisure and consumption is quite dynamic, so such a grand conclusion is complicated. How? Well, let's consider shopping itself as an illustration. Although we have no clear estimates of how many of us spend time wandering around the stores, a number of studies have pointed to the prevalence of shopping as a favorite pastime. In fact, when people are given more free time, participating in shopping tends to increase.

Visiting shopping malls is for many a preferred form of evening or weekend recreation. Shopping is fun—an experience—a fact not lost on retail marketing strategies. As an example, take the Recreational Equipment Inc.'s (REI) flagship store in Seattle, Washington. With a simulated rain shower to test rain gear, a glass-encased climbing wall to test climbing gear, a rough-and-tumble path through a forest to test mountain bikes and boots, and even an in-store ranger station, this outdoor equipment retailer reflects the growing trend of shopping as leisure.

But is shopping really leisure? If what we want are things, and things cost money, and money costs time (deGrazia, 1962), then are we experiencing leisure through shopping? This question leads us to the concept of the **harried leisure class**. First noticed by Steffan Linder in his 1970 book by the same title, the relevance of this idea today is stunning. Linder was the first economist to understand and predict the frantic pace of leisure in modern life. In his little book he pointed out that consumption takes time, and with increased levels of products and services, time for consumption has to be sped up. Linder considered this the antithesis of leisure. We have to work more, to be able to buy more things, and thus get into a hectic, never satisfied, materialistic frenzy.

Harried leisure class: Spending money for leisure, thus spoiling leisure by making us feel frantic

It is common wisdom that owning more and more material possessions will not necessarily bring happiness. Economists and psychologists who have spent decades studying the relationship between wealth and happiness, have generally concluded wealth increases human happiness when it lifts people out of abject poverty and into the middle class, but it does little to increase happiness thereafter (Gilbert, 2006). So, what if we were more conserving in our leisure consumption? Could we still have fun?

What would happen if we didn't want faster jet skis, easy travel to unusual places, and hundreds of music downloads? What would life be like if we engaged in only those activities that made a minimal demand on material goods, such as walking, yoga, reading, singing, and dancing? How would our health be affected if we chose the cheaper cross-country skiing over the more expensive downhill skiing, hiking over all-terrain motorbikes, or playing basketball at the park rather than at the club? Would recycling the medals we won in sport competitions, repairing and passing on to others toys our children have outgrown, and taking our own cup to the refreshment stand help the environment as well?

How Leisure Benefits and Harms an Economy

In spite of the delicate and sometimes conflicting balance between leisure and economics that we just illustrated through the concepts of economic development, capitalism, and consumption, there is no doubt that leisure has economic power. Yet, the dollars and cents of leisure's economic worth can be both positive and negative.

For example, the presence of leisure facilities and programs attracts businesses and industries to particular locales. Cultural and sporting events are good public relations for the corporations that support them, ultimately increasing profits. Well-planned leisure services can help reduce the costs of crime. Therapeutic recreation treatments return injured workers to the job, thus contributing to their company's and nation's productivity. And, according to a study of fitness and pay raises (Kosteas, 2012), exercising 3 or more times a week leads to 6% higher pay for men, on average, and 10% more for women. The pay hike is due, claims the study, to induced productivity boosts.

As well, and although it is difficult to estimate the number of people whose job income is leisure-related, available statistics suggest many occupations have something to do with the provision of leisure goods and services for others. For example, those in the entertainment fields, supervisors in city recreation agencies, managers in parks and forests, hospital recreation therapists, trainers at health and fitness facilities, employees of restaurants and hotels, wedding planners, bowling center managers, travel agents, and many more types of leisure-related employment provide benefits to an economy.

Figure 10.8. As an example of leisure related taxes, consider the city of Chicago. As of 2016, the streaming services (i.e., Netflix) tax is 9%, a taxi ride is taxed 15%, and the hotel tax is 17.4%. This tour of downtown also is taxed. © Patricia D. Setser

Leisure's positive impact on an economy can also be found in taxes and other governmental fees. Local, state or provincial, and federal revenues through taxes paid in connection with leisure contribute significantly to the economic health of a society. Each year, for example, the National Endowment for the Arts in the U.S. allocates millions of dollars in federal tax money to be used as matching funds by local arts organizations. The sources of these funds include sales taxes from the purchase of leisure goods and services, income taxes on wages earned in leisure-related jobs, property taxes on private and commercial leisure oriented properties, taxes on restaurant meals and hotel accommodations, etc.

On the other hand, sometimes leisure results in costs rather than benefits to both an individual's finances and a community's economy. For example, there is often decreased productivity of workers that happens around holidays, including the opening of baseball and hunting seasons; and leisure businesses are among the most susceptible to the whims of public taste. Financial headaches can also be caused by the seasonal nature of some forms of leisure, such as beach and ski resorts.

Frequently, members of a community must pay high costs to solve problems resulting from leisure. For example, there are about 144.1 million dogs and cats in the U.S. (Humane Society, 2016), and the cost to taxpayers for dealing with strays and removing fecal waste from public places amounts to millions of dollars per year. The U.S. Coast Guard comes to the rescue of an average of 114 people per day at a total cost of $680 million annually (Fagin, 2009). A Coast Guard patrol boat costs $1,147 per hour to operate, and if the rescue requires the use of a C-130 turboprop plane, the bill increases to a rate of $7,600 an hour.

Further, unintentional injuries from leisure pursuits affect millions of people, costing millions of dollars to treat and millions of dollars in lost wages, insurance payments, and lawsuits. For example, each year in the U.S. emergency departments treat more than 220,000 children ages 14 and younger for playground-related injuries, costing over $1.2 billion (Centers for Disease Control, 2012).

Box 10.7
In Profile

The Velvet Rope Economy

Behind a locked door aboard Norwegian Cruise Line's newest ship is a world most of the vessel's 4,200 passengers will never see. And that is exactly the point. In the "Haven," as this ship within a ship is called, about 275 elite guests enjoy not only a concierge and 24-hour butler service, but also a private pool, sun deck, and restaurant, creating an oasis free from the crowds elsewhere on the "Norwegian Escape." If Haven passengers venture out of their area to see a show, a flash of their gold key card gets them the best seats in the house. When the ship returns to port, they disembark before everyone else. (from Schwartz, 2016, p.1).

This has been labeled the "velvet rope economy." And, with disparities in wealth greater than at any time since the Gilded Age (and the time of the Titanic), the gap is widening between the highly affluent —who find themselves behind the velvet ropes of today's economy—and everyone else. Leisure service companies have become quite competent at creating extravagance and exclusivity for the select few.

More examples? When top-dollar travelers switch planes in Atlanta, New York, and other cities, Delta Airlines ferries them between terminals in a Porsche in what the airline calls a "surprise-and-delight service." Last month, Walt Disney World began offering after-hours access to visitors who want to avoid the crowds. In other words, if you are staying at one of the Disney hotels you qualify to have the Magic Kingdom to yourself. At SeaWorld, a family of four can jump to the front of the line and score the best seats for rides and shows for an extra $80, in addition to the basic $320 admission (Schwartz, 2016).

What We Understand About Leisure, Work, and Economics

Leisure, work, and economics are instrumentally related. That is, each has an impact on the others. From reading this chapter you should understand that:

1. Although work offers the rewards of money, self-esteem, personal interactions, and the sense of making a contribution to society, some people are dissatisfied with work. Therefore, should society place more emphasis on the values of leisure?
   Cite an example of how the values of leisure might be applied to the workplace:

   ____

   ____

2. There are basically three ways of answering this. One view is pro-leisure and maintains work is a less desirable human condition and leisure is needed to control or overcome its problematic effects.
   Based on the chapter discussion, describe the "pro-leisure" view of work and leisure:

   ____

   ____

3. Another, and opposite, view is pro-work, holding that work is the natural state of humans and leisure's role is in support of work.
   Based on the chapter discussion, describe the "pro-work" view of work and leisure:

   ____

   ____

4. The third view is a neutral one, maintaining all is well with both work and leisure, and healthy people need the rewards and satisfactions from both.
   Based on the chapter discussion, describe the "neutral" view of work and leisure:

   ____

   ____

5. Regardless of what it all means to society, and to us personally, the complicated web that is the leisure/work relationship has economic ramifications. For example, leisure is a mirror of a nation's level of economic development and its economic system.
   Select one of the economic systems discussed in the chapter and describe how it reflects leisure:
   ____
   ____

6. Sometimes consumption itself is viewed as a leisure experience.
   What is the difference between leisure consumption and leisure consumerism?
   ____
   ____

7. Leisure has both positive and negative economic consequences.
   Cite at least two positive and at least two negative economic consequences of leisure:
   ____
   ____

References

Aarssen, L. W., & Crimi, L. (2016). Legacy, leisure and the "work hard - play hard" hypothesis. *The Open Psychology Journal, 9*, 7–24. http://dx.doi.org/10.2174/1874350101609010007

Andreassen, C. S., Griffiths, M. D., Sinha, R., Hetland, J., & Pallesen, St. (May 18, 2016). The relationships between workaholism and symptoms of psychiatric disorders: A large-scale cross-sectional study. *PloS One, 11*(5). Retrieved from http://www.ncbi.nlm.nih.gov/pmc/articles/PMC4871532/

Bal, P. M., & Kooij, D. (2011). The relations between work centrality, psychological contracts, and job attitudes: The influence of age. *European Journal of Work and Organizational Psychology, 20*(4), 497–523.

Bank of America. (2016). *Leisure in retirement: Beyond the bucket list.* Retrieved from http://agewave.com/wp-content/uploads/2016/05/2016-Leisure-in-Retirement_Beyond-the-Bucket-List.pdf

Brennan, C. (September 9, 2008). Addicted to hard labour. *The Irish Times*. Retrieved from http://www.irishtimes.com/newspaper/health/2008/0909/1220629645968.html

Bureau of Economic Analysis. (May 27, 2016). Table 2.3.5. Personal Consumption Expenditures by Major Type of Product. Retrieved from http://www.bea.gov/iTable/iTable.cfm?reqid=9&step=1&acrdn=2#reqid=9&step=1&isuri=1

Bureau of Labor Statistics. (2012). Consumer expenditures–2011. U.S. Department of Labor. Retrieved from http://www.bls.gov/news.release/cesan.nr0.htm

Bureau of Labor Statistics. (2015). Employment and unemployment among youth summary. Retrieved from http://www.bls.gov/news.release/youth.nr0.htm

Bureau of Labor Statistics. (2016). Job openings and labor turnover–April 2016. Retrieved from http://www.bls.gov/news.release/pdf/jolts.pdf

Centers for Disease Control (CDC). (2012). Playground injuries: Fact sheet. Retrieved from http://www.cdc.gov/homeandrecreationalsafety/playground-injuries/playgroundinjuries-factsheet.htm

Charles, K. K., Hurst, E., & Roussanov, N. (September 2007). Conspicuous consumption and race. *National Bureau of Economic Research Working Paper No. 13392.* Retrieved from http://www.nber.org/papers/w13392

Cunningham, H. (1980). *Leisure in the Industrial Revolution*. London, UK: Croom Helm.

deGrazia, S. (1962). *Of time, work, and leisure*. New York, NY: The Twentieth Century Fund.

Dickens, P. (March/April 1991). Playing hard or hardly playing? *Executive Female, 46.*

Fagin, S. (December 19, 2009). Lessons of the Mount Hood tragedy: Who pays for search and rescue? TheDay.com. Retrieved from http://www.theday.com/article/20091219/INTERACT010102/912199999/0/SHANE

Gallup. (August 28, 2015). Americans' satisfaction with job aspects up from 2005. Retrieved from http://www.gallup.com/poll/184952/americans-satisfaction-job-aspects-2005.aspx

Gilbert, D. (2006). *Stumbling on happiness.* New York, NY: Vintage Books.

Goodale, T. L., & Godbey, G. (1988). *The evolution of leisure: Historical and philosophical perspectives.* State College, PA: Venture.

Griffiths, M. D. (2011). Workaholism: A 21st century addiction. *The Psychologist: Bulletin of the British Psychological Society, 24*, 740–744.

Hirschfeld, R. R., & Field, H. S. (2000). Work centrality and work alienation: Distinct aspects of a general commitment to work. *Journal of Organizational Behavior, 21*, 789–524.

Huizinga, J. (1938). *Homo ludens: Proeve Ener Bepaling Van Het Spelelement Der Cultuur* (Translation: *Homo ludens: A study of the play-element in culture*). Groningen, Wolters-Noordhoff cop. 1985. Original Dutch edition.

Humane Society of the United States. (2016). *Pets by the numbers.* Retrieved from http://www.humanesociety.org/issues/pet_overpopulation/facts/pet_ownership_statistics.html?referrer=https://www.google.com/

International Monetary Fund. (April 14, 2016). GDP Nominal Ranking. Retrieved from http://statisticstimes.com/economy/countries-by-projected-gdp.php

Keynes, J. M. (1930). Economic possibilities for our grandchildren. Reprinted in *Essays in Persuasion.* New York, NY: W. W. Norton & Co., 1963, pp. 358–373.

Kosteas, V. (June 2012). The effect of exercise on earnings: Evidence from the NLSY. *Journal of Labor Research, 33*(2), 225–250.

Kubota, K., Shimazu, A., Kawakami, N., Takahashi, M. Nakata, A., & Schaufeli, W.B. (2010). Association between workaholism and sleep problems among hospital nurses. *Industrial Health, 48*(6), 864–871.

Linder, S. (1970). *The harried leisure class.* New York, NY: Columbia University Press.

Mohsen, A. S. (October 19, 2015). Tourism industry now 6th largest GDP contributor, says Najib. *The Daily Sun.* Retrieved from http://www.thesundaily.my/news/1586311

Neulinger, J. (October, 1989). A leisure society: Idle dream or viable alternative, encroaching menace or golden opportunity. *J.B. Nash Lecture Series.* Boston, MA: American Association for Leisure and Recreation.

Parade Magazine & Yahoo/Finance. (August 31, 2012). Job happiness poll: Most Americans wish they could hit reset button on their careers. Retrieved from http://www.parade.com/what-people-earn/featured/job-happiness-poll-americans-wish-hit-reset-button-on-careers.html

Reid, D. (1995). *Work and leisure in the 21st century: From production to citizenship.* Toronto, ON: Wall and Emerson.

Robinson, J., & Godbey, G. (1997). *Time for life: The surprising ways Americans use their time.* University Park, PA: The Pennsylvania State University.

Saad, L. (August 29 2014). The "40-hour" workweek is actually longer. Gallup Poll. Retrieved from http://www.gallup.com/poll/175286/hour-workweek-actually-longer-seven-hours.aspx

Schor, J. B. (1992). *The overworked American: The unexpected decline of leisure.* New York, NY: Basic Books.

Schor, J. B. (2010). *Plenitude: The new economics of true wealth.* New York, NY: Penguin.

Schwartz, N. D. (April 23, 2016). In an age of privilege, not everyone is in the same boat. *The New York Times.* Retrieved from http://www.nytimes.com/2016/04/24/business/economy/velvet-rope-economy.html?_r=2

Smith, A. (1937). *An inquiry into the nature and causes of the wealth of nations.* New York, NY: The Modern Library. (Original work published 1776).

Snyder, B., & Jones, S. (November 11, 2015). Americans work hard, but people in these 15 countries work longer hours. *Fortune.* Retrieved from http://fortune.com/2015/11/11/chart-work-week-oecd/

Statistica. (2015). Consumer purchases of sports footwear in the U.S. from 2002 to 2015. Retrieved from http://www.statista.com/statistics/200802/sports-footwear-consumer-purchases-in-the-us-since-2004/

Torkildsen, G. (2005). *Leisure and recreation management* (5th ed.). New York, NY: Routledge.

Veal, A. J. (2012). The leisure society II: The era of critique, 1980-2011. *World Leisure Journal, 54*(2), 99–140.

Veblen, T. (1899). *The theory of the leisure class.* New York, NY: Macmillan.

World Tourism Organization (UNWTO). (2012). *UNWTO tourism highlights: 2012 Edition.* Retrieved from http://mkt.unwto.org/en/publication/unwto-tourism-highlights-2012-edition

World Travel and Tourism Council. (2015). Travel and Tourism Economic Impact: 2015 (World). Retrieved from http://www.wttc.org/-/media/files/reports/economic%20impact%20research/regional%202015/world2015.pdf

CHAPTER 11

The Freedom and Tyranny of Time

How do we know what time it is?

People view time according to their individual history, biology, and culture.

How does leisure depend on time?

Leisure is shaped by many time factors, including personal perceptions of free time, the amount of time available, the time requirements of activities, and a culture's time sufficiency.

Is time ever a problem for leisure?

While free time itself is a leisure expression, time can be problematic for leisure in modern societies because of tyrannies such as time urgency, time deepening, and even time-saving devices.

They lost a Friday. Citizens of the Pacific island nation of Samoa went to bed on Thursday night, December 29, 2011 and woke up Saturday morning, December 31. They lost a whole day of their lives. Why? Before this date Samoa was on the eastward side of the International Date Line, and afterward it had switched to the western side in order to be more aligned with its Asian trading partners. It had been out of alignment since 1892 when American traders persuaded it to shift from the western side to the eastern side of the date line to facilitate business with the west coast of the United States.

Shifting time by decree is not a new phenomenon. At the recent turn of the century, in a bid to be the first to greet the dawn of the new millennium, Pacific island nations engaged in a free-for-all of shifting time zones, date lines, and daylight saving times. The date line, which itself is an imaginary line drawn at a convention in 1884, zigzags along the 180-degree meridian. Travelers crossing the date line also lose a day of their lives going west and gain a day going east. Actually, "there is no legal reason why any country cannot declare itself to be in whatever time zone it likes," claims the Royal Observatory at Greenwich, the international arbiter of official world time (cited by Mydans, 2011).

Much ado about nothing? Not really; people take the idea of time very seriously. So seriously that they ascribe all kinds of actions to it. For example, we make time, make good time, hoard time, save time, waste time, take time, spend time, kill time, and of course, do time. At a party, we've had a good time or a bad time. There is summer time, nap time, supper time, time travel, and of course, Miller time. Time flies and, wow, time is money! And, as studied in Chapter 1, leisure is free time.

Figure 11.1. Many pastimes are very time conscious. For example, football is played by the clock. The game clock is a total of 60 minutes, out of which only 12 to 15 minutes contain actual playing.

But in studying the relationship between leisure and time, we'll discover there's much more to it than a free-time definition. Time not only is the "container" for leisure expression, but is also what makes leisure both possible and impossible. First, we'll compare the types of time, and their leisure significance. Then, we'll directly address whether leisure and time can be said to be compatible.

Types of Time

Many things affect leisure and time. One of them is the concept of time itself, so we begin here as a means of establishing a foundation. Most often we think of time as clock time. That is, time is measured as seconds, minutes, and hours. Also we typically refer to the weeks, months, years, decades, centuries, millennia, and so forth, of the calendar as time. Yet, these are not the only way to measure time. For example, there's universal time, international atomic time, sidereal time, terrestrial time, and Barycentric Dynamical Time. Even clock time hasn't always been the measuring standard. Let's trace this by comparing cyclical, mechanical, biological, and cultural time.

Cyclical Time

Our legacy of telling time perhaps began with **cyclical time**. Ancient cultures such as Incan, Mayan, Hopi, Babylonian, and Greek understood time as a wheel. That is, early humans considered time as part of the reoccurring and regular patterns of nature: the rising and setting of the sun, the tide coming in and going out, the passage of the seasons, and the location of the moon in the sky (Green, 1968).

Cyclical time: Time experienced as constant and returning

If we were able to experience cyclical time today it would mean we would sense that time is never lost or wasted, because just like the cycles of life, time repeats itself. Likely we would have no concept of needing to get control over time, we'd feel no responsibility for it. Life would not be thought of as a progression to the end.

Today, some world cultures still live according to cyclical time. For example, the Masai, a nomadic culture of Kenya, do not compartmentalize time into minutes and hours but instead schedule time by the rising and setting sun and the feeding of their cattle. The typical Masai day begins just before sunrise, when the cattle go to the river to drink. This period is called "the red blood period" because of the color of the sunrise. The afternoon is "when the shadows lower themselves." The evening begins when "the cattle return from the river." Seasons and months are determined by rainfall—a particular month lasts as long as the rains continue and a new month doesn't begin until the rains have ceased (Neuliep, 2011).

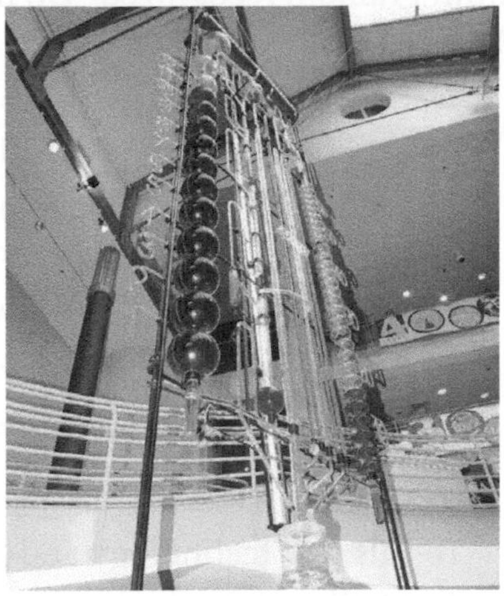

Figure 11.2. A contemporary water clock is in the atrium of the Indianapolis Children's Museum. Thirty feet tall, containing blue liquid that fills hour and 2-minute interval globes every 12 hours, the time piece is a central attraction for the museum. Source: Indianapolis Children's Museum, Indiana

As best we know, about 5,000 years ago, the great civilizations in the Middle East and North Africa began to perceive time differently. With emerging bureaucracies, these cultures apparently found a need to organize their time more efficiently. Instead of observing the stars, changes in seasons, and passing of day into night, devices were invented to measure the passage of time.

For example, the Egyptians were probably the first to divide their day into systematic parts. Obelisks (slender, tapering, four-sided monuments) were built as early as 3500 BC. Their moving shadows formed a kind of sundial, helping people partition the day into morning and afternoon. A few hundred years later, the Egyptians are credited with the invention of the water clock. Called clepsydras (water thieves), these were stone vessels with sloping sides that allowed water to drip out a small hole near the bottom, making it possible to tell time at night.

The earliest calendars also reflect a cyclical notion of telling time. Their original purpose was to show how many days until a certain important event takes place, such as the harvest or a religious festival. The earliest calendars must have had strong geographical influences as in colder regions the concept of the year was determined by the seasons, specifically by the end of winter. But in warmer regions, where the seasons are less pronounced, the Moon became the basic unit for calendar time reckoning. Most of the oldest calendars were, therefore, lunar calendars, based on the time interval from one new moon to the next—a so-called lunation. In some areas, however, it was not the moon, but rather other natural recurring events, such as the flooding of the Nile River, that formed the calendar.

Mechanical Time

It wasn't until the 14th century that mechanical clocks were developed (Priestly, 1968), but it took until the 17th century for Dutch scientist Christiaan Huygens to invent the balance wheel and spring assembly still found in some watches today. This improvement allowed portable clocks to keep accurate time to within 10 minutes a day—a feat increasingly important, first for the daily prayer and work rituals of monks in medieval monasteries, and later as a tool for industrialists to regulate the flow of production.

With the invention of the mechanical clock people's perception of time changed. Now set to the rhythm of a machine, and not nature, time became linear. This meant a period of time could pass, and when it passed, it could not be recovered. Unlike cyclical time, a linear notion of time meant it could

Mechanical time: Time paced by machine, enabling a precise division of the day into equal parts and a linear perception of its passing

no longer be accumulated—it could only be spent and wasted. Referred to as **mechanical time**, it demanded precision, punctuality, and reliability. Time was now vital to furthering a work-focused civilization (Cross, 1990). Time was now a resource to be used wisely. As the American statesman Benjamin Franklin recognized "Do not squander time, for that's the stuff of life" (in *Poor Richard's Almanac*, 1733 to 1757).

Box 11.1
Web Explore

Exploring Worldwide Clock Time

There are many fun tools available on the Internet to appreciate mechanical time around the world. Try these for starters:

http://www.timeanddate.com/worldclock/

http://www.timeanddate.com/countdown/newyear

http://www.timeanddate.com/time/map/

To this day, technology and the belief in the regularity of mechanical time have continued to sever our ties with nature. Lights and heating and cooling systems that turn on and off according to clock timers, have eliminated the need for paying attention to natural daily and seasonal cycles. Digital alarms wake us up in the morning, even if sunrise is still hours away. Wristwatches beep out the minutes it takes us to jog around the block. It is said that the future will even bring us nail watches, digital displays of time glowing from our finger nail. Today we live by completely artificial distinctions of time.

This inauthenticity has been extended, of course, by the rhythm of another machine—the computer. The computer works with the nanosecond as the basic time unit. At a billionth of a second, it is the measure of read or write access time to random access memory (RAM). Thus, a computer-driven concept of time speeds us up. Whereas the circle represented time for ancient peoples, and the straight line suggests society's experience of time since then, the double helix is considered the time-shape of the future (Rifkin, 1987). This spiral, with its feedback loops, suggests a computer-driven time experience that is not only linear but also simultaneous (which may help explain multitasking).

Further, sitting in front of computers, tablets, and smartphones all day, we're constantly confronted by a clock telling us what time it is. An overabundance of this can take us out of both the past and the future, and into a state of heightened "present hedonism" in which we're constantly focused on what's either right in front of us or coming immediately afterward (Gregoire (2014). "It's really minimizing the quality of life–the joy that we ought to be getting from everyday life" (Zimbardo & Boyd, 2008). Accordingly, here are three things psychologists suggest about how technology affects our perception of time (Gregoire, 2014; Zimbardo & Boyd, 2008):

1. Being connected can speed up your sense of time. It creates our personal "time zone," which creates a need for immediacy.
2. It can trap us in the next moment. We're not fully in the present because we're also anticipating the next moment.
3. The present orientation can make us more susceptible to instant gratification. We live in a time of temptation, and not being future-oriented harms our ability to act in the interest of more long-term goals.

Shifts in measuring time from cyclical nature to arbitrary machines are perhaps the most important changes in human life so far. In this sense, we certainly don't have "pastimes" anymore. Perhaps the first to call our attention to the implications of our time perceptions for leisure was Sebastian deGrazia in a classic study *Of Time, Work, and Leisure* (1962). "Clock time cannot be free," claimed deGrazia, and "because of this, few of us will ever experience the sublime state of leisure" (p. 310).

Biological Time

We also experience other types of time, which perhaps are able to put us more in touch with freedom in our daily lives. For example, we also live according to biological time. One source, photoperiodism, is an organism's (plants and animals) response to the length of day or night. Another example is endogenous rhythms, which are also common to many plants and animals, including humans.

Endogenous rhythms: Time generated within an organism

These **endogenous rhythms** are cyclical physiological functions. For example, the heart beats about 60 to 80 times per minute, and hunger occurs on about a 90-minute cycle. Endogenous rhythms prepare our bodies for forthcoming events: increases of the hormone melatonin after darkness prepares us for sleep; increases in deep body temperature in the morning heralds wake-up time. However, because we have become so dependent on external factors of timekeeping, such as the clock, computer, and television, we are not always able to experience time according to our endogenous rhythms.

Circadian clock: Daily rhythm of activity and rest

For example, one endogenous rhythm that is problematic today is the daily rhythm of activity and rest. This relies on our **circadian clock**, a cluster of nerves located on the hypothalamus in the brain, which tells time according to environmental cues—primarily light from the day/night cycle. Although unique for each of us, a typical single circadian cycle of activity and rest ranges between 20 and 28 hours.

Figure 11.3. People's body rhythms tend to fit into one of three general categories, called chronotypes. These are early, intermediate, and late. A person's category is determined by a combination of genetic, environmental, and social factors. In other words, there's a biological reason why some people can't sleep late and others can't get up early.

Many studies have demonstrated that when we live according to our circadian clock, we feel better. One reason is our natural circadian rhythm is experienced as comfort, even pleasure. This is also why we particularly appreciate such rhythmic experiences as music and poetry. Paying attention to our internal clock also means we can be at our best. For example, elite athletes have used circadian rhythm charting to help predict peaks in performance.

Abrupt changes in our circadian clock, such as jet lag resulting from air travel across time zones, have a detrimental effect on us. Also, as the latest studies have demonstrated, regularly using the artificial light from screens of computers and tablets before bed can tinker with the melatonin in the brain that promotes sleep. Researchers found that two hours of exposure to a bright tablet or computer screen at night reduced melatonin levels by about 22%, which not only causes sleep cycle disturbances, but also raises the risk of obesity, diabetes, and other disorders (Wood et al., 2012).

Cultural Time

Another type of time we live with is cultural time. That is, our social groups tell us what time it is. For example, on U.S. college campuses, if a professor is more than 10 minutes late for class, students begin to consider leaving, whereas in Brazil, university students define a professor's lateness as slightly over 30 minutes after the scheduled start of class (Levine & Wolff, 1985).

This suggests that time is not the same in every culture. Basically, groups are of two types in the ways they approach time. Similar to the differences between the cyclical and mechanical types of time, there are monochronic and polychronic groups. First understood by cultural anthropologist Edward Hall in 1959, **monochronic groups** of people are those who prefer to complete one task at a time. For them, task-oriented time is important. They value punctuality, keeping schedules, and completing tasks. They view time as if it were linear, that is, one event happening at a time. Examples of monochronic cultures include the United States, Canada, Germany, and Switzerland. On the other hand, **polychronic groups** of people are flexible about time schedules. They have a more socioemotional idea about time, that maintaining relationships and socializing are more important than completing tasks. For them, many things may happen at once. Latin America, the Middle East, and Africa are places where the polychronic orientation is more typical (Iowa State University Study Abroad Center, 2011).

Monochronic groups: Cultures in which time is organized sequentially; schedules and deadlines are valued over people

Polychronic groups: Cultures in which time is organized horizontally; people tend to do several things at once and value relationships over schedules

One example of how this cultural time distinction manifests in leisure is the activity of waiting in line. Americans collectively spend at least 37 billion hours a year waiting (Stone, 2012), and they do it mostly by forming lines according to order of arrival. But this is not universal. For example, in Israel (a monochromic culture), even though people wait for buses by stubbornly resisting forming lines, when the bus comes, they board according to the first-come principle as if they had been in line all along. However, since France is a polychronic culture, people do not honor any aspect of first-come-first served. For example, at the airports in France people form a large cone in front of the passport control desk, and make progress toward the front by attaching themselves to its sides rather than to its end.

Indeed, the fact that forming waiting lines is unknown or approached differently across cultures was a fact missed by the Walt Disney Company when it opened Hong Kong Disneyland. For example, in the first few weeks of the park's operation in 2005, officials noticed specific differences between Hong Kong visitors and those from mainland China. Since about 25% of Hong Kong residents had already visited a Disney theme park in the U.S., they were better able to participate in the park's queuing system. Visitors from mainland China, where only 1% had previously visited a Disney park, were unsure how the lines worked (Fountain, 2005).

Are Time and Leisure Friends?

Time is the most abundant and equally distributed of all resources—we all get exactly the same number of hours a day. Yet time is also considered the scarcest and most fragile of our resources. None of us feel we have complete control over our time or that we ever have enough time.

Time has been a major subject of not only philosophy, but also religion, sociology, anthropology, and the physical sciences, but defining it in a manner applicable to all fields of study has consistently eluded the greatest scholars. Even Aristotle, in the book *Physics*, asked the question, "In what sense, if any, can time be said to exist?" (cited in Barnes, 1984, p. 369). Nonetheless, understanding time continues to be important in contemporary life. Why? Time has become the framework for all our behavior. For example, in the English language the word is both a noun and verb. What is this paradox? The answer has something to do with how time and leisure relate.

To begin, leisure certainly takes place in time, and although estimates vary, for the majority of adults in developed societies, about 45 hours each week are available for leisure (Bureau of Labor Statistics, 2015a), amounting to more than four months a year of free time. How do we experience all this free time?

Time used for leisure is essentially shaped by four factors:

- Personal perceptions of free time
- Personal amounts of free time
- The time needs of leisure activities
- A culture's time sufficiency

First, people's perceptions of free time influence how they use it for leisure (Table 11.1). If free time is regarded as a privilege, it is likely to be used for pursuits perceived to be personally beneficial or socially constructive. Others may view free time as a chance for temporary escape from the physical and mental environment of work and daily routines. They regard it as an opportunity for getting away from it all. Still others see free time as neither a privilege nor an opportunity but as an empty space that, if left unfilled, becomes frightening. These are people who feel compelled from fear to keep busy, even in their free time. Finally, similar behaviors may arise from a perception of free time as a precious commodity. Stemming from feelings of guilt, every spare moment must be crammed with activity to be sure it is not wasted.

Figure 11.4. Buying, selling, fixing up, maintaining, driving, and showing classic cars is a popular pastime, especially for baby boomers. How do you choose to use your free time? © Patricia D. Setser

Table 11.1
Perceptions of Free Time

Free Time Perceived As:	Implications for Leisure	Example
Privilege	Seek personally beneficial or socially constructive pursuits	Volunteer to coach a youth soccer team
Opportunity	A chance for temporary escape from work and daily routines	Take a trip out of town for the weekend
Empty Space	Feel compelled to be busy even in leisure	Take a book with you to a musical concert
Precious Commodity	Not wanting to waste free time	Unable to spend the afternoon in a hammock

Quite related to perceptions of free time, leisure as experienced in time also depends on the amount of free time we actually possess. Whether the amount of free time people have is increasing or decreasing has been hotly debated because research findings on the question have conflicted. Yet even without study findings, it is clear to us all that some people have more free time than others. For example, notorious deficits in free time are typically ascribed to specific sectors of the population, such as married women who are employed outside the home with children living at home (Bureau of Labor Statistics, 2015b). The idea of **time famine** describes the condition of not having enough free time.

Time famine: Having insufficient free time

Box 11.2
The Study Says

Is Free Time Increasing or Decreasing?

Study One

Economist Juliet Schor published a study in 1992 entitled *The Overworked American: The Unexpected Decline of Leisure*. Her argument was that Americans are working longer; she claimed the average employed person worked an additional 163 hours a year in 1987 compared with 1969 (p. 29). This amounts to a loss of nearly one month of free time per year. The reasons for such changes, Schor suggested, is the endless work-and-spend cycle. Her findings claim we are spending our way through life. We work harder to be able to have the money to buy more.

Study Two

Leisure scholars John Robinson and Geoffrey Godbey published a study in 1997, and again in 1999 and 2008, that argued Americans actually have almost 265 hours more free time per year today than they did in the 1960s—that's five more hours per week. Their explanation was that we feel more rushed and stressed because we try to do many things all at once, having free time in only small segments rather than in a larger time period, such as a full weekend. Their findings also suggested we invest free time in activities that bring us minimal fulfillment, such as watching television, which also gives us a sense of time famine. Thus, the problem is not actually the amount of free time, but people's use of it.

Explaining the Contradiction

Which study is true? One way to answer this is to compare the ways used to collect information. Schor's findings are based on estimates of time use from various government reports. These documents track the market hours of full-time and part-time employees. Robinson and Godbey's findings are based on individual time diaries. Their project asked thousands of Americans to report their daily activities on an hour-by-hour basis. Since the two studies used different data sources, are the findings comparable? To help you make up your mind, see Schor's rebuttal to the contradiction at http://www.swt.org/putok.htm.

Also, supporting the Robinson and Godbey conclusions, a recent study (Saccaro, 2015) polled just over 1,000 working professionals and found that 65% are expected to be available outside of work both by e-mail and by phone. As a result, 45% feel they don't have enough free time; their job is colonizing their entire day, not just 9 to 5.

Source: Robinson & Godbey, 1997,1999, 2008; Schor, 1992

Leisure as experienced in time also depends on the amount of time an activity requires. For example, the game of *Monopoly* takes longer to play than *Dominos*, and a game of basketball is longer lasting than a game of croquet. Indeed, one of the complications of contemporary society is that people are choosing shorter, less absorbing leisure activities to match shorter blocks of free time (Godbey, 2006).

To illustrate, the trend in vacations is multiple 3-day excursions spread throughout the year rather than the traditional two-week trip in the summer. According to surveys, such "vacation deflation" is evidenced by the fact that only 14% of employees take a full two-week vacation each year (Athavaley, 2007). Another example is the game of golf. Golf has lost 5 million players in the last 10 years; 25 million golfers are likely to quit in the next few years (Preston, 2014). "And the 35-and-unders aren't even starting" (p. 16E). Why? One complaint revealed in interviews is that the game takes too long—four or more hours! (What would be wrong with four quiet, undisturbed hours in nature with friends?)

Temporal displacement: Altering the timing of events as reaction to adverse changes at a recreation site

Related, the concept of **temporal displacement** shows how people change the timing of specific leisure activities. Suppose boaters who in the past have frequented a particular lake become dissatisfied with the amount of boat traffic on the lake on weekends. If the boaters decide to switch their boating at the lake from weekends to weekdays, they have demonstrated temporal displacement. Spatial displacement is another way to change an unsatisfying recreational situation. This involves changing the location of the activity, such as to a different lake. Research has demonstrated that temporal displacement is the more common way to avoid recreation conflicts (Hall & Shelby, 2000).

Finally, the expression of leisure in time is a function of how much time a culture has. Referred to as a culture's **time sufficiency**, the amount of free time available affects the general welfare of people. First noted by Linder (1970), cultures can be categorized according to the amount of free time they have: they have either a time surplus or time scarcity (Table 11.2).

Time sufficiency: Amount of free time available to a culture

Table 11.2
Cultural Time Sufficiency and Leisure

Distinction	Time Surplus Culture	Time Scarcity Culture
Time	Time rich; much free or idle time	Time poor; no or little free time
Wealth	Poor	Rich
Production	Low	High
Work	Not dependent on mechanical time; no time-related work stress	Highly dependent on mechanical time; time stress causes illness
Leisure	Many holidays; popular recreation activities occupy large time blocks; much spontaneity; little consumption of special equipment	Few holidays; popular recreation activities occupy small time blocks; less spontaneity; much consumption of special equipment

While you might find it surprising, the least developed cultures tend to have a free-time surplus. This is because production and income are low enough that large portions of time remain unused. In fact, in time-surplus cultures where hurrying is not necessary, rushing is considered a sign of rudeness and poverty of spirit (Robinson & Godbey, 1997). As a result, leisure tends to be more spontaneous, lengthy, relaxed, and frequent. Time-surplus cultures also tend to designate a larger number of days as holidays.

Figure 11.5. The reality TV show The Amazing Race made a competition of traveling the world as quickly as possible. Source: CBS

For more developed cultures, on the other hand, there is typically a time famine. When the drive for time efficiency is dominant, free time is transferred to active use and becomes scarce. Punctuality becomes a virtue and rushing a sign of importance. For countries with time scarcity, leisure is less spontaneous and convenience becomes the rationale for choosing activities. In a study investigating time and cultural complexity, Chick and Shen (2007) concluded that "technological advancement and societal development do not necessarily and naturally lead to benefits when it comes to leisure" (p. 30).

Box 11.3
In Profile

The Slow Movements

In Japan there is a slow business school. Italy has a slow cities movement. Spain has a network of siesta salons. Originating in Austria is the Society for the Deceleration of Time, which sets speed traps for pedestrians and opposes daylight savings time. The slow family movement, the slow home movement (including decelerated décor), slow science, slow fashion, and slow travel are taking hold world-wide (go ahead, Google them). People are resurrecting the art of doing things more slowly.

For example, originating in 1989 as a response to the arrival of the first McDonald's in Rome, Italy the slow food movement is a fast-growing international organization with 100,000 members in 160 countries. Grouped in 1,300 local chapters called "convivials," they develop activities, projects and events at local, regional and global levels. The cause is to counteract fast food and fast life, the disappearance of local food traditions, and people's dwindling interest in the food they eat, where it comes from, how it tastes, and how food choices affect the rest of the world. "We believe that everyone has a fundamental right to the pleasure of good food and consequently the responsibility to protect the heritage of food, tradition, and culture that make this pleasure possible."

Source: Slowfood.com, 2015

Time Tyrannies

Even though time is a potentially "free" resource for leisure, time and leisure are not always friends, and adding to the woes just discussed are other disadvantages. Let's discuss such time tyrannies as time urgency, time deepening, and time-saving devices.

Time urgency: Feeling rushed

A truly contemporary condition, **time urgency** is a quickened pace of life—feeling rushed. It is to approach the day with speed and impetuosity. Although not everyone or not every culture experiences time urgency, according to the time diary studies of Robinson and Godbey (1997), the "always feel rushed" response on questionnaires has shown a gradual increase since 1965. Today only about 25% of Americans declare they almost never feel rushed (Pew Research Center, 2006).

People who perceive life in a time-urgent way engage in such self-defeating behaviors and thoughts as being excessively worried about schedules, keeping overly tight deadlines, and rushing when rushing is not necessary. Often called "hurry sickness," time urgency means being unreasonably tied to the clock, and can ultimately reduce effectiveness with more errors and lower quality results (Ashworth, 2015).

Box 11.4
By the Numbers

Top Time Wasters

1. Facebook
2. Personal grooming
3. Playing computer games
4. Television
5. Commuting

Sources: Summarized from multiple sources including Robinson, 2014 & Griffith, 2016

Time urgency can be particularly problematic for leisure. The consequences include participating hurriedly in an activity (visiting a park without getting out of the car) or substituting an activity that can be done more quickly (jogging instead of walking so to complete the mileage faster). How much real pleasure and satisfaction can be attained from learning to play the guitar in three easy lessons, eating dinner in less than 10 minutes, or traveling to Spain in a weekend? Time urgency in leisure might mean condensing a birthday party into a meal at a restaurant, spending only a few seconds in front of a painting in a museum, or becoming irritated when previous players don't leave the squash court within a minute of your reserved time.

So what's the tyranny in time urgency? Beyond losing the ability to savor the day, according to numerous medical studies, constantly being in a big hurry can kill you. For example, a study conducted at the University of California at San Francisco looked at 32 patients with heart disease. Thirteen of the patients exhibited symptoms of time urgency with accompanying episodes of decreased supply of blood to the heart muscle. Beyond heart problems, the stress felt by people with time urgency can also cause muscle pains, headaches, high blood pressure, irritable bowels, insomnia, phobias, depression, and anxiety. Your immune system may be weakened as well (Krishna, 2008).

Box 11.5
In Your Own Experience

Time Urgency Test

Check whether you rarely, sometimes, or almost always experience each statement.

	Rarely	Sometimes	Almost Always
I seem to do my best work under pressure.			
I'm frustrated by the slowness of people around me.			
I hate to wait or stand in line.			
I always seem to be rushing between places, projects, and events.			
I eat lunch or other meals while I work or study.			
I find it difficult to linger at the table after eating.			
I measure my self-worth by quantitative accomplishments.			
I feel I am often racing against time.			
I often interrupt people when they are talking.			
I sometimes suffer from a "racing mind."			

Give yourself 1 point for every "rarely," 2 points for every "sometimes," and 3 points for every "almost always" responses. Add the points up, and compare your score:

10-16 points – you are easy going and not experiencing time urgency.

17-23 points – you do like a degree of pressure in life and may need to guard against a tendency toward time urgency.

24-30 points – high time urgency; take steps now to reduce it in your life.

Time deepening: Doing multiple activities at the same time without fully experiencing any of them

Another contemporary time tyranny is time deepening. Originally based on Stefan Linder's 1970s idea about the harried leisure class (see Chapter 10), **time deepening** means doing more than one thing at a time in order to crowd a greater number of activities into the same amount of time (Godbey, 2003). For example, do you ever eat dinner, watch television, play a computer game, and text your friends all at the same time?

Figure 11.6. Texting while walking. Like distracted drivers, distracted walkers present a hazard. Some U.S. states are considering jail time and/or a fine for this activity.

Because of a computer-paced understanding of time, time deepening allows us to stack up activities as a way of making time "deeper." The notion of time deepening is the forerunner of today's multitasking. As with time deepening, multitasking is simultaneously doing as many things as possible, as quickly as possible, preferably marshaling the power of as many technologies as possible.

Since the 1990s, scientists have conducted experiments on the nature and limits of human multitasking. It has been shown, for example, that we (like a computer processor) are not really able to concentrate on multiple things at one time (Hallowell, 2007). Others have researched multitasking in specific domains, such as learning. For example, Mayer and Moreno (2003) concluded that it is difficult, and likely impossible to learn new information while engaged in multitasking. Similarly, another study on the effects of multitasking on academic performance found that using Facebook and text messaging while studying are negatively related to student grades (Junco & Cotton, 2012). Recent state laws also attest to the risks of multitasking and prohibit any use of electronics devices while driving.

Box 11.6 What Do You Say?

Multitasking Leisure

When it comes to being productive, studies have clearly demonstrated a lack of focus on only one task at a time is costly, not only to the results, but possibly to health and life as well. But, what could possibly be the harm in multitasking leisure? After all, the goal of leisure is not productivity, but rather fun—¬enjoyment, pleasure, freedom, intrinsic reward, happiness, humor, and many other benefits. Here are some examples of typical multitasked leisure expressions:

- Watching television and eating a meal
- Sending and receiving texts during a movie at the theatre
- Negotiating a business deal with other players during a round of golf
- Answering cell phone calls while eating in a restaurant with friends
- Listening to music while taking a walk in the forest
- Cooking a meal and answering e-mail

1. So, what's the harm? Is time deepening/multitasking advantageous or disadvantageous to leisure?
2. Are all the above examples equal in terms of their advantages or disadvantages? Why or why not?
3. Do you multitask during your leisure? If you do, how does it make you feel?

Finally, let's consider time-saving devices themselves in terms of leisure. You, or at least your children, will never know what it was like to be able to say "the check is in the mail" or have the luxury to "get back to you about it tomorrow." With surface mail delivery, we had at least a few days to a few weeks to sort out an issue. Then along came the fax machine, which meant that a same-day response could be expected. With e-mail the required response time was reduced to a few hours—and with instant messaging an immediate response is necessary.

The onset of the idea of a mechanical clock is what made efficiency truly possible in manufacturing and industry—higher production at lower costs. Efficiency has become the watchword for time-management strategies at work, with time-and-motion studies of organizational personnel and procedures revealing new ways to "work smarter." But this goal has steadily infiltrated other areas of life, including the home, for which such "time-saving" devices as the automatic dishwasher, microwave oven, and self-defrosting freezer have been widespread. And what is the reward of this efficient use of time?

A well-managed job is supposed to leave evenings, weekends, and holidays free for other activities. Thanks to time-saving devices in the kitchen, there should be ample time for family, community, civic, and leisure involvement. If we can more efficiently run our lives, then our leisure should be more time-rich, and thus enjoyable. Right? Yet, this promise has not been fulfilled. Why not?

Micro-boredom: Ever smaller slices of free time from which mobile technology offers an escape

One example of what has gone wrong is the new concept of **micro-boredom**. Just a decade ago, monotonous moments were just a fact of life. While standing in the checkout line at the grocer's, a funny incident from your day could come to mind, and a commute drive home after school or work could inspire ruminations about evening plans. These brief times of doldrums provide some of life's most quintessentially human moments. But no more. Increasingly, these empty moments are being saturated with productivity, communication, and the distractions offered by an ever-expanding array of time-saving mobile devices. What we used to call downtime is now increasingly filled with "mobisodes"—2-minute-long television episodes made for the cellphone screen, or a fit of Twitter and Facebook to turn a mundane moment into activity.

Why have time-saving devices actually cost us our time? Why has the promise of more leisure from them gone unfulfilled? One reason is the "Law of Unintended Consequences"—unforeseen negative by-products that undermine the planned benefits. For example, a time-saving device such as the computer certainly increases the range of possible functions, but it also devours more time (and produces larger quantities of paper) than previously. The relative ease and low expense of e-mail is proving to be an unexpected burden, as each morning the computer greets the office worker, teacher, and business manager with a large collection of messages that call for evaluation and urgent action.

What We Understand About Leisure and Time

Time and leisure are instrumentally related. That is, each has an impact on the other. Time not only is the "container" for leisure expression, but is also what makes leisure both possible and impossible. From reading this chapter you should understand the following:

1. The expression of leisure in time is a function of personal perceptions of free time, personal amounts of free time, the time requirements of particular pastimes, and the amount of free time available in a society.

   Discuss your own leisure interests in terms of these four perceptions of free time:

   ____

   ____

2. Cyclical time is that pace set by the rhythms of nature. In developed societies, it has been replaced by the concept of mechanical time—of life and leisure paced to the machine.
   Define cyclical time and mechanical time:
   ____
   ____

3. In the future, the computer may set an even faster and more artificial pace for life and leisure.
   Note some examples of this possibility in your own life:
   ____
   ____

4. Other types of time that affect our leisure are biological time and cultural time.
   Define biological time and cultural time:
   ____
   ____

5. There are unique tyrannies to leisure from time, including time urgency, time deepening, and time-saving devices.
   Are you experiencing any of these time tyrannies in your own life. If so, which one(s). If not, why not?
   ____
   ____

References

Ashworth, M. (2015). Always in a rush? Maybe it's time urgency. Psych Central. Retrieved from http://psychcentral.com/lib/always-in-a-rush-maybe-its-time-urgency/

Athavaley, A. (August 15, 2007). Vacation deflation: Breaks get shorter. *The Wall Street Journal*, D1 & D3.

Barnes, J. (1984). *The complete works of Aristotle.* Princeton, NJ: Princeton University Press.

Bureau of Labor Statistics. (2015a). American time use survey. Retrieved from http://www.bls.gov/tus/charts/#leisure

Bureau of Labor Statistics. (2015b). American time use survey. Retrieved from http://www.bls.gov/news.release/atus2.nr0.htm

Chick, G., & Shen, S. X. (2007). Time allocation and cultural complexity: Leisure time use across twelve cultures. *Proceedings of the 2007 Northeastern Recreation Research Symposium. Gen. Tech. Rep. NRS-P-23*, Newtown Square, PA: U.S. Department of Agriculture, Forest Service, Northern Research Station.

Cross, G. (1990). *A social history of leisure since 1600.* State College, PA: Venture.

deGrazia, S. (1962). *Of time, work, and leisure.* New York, NY: The Twentieth Century Fund.

Fountain, H. (September 18, 2005). The ultimate body language: How you line up for Mickey. *The New York Times.* Retrieved from http://www.nytimes.com/2005/09/18/weekinreview/the-ultimate-body-language-how-you-line-up-for-mickey.html?_r=0

Franklin, B. (1932). *The autobiography and selections from his other writing.* New York, NY: The Modern Library.

Godbey, G. (2003). Book review (Stefan Linder's *The Harried Leisure Class*). *Journal of Leisure Research, 35*(4), p. 478.

Godbey, G. (2006). *Leisure and leisure services in the 21st century: Toward mid-century.* State College, PA: Venture.

Green, T. F. (1968). *Work, leisure, and the American schools.* New York, NY: Random House.
Gregoire, C. (January 23, 2014). How technology speeds up time (and how to slow it down again). *The Huffington Post.* Retrieved from http://www.huffingtonpost.com/2013/12/06/technology-time-perception_n_4378010.html
Griffith, T. (2016) Top 20 time wasters and the top 5 worthwhile activities. Lifehack.org. Retrieved from http://www.lifehack.org/articles/productivity/top-20-time-wasters-and-top-5-worthwhile-activities.html
Hall, E. G. (1959). *The silent language.* Garden City, NY: Doubleday.
Hall, T., & Shelby, B. (2000). Temporal and spatial displacement: Evidence from a high-use reservoir and alternate sites. *Journal of Leisure Research, 32,* 435–456.
Hallowell, E. M. (2007). *Crazy busy: Overstretched, overbooked, and about to snap! Strategies for handling your fast-paced life.* New York, NY: Ballantine Books.
Iowa State University Study Abroad Center. (2011). Cultural differences: Time orientation. Retrieved from http://www.celt.iastate.edu/international/CulturalDifferences3.html
Junco, R., & Cotton, S. (2012). No A 4 U: The relationship between multitasking and academic performance. *Computers and Education, 59*(2), 505–514.
Krishna, R. M. (2008). Slow down, you move too fast. Integris Center for Mind, Body and Spirit. Retrieved from http://www.integris-health.com/INTEGRIS/en-US/Specialities/MindBodySpirit/Newsroom/MindMatters/TimeUrgency.htm
Levine, R., & Wolff, E. (1985). Social time: The heartbeat of culture. *Psychology Today, 19,* 28–30.
Linder, S. (1970). *The harried leisure class.* New York, NY: Columbia University Press.
Mayer, R. E., & Moreno, R. (2003). Nine ways to reduce cognitive load in multimedia learning. *Educational Psychologist, 38*(1), 43–52.
Mydans, S. (December 30, 2011). Samoa to skip Friday and switch time zones. *The New York Times.* Retrieved from http://www.nytimes.com/2011/12/30/world/asia/samoa-to-skip-friday-and-switch-time-zones.html
Neuliep, J. W. (2011). *Intercultural communication: A contextual approach.* Los Angeles, CA: Sage Publications.
Pew Research Center. (February 28, 2006). Who's feeling rushed? *A Social Trends Report.* Retrieved from http://www.pewresearch.rog/assets/social/pdf/Rushed.pdf
Preston, M. (May 27, 2014). From a pro, the mind-body link. *Sarasota Herald Tribune.* Retrieved from http://health.heraldtribune.com/2014/05/27/golf-pro-mind-body-link/
Priestly, J. B. (1968). *Man and time.* New York, NY: Dell.
Rifkin, J. (1987). *Time wars: The primary conflict in human history.* New York, NY: Henry Holt and Company.
Robinson, B. (April 12, 2014). Facebook: The world's biggest wast of time? *The Huffington Post.* Retrieved from http://www.huffingtonpost.com/billrobinson/facebook-the-worlds-bigge_b_4585457.html
Robinson, J., & Godbey, G. (1997, 1999, 2008 [2nd ed.]). *Time for life: The surprising ways Americans use their time.* University Park, PA: The Pennsylvania State University.
Schor, J. (1992). *The overworked American: The unexpected decline of leisure.* New York, NY: Basic Books.
Saccaro, M. (February 4, 2015). America's "free time" problem: Why nearly half of U.S. workers don't get enough. *Salon.* Retrieved from http://www.salon.com/2015/02/04/americas_free_time_problem_why_nearly_half_of_u_s_workers_dont_get_enough_of_it/
Slowfood.com. (2015). Terre Madre Salone del Gusto. Retrieved from http://www.slowfood.com/international/2/our-philosophy?-session=query_session:6C47D45618f442A10FrTDC152A0A
Stone, A. (August 18, 2012). Why waiting is torture. *The New York Times.* Retrieved from http://www.nytimes.com/2012/08/19/opinion/sunday/why-waiting-in-line-is-torture.html?pagewanted=all

Wood, B., Rea, M. S., Plitnick, B., & Figueiro, M. G. (2012). Light level and duration of exposure determine the impact of self-luminous tablets on melatonin suppression. *Applied Ergonomics*. Retrieved from http://www.sciencedirect.com/science/article/pii/S0003687012001159
Zimbardo, P., & Boyd, J. (2008). The time paradox: *The new psychology of time that will change your life.* New York, NY: Simon and Schuster.

CHAPTER 12

Is Leisure Fair?

Is there equity in leisure?

No. Barriers exist in contemporary societies to full fairness of opportunity in leisure.

What are examples of where inequity in leisure exists?

There is discrimination in leisure for women, persons with disabilities, gays and lesbians, ethnic and racial minorities, and others.

Does leisure have the potential to enable equity?

Yes, indeed! Leisure is an important context for creating fair opportunities for a high quality of life for everyone.

Is leisure a right or a privilege? Fundamental to discussing leisure's fairness, this simple question illustrates the quandary. When leisure is viewed as a privilege, it is something to be earned. But leisure can also be viewed as a right—something that is as essentially human and necessary as eating and sleeping. Thus, determining whether it is fair to charge fees to visitors to a national forest, or fair to prohibit women from joining a private country club, or fair for children who are abused in organized sport programs depends on leisure's position as a right or a privilege.

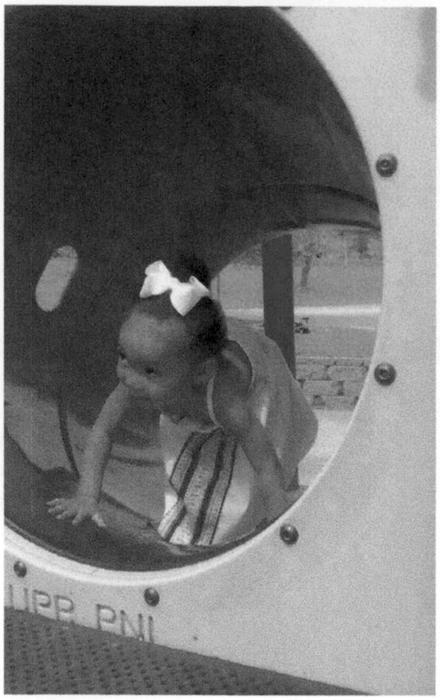

Figure 12.1. Is leisure a right of humanity or a privilege for those with means? © Patricia D. Setser, 2016

As a privilege, leisure is distributed unequally. When leisure is defined as free time or activity, for example, it is often viewed as a reward and thus a privilege for those who've earned it. As a privilege, leisure is a prize available only to qualifying people. Sometimes the qualifier is having enough money to pay for certain forms of leisure. Other times, it is the guilt-free sensation that, by the time the weekend is here, you have worked hard enough to take some time off.

As a right, on the other hand, leisure should be distributed equitably. Many societies believe in natural or inalienable rights—rights that are impossible to surrender. These are often described as life, liberty, and the pursuit of happiness. With these rights comes a commitment to equality—everyone has the same right to a good life. Accordingly, societies provide services considered vital to experiencing leisure.

In this chapter, we take the position that leisure is a right. Given this we first discuss how leisure both restricts and enables equity. Then we illustrate this through the examples of women, ethnic and racial minorities, gays and lesbians, and persons with disabilities.

Box 12.1
In Profile

Sport Team Mascots

What's your favorite sport team's mascot? Is it a bulldog, eagle, lion, longhorn steer, or cornhusker? Or maybe it is inspired by a Native American ethnic group, such as the Washington Redskins, Atlanta Braves, Edmonton Eskimos, Chicago Blackhawks, Florida State Seminoles, or Central Michigan University Chippewas. There is considerable controversy over the use of ethnic group mascots because some view them as disrespectful and offensive. Most notably, the National Congress of American Indians has issued a resolution opposing continued usage of Native team names, mascots, and logos. Some tribal entities have issued resolutions opposing usage as well. Conversely, certain tribes have granted permission to use their names for sport teams, as in the case of the Chippewa and Seminole tribes for Central Michigan University and Florida State University. Out of respect for the question of fairness in using ethnic group labels for mascots some teams have discontinued their use and selected other mascots. For example, after a protracted and bitter controversy over the logo "Illini" by the University of Illinois, the term has been removed from official university sanction, yet unofficially it is still widely used by students and fans.

Prohibitions and Permissions

Today in many contemporary societies there exists discrimination of opportunity according to gender, race, ability, religion, income, age, and other distinctions. Yet, of all the tools available to societies to create equity of opportunity, leisure is perhaps one of the most vital. Thus, leisure is both a hurdle to **equity** and an enabler of equity. For example, women feel more constrained by fear than men to participate in solo hiking (Coble et al., 2003), yet women are also now resisting societal notions and entering the traditionally male area of computer gaming (Bryce & Rutter, 2003).

Equity: Fairness

First, let's consider how leisure restricts equity. You are already well aware that, in general, certain pastimes are more likely to be pursued by people in certain age, gender, and other social groups. Is this by choice or prohibition?

A way of demonstrating leisure as prohibition is to cite incidences against participation for certain groups. For example, a study by Livengood and Stodolska (2004) evaluating the post 9/11 experiences of Muslim immigrants to the United States from Middle Eastern countries found that discrimination affected their leisure experiences by restricting the range of available leisure options and playmates. In another study (Barnett, 2007), the experience of trying out for cheerleading and the dance team was measured for high school girls. Findings indicated significant differences in positive and negative emotions, classroom attendance and performance, and feelings about self and school according to whether the girls were admitted or not to these activities.

There are several ways to consider such restrictions in leisure, including the conditions of discrimination and constraints. For example, much has been studied and written about **discrimination**. Stodolska (2005) proposed a model to explain individual discriminatory behavior. The model consists of three decision-making stages. First, an individual uses his or her own set of information to derive general beliefs about a group. Then he or she combines these preexisting beliefs with any new information received to form an attitude signifying the degree of hostility toward the group at a particular point in time. Finally, he or she weighs the internal benefits of discrimination against external consequences of such an action and chooses to act accordingly.

Discrimination: Unjust prejudicial treatment of different categories of people

According to Stodolska's model, acting in a discriminatory way against others is an individual decision. Shaw (2005), on the other hand, proposed that discrimination is also a societal decision. Her point is that in addition to individual prejudices, there are structural disadvantages experienced by certain groups. One source of societal structural disadvantages is power relations. Those who are discriminated against in leisure lack economic, social, and/or political power in the society. Shaw refers to this as a double discrimination. For those without societal power, leisure prohibitions pile on an additional disadvantage.

Another way to think about prohibitions in leisure is through the concept of **constraints**. In fact, the investigation of leisure constraints has become a major focus in research over the past several decades. Essentially, the numerous studies start with the question, "Why do some people not participate in leisure in general or in particular activities for which they might have a desire?" For example, a study by Nadirova and Jackson (2000) found the single most constrained leisure situation was the inability to participate as often as one would like. In another study, Jun and Kyle (2011) explored the role of personal identity in constraints for golfers and concluded the "homemaker identity" was the most conflicting with the "golfer identity."

Constraints: That which inhibits a leisure pursuit once an interest for it has been formed

A model has been developed to explain the concept of leisure constraints (Crawford & Godbey, 1987; Crawford et al., 1991; Godbey et al., 2010). It suggests leisure participation is dependent on negotiating through a hierarchy of structural, intrapersonal, and interpersonal barriers. The model claims that intrapersonal constraints have to be overcome first, followed by interpersonal and then structural in order to participate in desired leisure expressions.

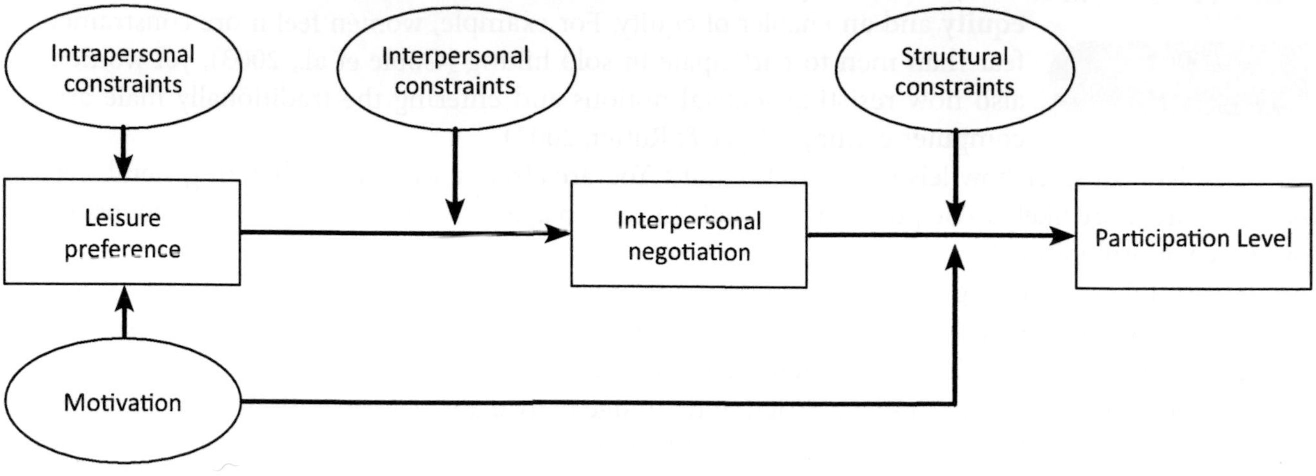

Figure. 12.2. A model of the leisure constraints concept used in a study by Jackson et.al., 1993.

Intrapersonal constraints are personal psychological attributes that constrain leisure involvement. Our own perception of our abilities, personality needs, religious beliefs, and prior socialization typically are cited as intrapersonal leisure constraints. For example, if prior socialization suggests men do not participate in group fitness classes, a particular man my feel constrained in participating even if he has an interest. Interpersonal constraints are those barriers arising out of social interaction with friends, family, and others. In a family, for example, interpersonal constraints may occur when spouses or partners differ in their leisure preferences (Jackson & Scott, 1999). Finally, structural constraints are typically architectural barriers, such as a recreation center that is inaccessible to a person using a wheelchair, or economic barriers, such as high fees charged for a youth sport program that prohibit economically disadvantaged children from signing up.

Figure 12.3. The Paralympic Games is a major international multisport event involving athletes with a range of disabilities. Paralympians strive for equal treatment with nondisabled Olympic athletes, but a large funding gap remains (Parkin, 2016).

Box 12.2
In Your Own Experience

Why Haven't You Taken a Cruise?

Mark each statement according to how likely it is to keep you from taking a cruise this year. Use the scale, Agree, Neutral and Disagree.

	Agree	Neutral	Disagree
1. Taking a cruise would be too expensive for me.			
2. I have special needs that cannot be accommodated on a cruise ship.			
3. I'm not able to leave my school, work, and/or family.			
4. My friends and family members are not interested in taking a cruise.			
5. I don't feel comfortable in a boat on the water.			
6. Ocean cruising is just not my thing.			

Scoring: items #1 and #2 represent structural constraints; items #3 and #4 are interpersonal constraints; items #5 and #6 are intrapersonal constraints.

While leisure contains factors that prohibit equitable individual and community lives, leisure can also enable equity. In fact, leisure can be one of the most powerful forces for equity. Leisure can be a means by which people who are homeless, unemployed, or migrant are incorporated into mainstream society. As well, community festivals are able to unify a widely diverse population through a common spirit of cooperation. And, as demonstrated every four years in the Olympic Games, leisure can call at least a temporary halt to international disagreements.

Inclusion: Valuing all people regardless of their differences

To harness leisure's equity powers, professionals in leisure services have focused on the concept of inclusion. **Inclusion** suggests that leisure service organizations provide mechanisms for people who have special life conditions, such as a physical disability, to participate according to typical circumstances and to help them become as independent as possible by joining the mainstream of society. Inclusion means the involvement and full acceptance of all people within the wide range of community settings. According to Schleien et al. (2003) inclusion involves three levels of acceptance ranging from a minimal physical level to an ultimate social level (Table 12.1).

Table 12.1
A Continuum of Leisure Inclusion

Level 1: Physical	Level 2: Functional	Level 3: Social
Access to buildings and programs	Opportunities to be successful within buildings and programs	Full and positive interactions with others through participation in activities

Diversity: Celebrating differences in people

Another concept that speaks to the ability of leisure to create equity—**diversity**—seems the antithesis of inclusion. A major conclusion from the most recent census of the population of the United States, for example, is that diversity has increased. For example, more than half of the growth in the total U.S. population between 2000 and 2010 was because of an increase in the Hispanic population, rising from 35.3 million in 2000 to 50.5 million in 2010 (U.S. Census, 2010). Beyond diversity of race and ethnicity, Americans also differ from one another more than ever before in terms of family type, household income, lifestyle, political beliefs, and other qualities.

As a result, it is important to support and protect diversity, because by valuing the mosaic of differences in individuals and groups and by fostering a climate where mutual respect is intrinsic, a better society for everyone is created. This can be done by way of **pluralism**—peaceful coexistence and interaction among people with different beliefs, customs, and lifestyles. For example, in 1971, the Canadian government referred to cultural pluralism, as opposed to multiculturalism, as the "very essence" of their nation's identity (Library and Archives Canada). In a pluralist culture, groups not only coexist side by side, but also consider qualities of other groups as traits worth having in the dominant culture.

Pluralism: A form of society in which minority groups maintain their independent cultural traditions

Sport is a ready source of examples of pluralism in leisure. For example, many sport teams accommodate training and scheduling to the fasting customs of athletes who are Muslim. Muslim athletes should fast from sunrise to sunset each day throughout the 30 days of Ramadan (Maughan et. al., 2012), and many teams make arrangements around this in order not to endanger the athletes' health.

As another example, in July 1996, the deciding game of the U.S. Cup soccer tournament was played in the Rose Bowl stadium in Pasadena, California. The contest matched the U.S. and Mexican national teams with important stars from both countries (Gramann & Allison, 1999). More than 98,000 spectators packed the stadium. Was this a testimony to a rising popularity of soccer in a traditionally non-soccer-playing country? Yes, in part, but this is not all of the explanation, because most of the fans were cheering for Mexico. Because of a large Mexican American population living in southern California, it was a home game for Mexico. In other words, the sport of soccer was able to maintain and even strengthen group identity within a diverse society. Latino cultural traditions were celebrated that day.

Examples

There are many more examples of how leisure is both a barrier to and an enabler of equity. To illustrate further the concepts of discrimination, constraints, inclusion, diversity, and pluralism just discussed, we focus on women, persons with disabilities, gays and lesbians, and racial and ethnic minorities.

Women

"The woman" has played many roles throughout history: mother, daughter, lover, and mate. She has also been prime minister, farmer, CEO, and scientist. Today women combine many of these roles, yet through the centuries, almost every society has developed definite ideas about what behaviors are appropriate for women. Some of these ideas have disappeared or changed greatly over time, but others have changed little or not at all.

Box 12.3
The Study Says

Gender and Leisure Deficits

Using data from the American Time Use Survey (2003-2012), this study examined how mothers' leisure varies by marital status. It was found that never-married mothers have more total free time than married mothers, yet the majority of never married mothers' leisure pursuits is passive and socially isolated. Further, un-partnered black mothers spend the most time in socially isolated leisure, such as time spent alone watching television.

Source: Passias, Sayer, & Pepin, 2015

What is the meaning of leisure for women? In developed countries, the differences between men's and women's use of leisure have narrowed. For example, rates of sport participation are converging, groups of women now enjoy girls' nights out in the same places as are frequented by groups of men, and men and women spend the same number of hours watching television every day (Roberts, 2010). So how has leisure been both prohibition and permission for women?

Feminism: The belief in and action toward political, economic, and social equality for men and women

One way of answering this is via the concept of feminism. **Feminism** is both an intellectual commitment and a political movement that seeks equity for everyone, regardless of gender. There are many different interpretations of feminism and disagreements about what exactly ought to be done about it, but basically topics in feminism include the body, work, family, and popular culture. And, within the past 30 years, a growing topic in feminism has been leisure.

In feminism, ideas of empowerment and social change are central. This is particularly poignant because both feminism and leisure are based on the qualities of choice and freedom. Yet, in many societies today, and in the past, leisure for women has itself been constrained because of a lack of empowerment and social action. This conclusion can be demonstrated through a quarter-century of research on women in developed cultures.

That is, our understanding about women's leisure has shown an evolution, progressively asking more and deeper critical questions. Earlier studies (1980-1989) revealed several initial understandings. According to an integrative review of research studies from that period (Henderson, 1990), leisure provided for women an opportunity to share a common world. That is, leisure settings and activities helped women be with others who shared their concerns. Other research revealed these concerns to include unstructured and fragmented leisure squeezed into brief time blocks around role and home obligations, fewer leisure opportunities for women when compared with men, and feelings of not deserving time off for themselves.

Figure 12.4. A women's bicycle racing team at Indiana University's "Little 500." A shorter version of the men's race, which was founded in 1951, women's teams have raced each other since 1988. Does this "separate but almost equal" program demonstrate equity for women's leisure? Courtesy Indiana University Foundation

Later, another review of research studies on women and leisure (Henderson, 1996) published from 1990 through 1995, debunked the common world of leisure idea and revealed there are actually multiple meanings of leisure for women. That is, there is a wide diversity among women who live in modern cultures about what leisure is and is not for them. This also broadened the feminist discussion to include what leisure can do for not only women, but men as well. In the later 1990s, studies broadened even further to include questions of race, social class, and age as related to gender and leisure.

According to the most recent review of research on women and leisure (Henderson & Hickerson, 2007), our understanding has transitioned from itemizing prohibitions on women's expression of leisure, to acknowledging what needs to be done about it. For the most part, studies carried out between 2000 and 2006 focused on how the benefits of leisure can overcome the constraints against it. For example, a study by Anderson et al. (2005) described the benefits of physical activity for girls with disabilities and how these benefits mitigated some of the constraints these girls faced because they were girls. In another study (Iwasaki et al., 2005), leisure was confirmed to be a means for addressing stress for women through coping.

This trajectory of progress in leisure for women is culture specific, of course. The balance of prohibition and permission is not always so evolutionary. For example, a study of Iranian women concluded that women had constraints due to the lack of opportunities within their communities. As well, specific cultural prohibitions based on traditional views, along with economic and personal home expectations were rated as more constraining to their leisure (Arab-Moghaddam et al., 2007).

Box 12.4 What Do You Say?

Gendered Toys?

In 2012, Hamleys (London's 251-year-old toy store) dismantled its pink girls and blue boys sections in favor of a gender-neutral store. Rather than floors dedicated to Barbie dolls and action figures, merchandise is now organized by types (soft toys) and interests (outdoor). Meanwhile, also in 2012, Lego launched a $40 million marketing campaign for its new Friends collection. The line features new, pastel-colored blocks that allow a budding Kardashian to build herself a café or a beauty salon (Orenstein, 2012). So, who has it right? Can equity be better achieved with gender-neutral or gender-specific toys?

1. Should gender be systematically expunged from playthings? Why or why not?
2. Do the sexes play differently? Studies suggest, for example, that children of both sexes appreciate stuffed animals and books, so should these types of play things be gender neutral?
3. Traditionally, toys were intended to communicate parental values and expectations, and to train children for their future adult roles. Does this add or subtract from a conclusion that toys should be gender neutral? How?

Persons With Disabilities

One billion people, or 15% of the world's population, experience some form of disability, with disability prevalence higher for developing countries. Further, one-fifth of the estimated global total, or between 110 million and 190 million people, experience significant disabilities (World Bank, 2016). For example, of the 5.4 million Americans with Alzheimer's, an estimated 5.2 million are age 65 and older (Alzheimer's Association, 2016). This means one in nine people age 65 and older has this progressive and fatal brain disease that causes problems with memory, thinking, and behavior severe enough to affect work, lifelong hobbies, and social life.

Disabling conditions: A physical, sensory, or mental impairment that substantially limits one or more life activity

Of course, a variety of **disabling conditions** is included in all these statistics. The largest number involves limiting basic physical activities, such as walking, climbing stairs, reaching, lifting or carrying. Other conditions include sensory, such as sight or hearing, as well as cognitive and emotional, which affects abilities to learn, concentrate, get along with others, and live independently.

According to a survey by the National Organization on Disability (2004):

- People with disabilities are twice as likely to have inadequate transportation (31% versus 13%), and a much higher percentage are without needed health care (18% versus 7%).
- People with disabilities are less likely to socialize, eat out, or attend religious services than their nondisabled counterparts.
- Life satisfaction for people with disabilities also trails, with only 34% saying they are very satisfied compared to 61% of those without disabilities.
- The severity of disability makes a significant difference with people having severe disabilities at a much greater disadvantage.

Disabling conditions cut across age, race, social class, gender, income, and educational backgrounds. But, as you know, leisure experiences and participation can provide unique and valuable opportunities that may result in numerous physical, social, and psychological benefits, as well as enhance overall quality of life. However, in order for these benefits to be gained by people with disabilities, leisure services must be both accessible and inclusive.

In response, during the 1960s in North America, a movement developed emphasizing the rights of people with disabling conditions. A significant turning point in Canada was the amendment of the Human Rights Act in 1974, which prohibits discrimination for employment for reasons of physical or mental disability (Searle & Brayley, 2000). Such official notice of the rights of persons with disabilities did not occur in the United States until 1990, with the passage of the Americans With Disabilities Act (ADA), which required public institutions to provide fuller and more equitable opportunities for accessibility to buildings, programs, jobs, and so forth.

Figure 12.5. The goal of inclusion is to create options that optimize leisure equity.

In applying these laws to leisure facilities, programs, and other services, the advocacy philosophy originally took the form of "separate but equal." Recreation programs in communities were instrumental in addressing the needs of persons with disabilities by establishing segregated programs. These were often labeled as programs for special populations. Later it was realized that segregation sometimes invited others to view persons with disabilities as different and worthy of pity. Now the focus is not simply on providing access to leisure resources through special programs, but also on enabling persons with disabilities to become full participants in community life (Bedini, 1990). As an inclusive philosophy, the goal is to create options that optimize leisure equity.

Box 12.5 Web Explore

What Does Disability Mean?

To understand more fully the role of leisure in the lives of persons with a disability, check out these talks presented at TED conferences: http://www.youtube.com/watch?v=YyBk55G7Keo and http://www.youtube.com/watch?v=dTwX-eZ4GkzI

At the core of inclusive leisure services are several fundamental principles about leisure and disability, namely self-determination, self-advocacy, normalization, and integration (Searle & Brayley, 2000).

First, one of the most significant ways persons with disabling conditions can be empowered through leisure is **self-determination** (Mahon & Bullock, 1992). Allowing people to make decisions for themselves, free from influence or interference, is important to everyone, and leisure settings and experiences are among the best sources for this. For people with disabling conditions, it is especially important to have the right to choose leisure. Similarly, **self-advocacy** means individually and as a group, people with disabling conditions are allowed to speak for and on behalf of themselves. In the past 30 years, a great deal has been accomplished to facilitate equal

Self-determination: Defining goals for oneself and taking the initiative to achieve them

Self-advocacy: Speaking on behalf of oneself

rights for people with special needs, yet until recently, much of what was proposed was by people without disabilities. Self-advocacy gives people with disabilities their own voice, and leisure settings and experiences are among the best sources for this.

Normalization: The availability of typical leisure experiences

Integration: Enabling persons with and without disabilities to participate together

The principle of **normalization** does not mean making persons with disabling conditions "normal." Instead, it refers to the provision of typical experiences so that those with disabilities can maintain or develop leisure interests along with their own peers. One of the outcomes of normalization is **integration**, which requires both social interaction and social acceptance (Bullock & Howe, 1991). Based on the idea of integrity, integration encourages "to be yourself among others" (Fullwood, 1990, p. 3.)

Gays and Lesbians

In the past, throughout much of the world, religious and governmental authorities have condemned gays and lesbians. Until more recently in the United States, for example, homosexuality was categorized as a form of mental illness by the psychiatric profession and as a crime by law enforcement. Change began in the 1960s as civil rights movements worked to remove some of the discriminatory laws.

Today, while the exact proportion of the contemporary population that is gay, lesbian, bisexual or transgender has been difficult to estimate reliably (roughly 4% to 10%), an increasing visibility in many cultures means they are no longer thought of as counterculture. In particularly the last few decades, there has been a trend toward increased recognition and legal rights, including for civil unions and marriage, adoption and parenting rights, and equal access to health care. For example, in 2016, same-sex marriage was legal in 23 countries of the world, including Argentina, Belgium, Canada, Denmark, Iceland, Netherlands, Norway, Portugal, South Africa, Spain, Sweden, and the United States (Marriage Equality News, 2016). Meanwhile in 2016, a total of 77 countries in the world still had laws declaring homosexuality to be illegal and of these, 10 still find it to be punishable by death (Bearak & Cameron, 2016).

In terms of leisure, gays and lesbians have become an important consumer market in many economies, including in tourism. For example, Gay Days at Walt Disney World in Orlando, Florida, annually draws some 170,000 visitors. While not officially sponsored by Walt Disney Company, the event is possible because of the park's official policy not to discriminate against anyone's right to visit the parks, and over the years it has become more involved in working with the event coordinators. This is because niche tourism marketed to people who want to travel to gay destinations is economically beneficial. As an industry, it includes travel agents, tour companies, cruise lines, special events, travel advertising, and promotions campaigns. For example, based on tourism industry data, the annual economic impact of gay and lesbian travelers is approximately $65 billion in the U.S. alone (World Tourism Organization, 2016).

In spite of this, gays and lesbians, including in the United States, continue to be discriminated against in the domains of family, employment, religion, housing, health care, and leisure. While recreation facility and program use has been shown to enhance a sense of community belonging, and thus is a coping mechanism for feelings of marginalization (Kalbfleish et.al., 2016), some leisure service organizations have explicitly refused participation to gay and lesbian individuals. These include recreation and social clubs sponsored by religious denominations, fraternities and sororities, and some school extracurricular activities.

To illustrate, on February 6, 2002, the Boy Scouts of America (one of the largest private youth organizations in the U.S.) adopted a resolution stating gays were unacceptable role models for scout youth, a policy reaffirmed again in 2012 after a 2-year internal evaluation (Boy Scouts of America, 2012). Then on May 23, 2013, the BSA's National Council approved a resolution to remove the restriction denying membership to youth on the basis of sexual orientation alone, but the policy for adult leaders remained in place until July 27, 2015. Obviously, this membership debate (and accompanying litigation) was the result of a conflict between the organization's stated mission and a changing society.

Figure 12.6. The Boy Scouts of America recently decided not to discriminate against gay members and leaders. The 2016 Pride March in New York City.

Because gays and lesbians remain marginalized in leisure, researchers have focused on the coping strategies used when faced with such discrimination. Particularly, social support has been highlighted as an important stress-coping resource (Haas, 2002) and emphasizes the significant role of leisure. For example, in a study on the lives of older lesbians, Jacobson and Samdahl (1998) found that to cope with their experiences of discrimination, these women actively created private safe leisure spaces for themselves (such as in softball leagues)—an alternative community providing support and validation. Further, in a study on gay tourists, Pritchard et al. (2000) concluded the need for safety, to feel comfortable with like-minded people, and to escape to specifically gay spaces were key influences on their choice of vacation destination. As well, studies of participants in the Gay Games report them as full of the "joy of being wholly who they are" (Deane-Young, 1994, p. 11).

Yet in studying gays and lesbians in sport, Anderson (2002) sees this as a form of self-marginalization, refusing to challenge the discrimination, and cites the creation of the Gay Games as a prime example. Jarvis (2006) suggests that gay sport has largely avoided challenging what he terms the "cultural conservatism" of sport.

Racial and Ethnic Minorities

In North America, increasing diversity in ethnicity and race has been so dramatic that certain groups are on the verge of losing their minority status. For example, Stodolska and Walker (2007) noted that minority populations in Canada are growing at a significant rate, and in the state of Hawaii non-White ethnic groups account for about 75% of the population, with the largest being those of Asian descent at about 55%. Hawaii is one of four states, along with the District of Columbia, with majority minority populations, but the numbers are likely to grow until racial and ethnic minorities will make up the majority of the entire U.S. population by 2050 (*Star-Bulletin*, 2008).

What do we mean by race and ethnicity? Definitions of what constitutes an ethnic or racial group are subject to much discussion and study, and the terminology used to describe them has changed over time. Let's consider **ethnicity** first. Membership in any ethnic group is something that is subjectively meaningful to the person. For example, the ethnicity data collected by the United States Census Bureau is self-identified. Individuals respond to the survey according to the group with which they most closely identify. They may base this on any number of factors, including their nationality, country of birth, language spoken at home, parents' country of birth, geographical origin, and/or religion.

Ethnicity: A social construction indicating common cultural, ancestral, and/or language traits

Box 12.6
By The
Numbers

Most Spoken Languages

Language is one indicator of ethnicity. Here are the most widely spoken languages in the world:

1. Chinese (includes 13 dialects) = 1,197,000,000
2. Spanish = 414,000,000
3. English = 335,000,000
4. Hindi = 260,000,000
5. Arabic (includes 18 dialects) = 237,000,000

Source: Infoplease, 2016

Race: Self-defined distinction usually based on physical characteristics

The U.S. Census Bureau also counts people according to self-identified **race**. Residents choose one or more races with which they feel most closely connected. It is important to distinguish that the racial categories used do not reference particular biological, genetic, anthropological, or even scientific characteristics because race also generally reflects a social definition, even though race also reflects physical characteristics, including skin color, eye color, hair color, and bone/jaw structure.

Given the increasing ethnic and racial diversity of North America, you might rightly conclude that there are likewise increasing challenges and opportunities in leisure. Accordingly, leisure has been a tool that both hinders and enables ethnic and racial diversity. For example, those who define themselves as Hispanic and Black are much less likely to read for leisure (U.S. Census Bureau, 2007). Is this because of a prohibition, or is this by choice?

Over the past 40 years, scholars have produced a voluminous body of literature examining leisure meanings according to racial and ethnic distinctions. For example, while ethnic and racial minorities are still constrained by socioeconomic status, limited access to quality recreation resources, discrimination, and lack of information, Stodolska (2015) has produced numerous studies that point to many benefits from leisure to minorities, including facilitating interracial/intergroup contacts, creating opportunities for learning and cultural exchange, helping to strengthen bonds within ethnic communities, and facilitating preservation of ethnic culture. Specifically, the focus of many studies has been on neighborhood/community-based leisure— such as, how access to urban parks is affected by racial and ethnic identities. Similarly, ethnic and racial group use of the outdoors and forest-based recreation has been a common theme of studies, as has race and ethnicity in sports and youth development (Floyd et al., 2008).

Box 12.7
The Study Says

What About Baseball?

In 1975, 27% of the players in major league American baseball were African American. By 2010, African Americans numbered only 8% (Nightengale, 2012). Today, African Americans comprise less than 3% of the players at the highest competitive levels of youth baseball and 3% of NCAA Division I baseball players. African Americans also constitute less than 5% of spectators at major league parks.

Why? According to studies, basketball has become the preeminent sport in African American groups. The studies contend this has been brought about by four factors: encouragement by authority figures to pursue basketball, the portrayal of basketball in the media as a form of empowerment, the abundance of black role models in basketball, and the perception of high and fast social mobility through basketball.

Source: Ogden & Hilt, 2003

There are several theoretical perspectives available to help make sense of the race, ethnicity, and leisure relationship as well. One perspective that has been rather long standing, but is still used today to explain ethnic/racial leisure distinctions is termed marginality. The thesis of **marginality** suggests ethnic and racial differences are due to a group's marginal position in society. For example, over the years, research has found differences between Whites and Blacks in their interests in outdoor recreation. In general, members of ethnic minority groups participate less frequently (Gramann & Allison, 1999). Marginality would explain this difference as Blacks feel more alienated from the dominant culture that participates in it. Thus, they self-segregate from certain pastimes.

Marginality: Being on the margins of the dominant culture

Figure 12.7. Nicodemus, Kansas. In the 1870s, this little town witnessed great movements of African Americans from the horrors of Reconstruction in the South. In 1996 Nicodemus was established by the National Park Service as a national historic site. Source: Library of Congress. Early area homestead, circa 1885.

Some studies have argued, however, that the marginal status of racial and ethnic groups in leisure is due to opportunity discrimination (Washburne, 1978). As applied to outdoor recreation participation, in particular, this maintains the ethnic/racial differences are due to the cost of participation and the geographical location of resources—that historically the dominant groups have had a larger discretionary income and greater access to outdoor recreation sites. Others (cf. Floyd, 1998) have rejected a marginality explanation specifically due to socioeconomic differences within ethnic groups—not everyone who identifies themselves with a minority group lacks resources.

What We Understand About Leisure Equity

Our pastimes are a tool both for and against equity for people. For such groups as women, persons with disabilities, gays and lesbians, and ethnic and racial minorities the following points can be made about leisure and equity:

1. Leisure is not yet equitable; constraints to participation exist.
   Select one of the groups discussed and illustrate this conclusion:

   ____

   ____

2. Leisure has the potential of providing equality of opportunity.
   Select one of the groups discussed and illustrate this conclusion:

   ____

   ____

3. This can be accomplished through such principles as inclusion and celebration of diversity.
   Define each of these concepts and describe how they are forces for equity in leisure:

   ____

   ____

References

Alzheimer's Association. (2016). Quick facts. Retrieved from http://www.alz.org/facts/

Anderson, E. (2002). Openly gay athletes: Contesting hegemonic masculinity in a homophobic environment. *Gender and Society, 16*, 860–877.

Anderson, D. A., Bedini, L. A., & Moreland, L. (2005). Getting all girls into the game: Physically active recreation for girls with disabilities. *Journal of Park and Recreation Administration, 23*(4), 78–103.

Arab-Moghaddam, N., Henderson, K. A., & Sheikholesclami, R. (2007). Women's leisure and constraints to participation: Iranian perspectives. *Journal of Leisure Research, 39*(1), 109.

Barnett, L. A. (2007). "Winners" and "losers": The effects of being allowed or denied entry into competitive extracurricular activities. *Journal of Leisure Research, 39*(2), 316–344.

Bearak, M., & Cameron, D. (June 16, 2016). Here are the 10 countries where homosexuality may be punished by death. *The Washington Post*. Retrieved from https://www.washingtonpost.com/news/worldviews/wp/2016/06/13/here-are-the-10-countries-where-homosexuality-may-be-punished-by-death-2/

Bedini, L. A. (October 1990). Separate but equal? Segregated programming for people with disabilities. *Journal of Physical Education, Recreation and Dance, 40*, 40–44.

Boy Scouts of America. (July 2012). News release. Retrieved from https://www.documentcloud.org/documents/400600-boy-scots-of-america-statement-reaffirms-ban-on.html

Bryce, J., & Rutter, J. (2003). Gender dynamics and the social and spatial organization of computer gaming. *Leisure Studies, 22*(1), 1–15.

Bullock, C. C., & Howe, C. Z. (1991). A model therapeutic recreation program for the reintegration of persons with disabilities into the community. *Therapeutic Recreation Journal, 25*(1), 7–17.

Coble, T. G., Selin, S. W., & Erickson, B. B. (2003). Hiking along: Understanding fear, negotiation strategies and leisure experience. *Journal of Leisure Research, 35*, 1–21.

Crawford, D., & Godbey, G. (1987). Reconceptualizing barriers to family leisure. *Leisure Sciences, 9*, 119–127.

Crawford, D., Jackson, E. L., & Godbey, G. (1991). A hierarchical model of leisure constraints. *Leisure Sciences, 13*, 309–320.

Deane-Young, P. (1994). *Lesbians and gays in sports*. New York, NY: Chelsea House.

Floyd, M. F. (1998). Getting beyond marginality and ethnicity: The challenge for race and ethnic studies in leisure research. *Journal of Leisure Research, 30*, 3–22.

Floyd, M. F., Bocarro, J. N., Thompson, T. D. (2008). Research on race and ethnicity in leisure studies: A review of five major journals. *Journal of Leisure Research, 40*(1), 1–22.

Fullwood, D. (1990). *Chances and choices: Making integration work*. Baltimore, MD: Brookes.

Godbey, G., Crawford, D. W., & Shen, X. S. (2010). Assessing hierarchical leisure constraints theory after two decades. *Journal of Leisure Research, 42*(1), 111–134.

Gramann, J. H., & Allison, M. T. (1999). Ethnicity, race, and leisure. In E. L. Jackson & T. L. Burton (Eds.), *Leisure studies: Prospects for the Twenty-first century* (pp. 283–298). State College, PA: Venture.

Haas, S. M. (2002). Social support as relationship maintenance in gay male couples coping with HIV or AIDS. *Journal of Social and Personal Relationships, 19*, 87–112.

Henderson, K. A. (1990). The meaning of leisure for women: An integrative review of the research. *Journal of Leisure Research, 22*(3), 228–243.

Henderson, K. A. (1996). One size doesn't fit all: The meanings of women's leisure. *Journal of Leisure Research, 28*(3), 139–154.

Henderson, K. A., & Hickerson, B. (2007). Women and leisure: Premises and performances uncovered in an integrative review. *Journal of Leisure Research, 39*(4), 591–610.

Infoplease. (2016). Most widely spoken languages in the world. Retrieved from http://www.infoplease.com/ipa/A0775272.html

Iwasaki, Y., MacKay, K., & Mactavish, J. (2005). Gender-based analyses of coping with stress among professional managers: Leisure coping and non-leisure coping. *Journal of Leisure Research, 37*, 1–27.

Jackson, E. L., Crawford, D. W., & Godbey, G. C. (1993). Negotiation of leisure constraints. *Leisure Sciences, 15*: 1–11.

Jackson, E. L., & Scott, D. (1999). Constraints to leisure. In E. L. Jackson & T. L. Burton (Eds.), *Leisure studies: Prospects for the Twenty-first century* (pp. 299–322). State College, PA: Venture.

Jacobson, S., & Samdahl, D. M. (1998). Leisure in the lives of older lesbians: Experiences with and responses to discrimination. *Journal of Leisure Research, 30*, 233–255.

Jarvis, N. (2006). Ten men out: Gay sporting masculinities in softball. In J. Caudwell (Ed.). *Sport, sexualities, and queer theory* (pp. 62–75). London, UK: Routledge.

Jun, J., & Kyle, G. T. (2011). The effect of identity conflict/facilitation on the experience of constraints to leisure and constraint negotiation. *Journal of Leisure Research, 43*(2), 176–204.

Kalbfleisch, L., Mock, S. & Hilbrecht, M. (July 11, 2016). LGB discrimination and diminished sense of belonging: The role of community leisure facility use as a buffer. *3rd ISA Forum of Sociology, Vienna, Austria.* Retrieved from https://isaconf.confex.com/isaconf/forum2016/webprogram/Paper82942.html

Library and Archives Canada. (8 October 1971). *Canadian Multicultural Policy 1971.* Parliament. House of Commons. Debates, 28th Parliament, 3rd Session, Volume 8.

Livengood, J. S., & Stodolska, M. (2004). The effects of discrimination and constraints negotiation on leisure behavior of American Muslims in Post-September 11 America. *Journal of Leisure Research, 36*(2), 183–208.

Mahon, M. J., & Bullock, C. C. (1992). Teaching adolescents with mild mental retardation to make decisions in leisure through the use of self-control techniques. *Therapeutic Recreation Journal, 26*, 9–26.

Marriage Equality News. (June 26, 2016). Marriage equality. Retrieved from http://www.lgbtqnation.com/tag/gay-marriage/

Maughan, R. J., Zerguini, Y., Chalabi, H., & Dvorak, J. (2012). Achieving optimum sports performance during Ramadan: Some practical recommendations. *Journal of Sports Science, 12*(30), 109–117.

Nadirova, A., & Jackson, E. L. (2000). Alternative criterion variables against which to assess the impacts of constraints to leisure. *Journal of Leisure Research, 32*(4), 396–405.

National Organization on Disability/Harris Survey of Americans with Disabilities. (2004). *Landmark disability survey finds pervasive disadvantages.* Retrieved from file:///C:/Users/Ruth/Downloads/NationalOrganizationonDisabilityHarrisSurvey%20(1).htm

Nightengale, B. (April 15, 2012). Number of African-American baseball players dips again. *USA Today.* Retrieved from http://usatoday30.usatoday.com/sports/baseball/story/2012-04-15/baseball-jackie-robinson/54302108/1

Ogden, D. C., & Hilt, M. L. (2003). Collective identity and basketball: An explanation for the decreasing number of African-Americans on America's baseball diamonds. *Journal of Leisure Research, 35*(2), 213–227.

Orenstein, P. (January 1, 2012). Does stripping gender from toys really make sense? *The New York Times.* Retrieved from http://www.nytimes.com/2011/12/30/opinion/does-stripping-gender-from-toys-really-make-sense.html?_r=0

Parkin, B. (September 2, 2016). Rio paralympics race to assemble financing in days before games. *The Wall Street Journal.* Retrieved from http://www.wsj.com/articles/rio-paralympics-race-to-assemble-financing-in-days-before-games-1472853626.

Passias, E., Sayer, L. C., & Pepin, J. R. (2015). Who experiences leisure deficits? Mother's marital status and leisure time. Time Use Lab, University of Maryland. Retrieved from http://www.timeuselab.umd.edu/uploads/1/8/7/9/18797564/mom_leisure_--_draft.pdf

Pritchard, A., Morgan, N. J., Sedgley, D., Khan, E., & Jenkins, A. (2000). Sexuality and holiday choices: Conversations with gay and lesbian tourists. *Leisure Studies, 19*(4), 267–282.

Roberts, K. (2010). *Sociology of leisure.* Retrieved from www.sagepub.net/isa/resources/pdf/Leisure.pdf

Schleien, S. J., Green, F. P., & Stone, C. F. (2003). Making friends within inclusive community programs. *American Journal of Recreation Therapy, 2*(1), 7–16.

Searle, M. S., & Brayley, R. W. (2000). *Leisure services in Canada: An introduction.* State College, PA: Venture.

Shaw, S. (2005). Discrimination is a societal issue too: Moving beyond individual behavior. *Leisure Sciences, 27*(1), 37–40.

Star-Bulletin Staff. (May 1, 2008). Hawaii's ethnic diversity still tops. *Star-Bulletin.* Retrieved from http://starbulletin.com/2008/05/01/news/story10.html

Stodolska, M. (2005). A conditioned attitude model of individual discriminatory behavior. *Leisure Sciences, 27*(1), 10–20.

Stodolska, M. (2015). Recreation for all: Providing leisure and recreation services in multi-ethnic communities, *World Leisure Journal, 57*(2), 89–103.

Stodolska, M., & Walker, G. J. (2007). Ethnicity and leisure: Historical development, current status, and future directions. *Leisure/Loisir, 31*, 3–26.

U.S. Census Bureau. (May 26, 2007). Facts for features. Retrieved from http://www.prnewswire.com/cgi-bin/stories.pl?ACCT=104&STORY=/www/story/05-29-2007/0004597318&EDATE

U.S. Census Bureau. (2010). 2010 census shows America's diversity. Retrieved from http://2010.census.gov/news/releases/operations/cb11-cn125.html

Washburne, R. F. (1978). Black underparticipation in wildland recreation: Alternative explanations. *Leisure Sciences, 1*, 175–189.

World Bank. (2016). Disabilities overview. Retrieved from http://www.worldbank.org/en/topic/disability/overview

World Tourism Organization (UNWTO). (2016). *Global report on LGBT tourism: Volume three.* Retrieved from http://www.e-unwto.org/doi/pdf/10.18111/9789284414581

Leisure Systems

CHAPTER 13

Why are leisure systems important?

As you already know, having access to leisure resources is imperative to the lives of individuals, communities, and entire societies. Delivery systems for these resources assist with this access.

What are the types of organized leisure systems?

Leisure resources are usually grouped into the categories of sports, cultural arts, outdoor recreation, travel, hobbies, social recreation, and others.

Who sponsors these leisure systems?

They are sponsored by public, private, and commercial agencies.

How do I prepare for a career within a leisure system?

Both formal education in a college or university, and practical experience with leisure sponsors are important steps to securing a professional position in the leisure services fields.

Where do places for leisure come from? How are they cared for so we may use them? Who manages our gymnasiums, playgrounds, art centers, concert halls, health clubs, campgrounds, and resorts? What makes it possible for us to have forests, gardens, parks, trails, reservoirs, and beaches? These and many other leisure resources are managed by a varied collection of agencies, organizations, and companies. Funds are generated, personnel hired, facility and program services offered, and people are served by hundreds and thousands of these efforts, big and small—all focused on leisure. This is called a **leisure service delivery system**.

Leisure Service Delivery System: A means for providing leisure products and services to the public

Of course, many pastimes are experienced in informal ways, such as reading a book, walking around the neighborhood, and socializing with friends. However, other pastimes require or are made better by a more formal organization that provides facilities, equipment, leadership, instruction, schedules, and other support. Even such independently experienced activities as reading, walking, and socializing require the provision of safe, attractive, and accessible areas to be fully enjoyed.

Figure 13.1. Maiden voyage of "Harmony of the Seas," the world's largest cruise ship launched in May 2016. As an example of a leisure service delivery system, the cruise industry provides $119.9 billion annually to the world economy, adds $19 billion to U.S. wages and salaries annually, hosted 22 million passengers in 2014, and typically debuts 22 new ships each year (Cruise Forward, 2014).

Since leisure service delivery systems are broad, varied, and numerous, in our final chapter we survey some of the typical ways resources for leisure are managed. We begin by reviewing the theme of leisure in a utilitarian role by exploring why leisure service delivery systems are important. Next, ways of structuring services according to type of leisure expression are presented. These include tourism, cultural arts, sports, and outdoor recreation. Finally, ways of organizing leisure services according to type of sponsorship (public, private, and commercial) are discussed, along with how to secure a professional position with a leisure services sponsor.

Why Leisure Systems Are Important

At Yale University Law School, classes, professors, computer labs, textbooks, and other resources help students succeed. There is also Beau. Yale, renowned for competitiveness and its Supreme Court justices, has a program in which students can check out a "therapy dog." Stressed-out students can play with Beau (a labrador and basset hound mix) as he hangs out at the library. (The Yale Med School's therapy dog is Finn.) It is well known that playing with a dog results in "increased happiness, calmness and overall emotional well-being" stated Blair Kauffman, the law librarian (Williams, 2011).

Beau is a great example of a leisure resource. His puppy play has a specific function. Part 3 of this text has focused on the functional side of leisure: its ability to be a tool for accomplishing other things beyond itself, including being more successful in law and medical school. This chapter concludes the text, then, with the specific means by which this functional role for leisure is accomplished.

From Chapter 1 you remember that in ancient societies leisure served purposes greater than its own expression. As societies became more complex, they became even more reliant on leisure as a tool for solving problems and creating **public good**. This is leisure's utilitarian role—it serves a specific and needed function.

Public good: For the benefit or well-being of everyone

Today, as a public good, leisure is key to not only individual health and wealth, civic celebrations, and family vitality, but also in counteracting deprivation and improving social communication and cooperation. Leisure is useful in creating higher quality lives: It enhances life's livability. Although leisure is far from being a perfect solution for social, political, economic, and environmental difficulties, it is a major contemporary problem solver. It accomplishes this by creating "community." That is, unified groups of people are able to take life-sustaining actions because members work together to take care of each other. It is through community that we demonstrate leisure's ability to accomplish so much.

How is this accomplished? A community system of leisure provision ensures people have access to the resources they need and want. Essentially, leisure systems are important because they provide capital. In an earlier chapter in Part 3, we presented the case for leisure's contribution to economic capital; here we add to that the ideas of social and cultural capital.

Social capital: The value of social networks; transactions are marked by reciprocity, trust, and cooperation for a common good.

Social capital refers to the benefits of cooperation between individuals and groups. That is, social networks of people have value. This is not a particularly new idea as it was probably Alexis de Tocqueville who in the early 19th century first observed that Americans were prone to meeting at as many gatherings as possible to discuss all possible issues of state, economics, or the world that could be witnessed. This high level of transparency, he reasoned, caused greater participation from the people and thus allowed for democracy to work better (Putnam, 2000).

That is, by engaging with each other in a meaningful and collective way, people provide communal health for each other. Social capital is anything that facilitates this action by generating networks of reciprocal relationships. Since de Tocqueville, many have studied social capital. Robert Putnam (2000) described social capital as a key component of not only feeling connected in a society, but also of building and maintaining a productive community for all. Leisure resources, such as social clubs, sport leagues, choruses, camps, and even tour groups are examples of social capital.

Box 13.1 What Do You Say?

Is Social Capital in Trouble?

Research by Robert Putman (1995) documented that such community networks as the Parent Teacher Association, League of Women Voters, and Canadian Red Cross have experienced decreasing participation in recent years. Does this mean a decline in social capital in North America? Putnam explains that people are not participating as much as they used to in making their communities good places to live, citing a roughly 25% decline in the time spent in informal socializing and face-to-face visiting since 1965, and nearly a 50% decline in memberships in clubs and organizations. Some critics disagree with Putnam, however. They argue Putnam's research ignored grassroots political groups, religious organizations, and youth sports leagues. Also, Stengel (1996) proposed people may be redefining the forms and nature of their participation in the community. For example, more of the efforts of social capital may now be done on mobile devices, and therefore not be as visible. As well, though still a very new notion, some consider that millennials are beginning to center social capital around their work: turning the office into a source of friendships, meaning, and social occasions (Brooks, 2016).

1. In your own community have you noticed a decrease in social capital? How or how not?
2. What if such organizations as the garden club disappear in your town? Or, if student government and club sports disappear on your campus? Do they really matter?
3. Do you agree or disagree with Godbey (2006) who claimed the consequences of a loss in social capital include a loss of democracy, increased alienation and loneliness, and a decreasing ability to solve problems? Why or why not?

Cultural capital: Personal assets, such as education, intellect, dress, or physical appearance that promote social mobility

Another form of capital that explains the importance of leisure systems is cultural capital. **Cultural capital** is the knowledge, experience, and connections we acquire in life that enable us to succeed. This is our "life advantage" that comes from our families, schooling, and to the point, our leisure. Beyond economic means, cultural capital is what gives us our status in society.

Cultural capital is a concept that has gained widespread popularity since it was first articulated by Pierre Bourdieu and Jean-Claude Passeron in their 1973 article, *Cultural Reproduction and Social Reproduction*. They considered cultural capital to be the reason some children fail at school and some adults lack success in occupations. Their view was that people need to possess the behaviors and knowledge that are the most highly regarded in their society in order to succeed there. In other words, cultural capital is having the social "currency" of a culture.

This idea has been studied widely. For example, some studies (cf. Dumais, 2002) suggest cultural capital includes a linguistic advantage; others (cf. Mohr & DiMaggio, 1995) have identified it as participating in the highbrow tastes and styles of the dominant in-power culture. Many studies have investigated leisure's role in cultural capital. Katsillis and Rubinson (1990) found high school students' attendance at lectures, the theater, museums, and galleries to be positively related to their success in school. In a study by Downey and Powell (1993), those eighth graders who were more successful in school participated in scouting, hobby clubs, Boys' & Girls' clubs, non-school team sports, 4-H, and other recreation programs. Stempel (2005) concluded from his data that the dominant social classes use strenuous aerobic sports, moderate levels of weight-training, and competitive sports as capital for advancement in society. Participating in a diversity of leisure activities was found by Stalker (2011) to be an important indicator of cultural capital.

Leisure Resource Types

What exactly are the leisure resources of a community that provide opportunities for gaining social and cultural capital? There are so many that listing them all would take so many pages we'd call it a book. The variety is limited only by imagination, because leisure interests are as broad as humanity itself. For fun, people collect stamps, run marathons, fly airplanes, zentangle (drawing images from repetitive patterns), bake cookies, climb mountains, take photographs, watch football games, collect swizzle sticks, plant flowers, roast marshmallows, and race around poles and barrels.

Figure 13.2. Poles and barrel racing is a rodeo event that combines the horse's athletic ability and the horsemanship skills of a rider in order to maneuver a horse in a pattern around the poles or barrels in the fastest time. Susan Olgier competing with Abby. © Patricia D. Setser

While even classifying experiences that offer leisure meaning and value is itself a difficult task, and the means of the classification are arbitrary, people's pastimes can be grouped by the activity types listed in Table 13.1. The categories of sports and games, cultural arts, outdoor recreation, travel and tourism, hobbies, and social recreation are not all-inclusive, but they are useful for describing the common types of organized leisure services provided in many contemporary societies.

Table 13.1
Types of Leisure Resources

Category	Subcategories	Examples
Sports and Games	Individual Dual Team	Gymnastics, ice skating, solitaire, badminton, wrestling, chess, volleyball, water polo, charades
Cultural Arts	Music Fine arts Dance Drama	Guitar lessons, karaoke, filmmaking, ceramics, painting, ballroom dance, rhythm games, mime, storytelling, stage shows
Outdoor Recreation	Camping Nature-oriented Conservation Adventure Outdoor sports	Backpacking, RVing, stargazing, bird watching, gardening, wildlife planting, spelunking, extreme skiing, fishing, horseback riding
Travel and Tourism	Group tours Cruises Ecotourism Destination focused	Package tours, theater trips, fieldtrips, ocean and river cruises, volunteering to count zebras, theme parks, resorts, adventure travel
Hobbies	Collecting Making and tinkering Arts	Poetry writing, puzzles, reading, autographs, dolls, coins, model building, cooking, sewing, knitting
Social Recreation	Parties Clubs Eating events Visiting events	Holiday, birthday, poker, meetings, coffee houses, drop-in, picnics, cookouts, potlucks, coffee breaks, Internet chat rooms

From this list, we now explore tourism, cultural arts, outdoor recreation, and sports a bit more. The question we ask is, "What are the resources for these pursuits?"

Tourism

Tourism is travel for recreational purposes. It is the short-term movement of people to destinations outside where they ordinarily live and work. We travel to lose ourselves and we travel to find ourselves. While people have traveled from earliest times to escape danger, worship deities, or extend an education, today travel purposes are as wide as all interests. For example, the list might include agritourism, birth tourism, food tourism, geotourism, marijuana tourism, heritage tourism, medical tourism, sex tourism, war tourism, and wildlife tourism. Travelers today go on cruises and organized tours, make pilgrimages to religious sites, and sign up for fantasy camps. They go dog sledding, participate in fly-in hiking, take glacier tours, and go glamping.

Figure 13.3. Glamping is "glamorous camping." Not in the least bit rustic, a new tourism service makes it possible to have more than the comforts of home and also be close to nature.

As well, the geographic spread of tourism continues to widen as all parts of the world are now accessible to tourists. While some destinations are not considered safe or are very expensive to get to, intrepid tourists still go. For example, while difficult to accurately count, in 2014 Afghan embassies issued about 20,000 tourist visas, and bookings for adventure trips there have been doubling annually (Gordon, 2014). The most visited site in Afghanistan is Tora Bora, the cave complex where Osama bin Laden slipped away from invading U.S. forces in 2001 (Gutcher, 2012). And, as another example, the number of tourists to Antarctica for the 2015/2016 season is expected to be 40,029, each paying upwards of $35,000 for the trip (O'Flaherty, 2015).

Overall, the tourism industry is often described as one of the world's largest export businesses (even though the customer travels there), and a complex network of agencies is required to support it. Since leisure travel involves a composite of activities, services, and industries, including eating and drinking establishments, transportation, accommodations, entertainment, events and attractions, and others, the delivery of travel experiences must operate as a coordinated enterprise. For example, the success of the resort business on the island of Antigua depends not only on the marketing efforts of travel agents worldwide, the availability of transportation to and within the island, housing and restaurants, but also retail shops, charter boats, diving and snorkeling guides, golf courses and personnel, babysitters, musicians, gardeners, and even weather forecasters. Taken together, these are referred to as the **tourism system**. The exact mix of agencies and services within a tourism system for a particular locale depends, of course, on the type of tourism available there.

Tourism system: An industry created to serve tourists

Box 13.2
Web Explore

Amazing Hotels

One member of the tourism system is lodging. To demonstrate the point that lodging accommodations not only support tourism but also are often the very reason for the trip, check out some unusual hotels:

Kokopelli's Cave Bed and Breakfast: https://kokoscave.com/

The Ice Hotel of Quebec: http://www.hoteldeglace-canada.com/

Jules Undersea Lodge in Key Largo: http://www.jul.com/

Crane Hotel, Harlingen, Netherlands: http://faralda.com/

Cultural Arts

The term *art* refers to a diverse range of activities that appeal to the senses. It most often refers to the visual arts, including painting and sculpture, but also is applied to other art forms that stimulate other senses, such as music, dance, and drama. Cultural art program and facility services are an integral part of a community's quality of life. Indeed, summer day camp programs for children are just as likely to include crafts and dance as swimming and games. Members of senior adult centers can sign up to learn to play the oboe. Haiku poetry is taught to youth offenders in jail, football players take ballet classes, and executives join potters cooperatives.

Communities everywhere have orchestras, dance companies, theater groups, and art fairs. Voluntary organizations sponsor photography clubs and quilting guilds. Army bases provide rap practice rooms, shopping malls feature art exhibits, and your university's string quartet perhaps performs weekly at noon on the campus lawn. To illustrate the pervasiveness of cultural arts services, there are more than 55,000 art museums in 202 countries in the world (ICOM, 2014), and more than 13 million people attended Broadway Shows in New York City in the 2015–2016 season (Broadway League, 2016).

In fact, the options for cultural art resources are limitless, thus the challenge is to coordinate them to ensure their adequate distribution. One solution is **community arts councils**. In many communities, special interest organizations in the arts are coordinated or assisted by a comprehensive agency that helps promote their efforts to provide arts services. As nonprofit organizations, community arts councils promote and support all forms of cultural arts for all ages. They often fund artists and art organizations, provide special programs and events, and sponsor art education classes. For example, BEAD (Bloomington Entertainment and Arts District) in Bloomington, Indiana, works with galleries; live music and performing arts venues; over 90 restaurants; and 100 specialty shops, parks, hotels, and neighborhoods "to bring the business and creative sectors together to advance commerce and culture, build community, and spur arts development" (https://bloomington.in.gov/bead).

Community Arts Council: A collective method of art-making, engaging professional artists and self-defined communities through collaborative artistic expression

A **cultural arts center** represents another way communities are able to promote and assist in the provision of arts services. These are multiple-purpose facilities often sponsoring dramatic, dance, and musical performances. In many communities, cultural arts centers provide one or more stages, an art gallery, and rehearsal and workshop areas under one roof. One of the first multiple-purpose cultural arts centers was New York City's Lincoln Center for the Performing Arts. Founded in 1962, the Lincoln Center's buildings and auditoriums cover 16 acres. It supports 12 independent arts organizations including the Metropolitan Opera, the New York Philharmonic Orchestra, The Juilliard School of Music, The New York City Ballet, and the Film Society of Lincoln Center. In a typical year, the center hosts over 5,000 performances featuring over 3,000 artists (http://www.lincolncenter.org/).

Cultural Arts Center: An organization, building, or complex that promotes the arts; it can be neighborhood arts organizations, private facilities, government-sponsored, or activist-run.

Sports

Even only a casual observation of the average community demonstrates the priority of sport resources. Basketball hoops above garage doors, tennis courts behind apartment buildings, city swimming pools, private golf courses, and of course, softball diamonds can be found everywhere. In fact, you are hereby challenged to find even one town in the U.S. that does not have at least one softball facility! This is because according to the U.S. Census Bureau (2012), about 12 million Americans play amateur softball. Each year, new highs are reached in attendance at sporting events, new teams and leagues in both amateur and professional sports are established, and new sports soar to popularity (pickleball anyone?).

Figure 13.4. Pickleball is claimed to be the fastest growing sport in North America. It combines elements of tennis, badminton and ping-pong, and can be played indoors and outdoors on a modified tennis or badminton court. Required equipment are a paddle and plastic ball. © Ruth V. Russell, 2016

Many agencies and organizations provide resources for sport participation and spectating. Athletic clubs, community centers, Boys' & Girls' clubs, YMCAs, commercial stadiums and tracks, hotels, camps, cities, schools, churches, military bases, and many others are examples. Governmental sponsors most likely provide programs in team sports, such as basketball, soccer, and softball; whereas private sport and fitness clubs typically offer individual sports, such as jogging, weight lifting, golf, tennis, boating, and swimming.

Even the home is an important sport resource: exercise apparatus and portable swimming pools are common. Perhaps the largest growth in sport participation at home now comes via the computer in the form of sport video games and Internet-based fantasy sports. For example, according to the Fantasy Sports Trade Association (2016), it is estimated that 57 million people aged 12 and above in the U.S. and Canada played fantasy sports in 2015. Participation has grown over 60% in the past four years, with 20% of all males in the U.S. playing fantasy sports.

Sports are offered not only in a wide range of facilities and programs but to a broad range of participants as well. Communities offer sport services for the novice and the highly skilled, for the young and the old, for women and girls, as well as men and boys. For example, in St. Petersburg, Florida, a softball league has a minimum age requirement of 75 years. They call themselves "Kids and Kubs," and they've been playing regular seasons since 1931. Sports for people with disabilities are also a major service provision with numerous organizations, providing such sport opportunities as golf, downhill skiing, tennis, and basketball.

Box 13.3
By The
Numbers

Retiring Jersey Numbers

Retiring the number of an athlete is an honor a team or league bestows, usually after the player has left the team. Once a number is retired, no future player from the team may wear that number. The first number officially retired by a team in a professional sport was that of hockey player Ace Bailey, whose number 6 was retired by the Toronto Maple Leafs in 1934. Here are some other examples of retired jersey numbers:

Gerald Ford's #48 was retired by the University of Michigan football squad when he became president

Joe Green, #70, from the Pittsburgh Steelers football team

Peyton Manning, #18, when released by the Indianapolis Colts football squad

Lou Gehrig, #4, after retiring from the New York Yankees baseball team due to illness

For the "Sixth Man," #6, retired from the Sacramento Kings and Orlando Magic basketball teams

Wayne Gretzky, #99, retired league-wide by the National Hockey League

Box 13.4
In Profile

ESPN

ESPN (Entertainment and Sports Programming Network) is a U.S.– based global cable and satellite television channel owned by The Walt Disney Company and the Hearst Corporation. As of 2015, ESPN is available to approximately 94 million paid subscribers in the U.S. alone. It also broadcasts in more than 200 countries. While ESPN has been one of the most successful sports networks, there has been much criticism, including accusations of biased coverage, conflict of interest, and mishaps of individual broadcasters and analysts. Yet, the network has been a part of popular culture since its inception in 1979. Many movies with a sports theme have included ESPN announcers into their storylines, and numerous jokes made by comedians (see George Carlin, Jimmy Fallon, and Saturday Night Live, for example) have parodied it with fictional outlandish sport events. There are at least 22 children who are named after the network.

Source: Wikipedia, 2016

Sport is everywhere. As a wildly popular activity to both play and watch, sport is an undeniably worthwhile leisure resource for communities. However, communities must also assume responsibility for issues associated with sport that are not at all positive. Sports are plagued by questions of injury, violence, racism, and sexism. For example, the sport of boxing has been described as opponents throwing punches at each other with the result decided when one of the opponents is deemed incapable to continue.

Perhaps the biggest concern in sport today comes from its potential for wielding power. While sport participation is central to the development of children and youth and provides opportunities for adults to stay active and healthy, and while sport spectating inspires social bonding and tension relief for a community's citizens, sport is also part of a large social system that is used for political, economic, and personal gain, and sport sponsors must remain vigilant for this.

Outdoor Recreation

People join hiking clubs, go fishing, and make reservations months ahead to vacation near the ocean. Normally sedentary and prosaic adults spend their weekends climbing rocks, exploring caves, or following soaring bald eagles. Caring for plants provides therapy to patients in a skilled nursing center. Summer campers learn to overcome their fears of snakes. Indeed, the out-of-doors is a prime resource for leisure. Forests and soil, sunshine and rain, rivers and sky, the hills, prairies, and lakes are more than just pleasant places in which to play. In the outdoors, people participate more intimately in their own ecology. They go outdoors to repair what happens to them indoors.

Such romantic ideas about nature are very old ones in many societies, including in the United States. As European settlers moved west in the early 1800s, their relationship with wilderness shifted. As it became less hostile, in their collective minds it began to represent the unique value of their new country. Assisted by the artists and writers of the time, a new reverence for nature emerged. The novels of James Fenimore Cooper, for example, described those who lived on the frontier as pure of heart and noble in deed. Such poets as Ralph Waldo Emerson swore undying love to nature, and artists Thomas Cole and Thomas Moran made forays into the thick woods to paint their majestic beauty.

As the century progressed, such romanticizing of nature led to concern for its destruction. In the face of increasing industrialization and urbanization in the later decades, one solution seemed to be parks. The need for open spaces for leisure was felt first in the larger cities. Following the example of William Penn, who set aside five undeveloped squares for a park in Philadelphia in 1682, and James Oglethorpe, who designed public gardens and squares in Savannah, Georgia in 1733, New York City planners provided the grandest example of the park solution at the time: Central Park, designed by Frederick Law Olmsted and Calvert Vaux in 1853.

Figure 13.5. Snowmobiling in Yellowstone National Park. Even in winter visiting the park is popular. In February, for example, close to 36,000 tourists come to the park (NPS, 2016).

Concern for the care of the natural heritage also began to be answered by government. In 1865, Congress set aside Mariposa Big Tree Park for the state of California. The intention was to preserve significant natural resources for the enjoyment of future generations. New York, Michigan, Minnesota, and New Jersey followed this lead and claimed open spaces for the benefit of their citizens as well. Later, thanks to the continued reports of explorers and artists, the United States Congress established Yellowstone National Park in 1872.

As of 2015, there were 25,800 protected areas covering 499,800 square miles that were available for outdoor recreational use in the United States. This is 14% of the total land area, and also one-tenth of the protected land area of the world. The U.S. also had in 2015 a total of 787 protected marine areas, covering an additional 490,893 square miles, or 12% of its total marine area (World Data Base, 2015). These protected areas are managed by federal, state, county, and municipal governments and include the provision of parks, forests, nature preserves, zoos, botanical gardens, camps, lakes and reservoirs, nature centers, resort ranches, marinas, ski slopes and trails, horse trails, picnic areas, campgrounds, rivers, and beaches. In the typical U.S. community, there is one park per every 2,277 residents, averaging 9.5 acres of park per 1,000 residents (NRPA, 2016a).

These outdoor resources are very good for our health. For example, one study (James et. al., 2016) found that people who live near "greener" areas have a lower risk of mortality. Specifically, places with more vegetation, such as parks, are less polluted, encourage people to exercise and engage with other people, and visually enhance daily experience—and particularly reduce the risk of respiratory disease, cancer, and kidney disease. This effect held in the study regardless of income, weight, or smoking status, and also for both urban and suburban locations.

Leisure Resource Sponsors

Leisure resources may also be classified according to the type of sponsor. For example, federal, state/provincial, and local governments provide leisure resources and so do nongovernmental, nonprofit agencies. Private clubs and commercial for-profit businesses also provide for the pastime needs of people. Employers often offer facilities and programs for leisure as an employment benefit. Colleges and universities accommodate the sport, social, and cultural arts interests of students and faculty. Recreation services are part of the treatment for residents of correctional institutions, as well as patients in hospitals.

Box 13.5
In Your Own Experience

Community Inventory

Today organized leisure services are pervasive. There are several ways of proving this claim. One way is to inventory your own community. Have some fun and try this: walk down to your nearest city bus stop. Get on (better pay the fare, too). Ride the bus for its entire route, until you return to the stop where you originally boarded. While you ride and enjoy the passing scenery, keep a tally of the leisure organizations, facilities, and services you see from the bus window. How many parks, playgrounds, community centers, public gardens, golf courses, art centers, museums, and so forth do you count? Do you pass a YMCA, a Boys & Girls club, a community arts agency, and a country club? How about commercial leisure places, such as restaurants, bars, arcades, movie theaters, and a bowling center? Bring your tally back to class and share with classmates. Try to organize your list according to the categories in Table 13.2. Discuss your reaction to what you observed. Point out the utilitarian role of these leisure resources?

To help you grasp these numerous sponsors, we consider them according to three broad categories. First, public agencies are government sponsored and equitably available to all people. Although there is overlap in distinguishing them, private agencies are those who provide facilities and programs to members or selected elements of the population at-large, and commercial agencies provide leisure services as a business. Table 13.2 compares these categories of service sponsors.

Public Agencies

Of all the types of sponsors of leisure services, governmental agencies have the unique distinction of being the following:

- The first type of organization to be formally recognized as responsible for serving the public's leisure needs

- The only type of organization that is responsible for providing services on an equal basis to the entire population of a locale
- The only type of organization that has the power to secure, hold, protect, and open for use the natural resources upon which much of our leisure depends

Table 13.2
Leisure Service Sponsor Types

Type	Examples	Purpose	Services	Funding Source
Public	Monroe County (IN) Parks and Recreation Department, Arkansas State Parks, the National Park Service, U.S. Army MWR	To see that all citizens are equitably able to experience a high quality of life	Wide variety, with focus on outdoor recreation, cultural arts, and sports	Government taxes, bonds, user fees, gifts, and grants
Private	YMCA, Girls Inc., Moffitt Cancer Center Dog Therapy, condominium fitness center, University of Florida RecSports, Cummins Engine Golf Club	To meet the leisure needs of members, or other subselection of the population	Wide variety, with focus on social recreation, sports, hobbies, and voluntary service	Member dues, merchandise sales, the United Way, HOA dues, donations, and grants
Commercial	Walt Disney World, Bubba's Burgers, Kilroy's Bar, Suburban Bowling Center, Jellystone Park Camp Resort, Indianapolis Colts	To sell leisure experiences in order to make a profit	Wide variety, with focus on entertainment, sports, travel, and cultural arts	Paying customers

The primary function of government is to serve citizens' needs. Accordingly, government is the means by which people's leisure needs are met without regard to ability to pay, gender, race, occupational status, housing type or location, age, or any other distinction that can restrict access. This is perhaps best illustrated by the leisure services provided by local governments.

City, town, county, township, school district, and other governmental agencies operating at the local level of a community serve the broadest needs and largest clientele. Because they are that level of government closest to the citizens, they are better able to respond directly to the needs of the people. For example, after years of passing laws against loitering, cities from New York to Atlanta to San Francisco are creating new "parklets" where passersby are encouraged to sit and stay awhile—this is a function only a local government can provide.

Public recreation agencies at the local level are often referred to as **municipal recreation**. Municipal recreation and park departments acquire, develop, and maintain facilities needed for local citizens, as well as provide the skilled leadership and program structure for the use of these facilities. For example, most cities provide softball and baseball diamonds, tennis courts, swimming facilities, basketball courts, playing fields, picnic areas, playgrounds, and community centers, as well as directors, supervisors, and other professional staff to plan programs for and manage these facilities.

Municipal recreation: Leisure services sponsored by local governments, such as a city

Medium to large communities may also have gymnasiums, golf courses, auditoriums, outdoor theaters, bike and walking trails, fitness centers, dog parks, nature centers, skate parks, and cultural arts centers. Some also provide such special-interest leisure opportunities as zoos, aquariums, arboretums, campgrounds, ice arenas, and velodromes.

Figure 13.6. Aquariums are facilities where animals are confined within tanks and displayed to the public, and in which they may also be bred. Such facilities include public aquariums, oceanariums, marine mammal parks, and dolphinariums. Worldwide, over 200 aquariums are available to visit.

Local government leisure organizations typically work closely with other branches of local government, such as the police department, to develop effective programs to solve social problems. They also cooperate with other community organizations, as well as state and federal authorities, to develop comprehensive, long-range service plans.

Another level of government that serves as a leisure services sponsor is the state or provincial government. In the U.S., even though the Tenth Amendment to the Constitution gives states powers in such areas as public education, welfare, and health services, the idea that leisure services are a state responsibility didn't take hold until the 1960s and 1970s. Today, however, and even with recent cutbacks in budgets, states remain a viable leisure services sponsor.

This is because states are able to function in ways not possible for local governments. For example, the functions of the state government in sponsoring leisure services can be summarized as (Maclean et al., 1985):

- **Enactment of enabling legislation**. States give local governments the legal authority to operate recreation and park services. Such enabling legislation gives city, county, and other local authorities the power to acquire properties, employ personnel, and impose taxes to support leisure services.
- **Direct provision of leisure services**. States operate a network of parks, forests, and recreation areas. These resources typically include nature preserves, historical monuments, beaches, campgrounds, rest areas, and parks.
- **Education**. States also sponsor educational services related to leisure, including publications, traveling exhibits, workshops, conventions, and outreach programs in schools. State-affiliated colleges and universities also offer professional curriculums that prepare students for careers in leisure services, as well as direct recreation resources to students, faculty, and staff.
- **Promotion of tourism**. State departments of commerce, planning, highways, natural resources, and tourism typically make special efforts to attract visitors to the area. They conduct marketing research and promotions campaigns focused on getting their share of the tourist dollar.
- **Regulations**. State standards affecting leisure are of two types: those protecting participants and those protecting resources. Those protecting participants include regulations for safety, cleanliness, and health in camps, resorts, swimming pools, and restaurants. Regulations protecting leisure resources pertain to water pollution, fire dangers, and soil conservation.

Federal governments, in turn, manage leisure resources that are further away from the daily life of citizens, but are of greater significance in terms of heritage or beauty than those managed at state and local government levels. In the United States, for example, the federal government provides a broad assortment of services. While difficult to count from election to election, there are more than 90 departments, bureaus, commissions, councils, divisions, and authorities at the federal level having at least some responsibility for leisure provisions. As you can imagine, coordination among these many agencies has been difficult. Overall, the complexity of federal level efforts to support leisure services can be summarized into six functions (Maclean et al., 1985):

- **Ownership and management of land, water, and wildlife for leisure.** In the U.S., out of 2.27 billion acres of land, the federal government owns and manages 28%. It administers these public lands that are used for recreation primarily through The National Park Service, which runs the National Park System; the U.S. Forest Service, which manages the National Forests; the Bureau of Land Management, which manages other public lands; and the Fish and Wildlife Service, which administers the National Wildlife Refuge System. National Monuments are assigned a managing agency at the time of their designation by the President. In Canada, the majority of all lands are held by governments in the name of the monarch and are called Crown Lands. About 89% of Canada's land area is Crown Land, and of this the federal government manages 41%. Most federal Crown Land is in the territories (Northwest, Nunavut, and Yukon).
- **Grants to state and local governments**. Several federal agencies make financial grants to lower level governments for purchasing land, facilities, training, and programs in leisure. For example, the federal government awards grants of up to $50,000 for developing services in correctional institutions.

Military recreation: In the U.S., leisure services sponsored by the Department of Defense; community recreation for military personnel and their families living on military bases

- **Direct program operation.** While this function is more likely the responsibility of local governments, some federal agencies operate leisure services directly for participants, such as in **military recreation** through "Morale, Welfare, and Recreation (MWR)" services supported by Congress as well as user fees.
- **Research.** The federal government supports a broad spectrum of research about leisure ranging from outdoor recreation trends to the status of urban recreation. For example, monies are available to collect and analyze data leading to increasing the inclusion of persons with developmental disabilities into the community.
- **Regulation.** Federal regulations affecting leisure systems include standards for hunting and fishing, boating safety, the impact of leisure activities on the environment, and architectural accessibility for persons with disabilities.
- **Advisory services.** In the U.S., more than 30 federal organizations offer technical assistance for local agencies. For example, The President's Council on Fitness, Sports and Nutrition provides consultation and publications to schools, municipal recreation and park departments, and youth organizations who wish to introduce or improve physical activity and sports programs.

Private Agencies

Government-sponsored leisure systems are just one slice of the leisure resource pie. Another type of sponsor of leisure service organizations is private. These are the social, civic, religious, political, fraternal, labor, conservation, special interest, and youth-serving agencies that provide for the pastime needs of members and/or specific populations or people. Almost all of us have been touched at some point in life by this type of leisure service agency. Have you ever been a Girl Scout or a Big Brother? Have you been a member of the YMCA, or 4-H, a country club, or fraternity or sorority? Did you play baseball in Little League? Does anyone you know belong to Kiwanis, the Nature Conservancy, the Catholic Youth Organization, or Bass Unlimited?

Private leisure organizations range from small groups of people gathered to express a particular leisure interest, such as your grandfather's poker club, to complex international organizations with thousands of members, such as the Girl Scouts. A tidy system of categorizing this wide range does not exist, but it may be useful to consider them according to those that are private leisure dominant organizations, private secondary leisure organizations, and quasi-private organizations (Table 13.3).

First, private leisure dominant organizations exist primarily to serve the leisure interests of their members. For example, social clubs, country clubs, college alumni clubs, and poker clubs provide for members' social needs. Clubs promoting drama, music, the fine arts, and hobbies are also extensively available. Some of these organizations own extensive facilities, such as retreat centers, clubhouses, dining rooms, libraries, studios, practice rooms, and game rooms.

Table 13.3
Types of Private Leisure Service Organizations

Category	Examples	Description
Leisure dominant	Country clubs, college alumni clubs, poker clubs, The Appalachian Trail Conservancy	Sole purpose is to serve the leisure needs and interests of members.
Leisure secondary	Condominium management associations, religious organizations, employee recreation services	Primary purpose is something other than leisure, but leisure services are offered in support of the primary purpose.
Quasi-private	4-H clubs, YMCA, campus recreation	Nongovernment and nonprofit with mostly open membership with some public and/or government funding.

Other examples include organizations focused on sports. Thousands of private sporting clubs were formed in the late 1800s, and there remains many golf, tennis, cricket, bowling, swimming, sailing, skiing, and track and field clubs today. While some sports clubs have no facilities of their own and use public facilities, others control extensive properties, including marinas and playing fields.

Further, outdoor recreation is often the main service of private leisure-dominant organizations, including hiking, bicycling, mountaineering, and camping and RVing clubs. For example, the Appalachian Trail Conservancy is a 90-year-old private organization made up of members dedicated to the conservation of the 2,175-mile Appalachian National Scenic Trail, a 250,000-acre greenway extending through 14 states from Maine to Georgia.

Another category of privately sponsored agencies is the secondary leisure organization (Table 13.3). These agencies contribute to the supply of leisure opportunities, even though their primary purpose is something else. For example, residential management associations, composed of owners of houses or condominiums, exist primarily to maintain and manage shared residential facilities, such as parking, trees, lawns, and so forth, but sometimes also shared recreation resources, such as swimming pools, tennis courts, and party rooms. Religious organizations are another example of private secondary leisure sponsors. In support of a religious or denomination creed, often leisure facilities include gymnasiums, camps, and resort locations.

Employee recreation: Leisure services sponsored by companies as an employee benefit

Also, corporations and industries represent an example of the private secondary leisure category. **Employee recreation** services provide facilities and programs ranging from holiday events, sport leagues, and summer camps, to charter travel arrangements, stores, fitness centers, and even stress management and weight control classes—all aimed at building a sense of camaraderie and loyalty among company employees. The payoff for the company, of course, is healthier employees, which both increases work productivity and decreases insurance costs (Russell & Jamieson, 2008).

Perhaps the Amazon company is taking employee perks to a whole new level! In July 2016, construction began for a greenhouse in downtown Seattle that is meant to be a refuge for office employees. Constructed as a trio of spheres, it will house more than 3,000 species of plants, many of which are endangered. The spheres will contain tree houses joined by a series of suspension bridges. Amazon hopes its employees will host meetings in the tree houses (Wingfield, 2016).

Finally, a large collection of private organizations can be grouped under the heading of quasi-private (Table 13.3). These represent a special kind of private leisure resource, because while they exist to serve the needs and interests of their members, they also receive support from the public at-large or a governmental agency. Such organizations as 4-H clubs and YMCAs (originally the Young Men's Christian Association) may receive government grants or public donations, and although they may have membership policies, participation cannot be denied on account of race, religion, ethnicity, sexual orientation, or income level. For example, there are 4-H clubs for urban residents, and people of any or no religious affiliation, as well as women, are welcome to join the YMCA.

Campus recreation: Leisure services sponsored by colleges and universities for students and the campus community

Perhaps we can cite **campus recreation** as another example. Regardless of whether a college or university is privately or state affiliated, the leisure services offered on campuses are open not only to students, but often also to faculty, staff, and the broader community. For example, serving over 25,000 students, recreation services at the University of Nebraska at Lincoln include fitness, outdoor adventures, intramural sports, swimming lessons, ballroom dance, and many others to help current students cope with academic pressures as well as recruit new students—providing a vibrant campus community all around.

Commercial Agencies

In contemporary societies, people are willing (and often eager) to pay for leisure services. In fact, commercial sponsorship of leisure is one of the largest and fastest growing areas of the leisure resource system. Commercial leisure organizations sell leisure experiences to make a profit. Total expenditures for commercially sponsored pastimes far exceed those for services offered by public and private agencies.

Figure 13.7. Wave pool and water park at the West Edmonton Mall, Edmonton, Canada.

Leisure resources operated for commercial purposes include ski resorts, water parks, campgrounds, bowling centers, riding stables, health spas, hotels, restaurants, theaters, casinos, theme parks, sport stadiums, and music halls. In some cities, regions, states, and even nations, commercial leisure organizations are the primary industry.

In spite of this variety, certain types of pastimes are regarded the domain of commercial sponsorship. For example, commercial agencies are more likely to be associated with entertainment, popular culture, spectator sport, theme park, food and drink, and shopping facilities and programs. As a frequently glamorous resource for leisure, commercial services provide a magnitude of opportunities that round out the services offered by public and private sponsors. This is because commercial enterprises are able to offer activities considered too expensive for public and private sponsors, and often more unique than people's everyday leisure expressions.

Commercial leisure organizations are also able to respond quickly to current trends and often more willing to take speculative risks, thus creating demands for new leisure resources. A good illustration of this is the wave pool. Commercial developers introduced the idea into the United States and demonstrated its ability to entice patrons to stay longer, return more often, and pay higher admission charges than conventional swimming pools (Chubb & Chubb, 1981). As a result, some public agencies such as cities, now offer wave pools as standard services.

In spite of the many benefits of commercial recreation, there are also criticisms. A prime complaint is the profit motive itself. Commercial establishments have been blamed for being too tempted by making money and thus disregarding the overall welfare of people. By actively advertising, they can create demands where none previously existed. Some commercial leisure resources (such as bars and adult bookstores) have also been blamed for the demise of a positive moral order in society.

Those criticisms that ring true are, however, controlled. Such regulations as legal and trade boundaries, competition, and public opinion indicate what is appreciated from what is not tolerated in commercial recreation. For example, a dishonest operation is likely to have to close when a responsible competitor opens for business.

Therapeutic Recreation

To conclude this section of the chapter, there is one more form of leisure resource that actually combines everything we've discussed. **Therapeutic recreation** (TR) services seek to restore or rehabilitate in order to improve the well-being of persons with illnesses or living with disabling conditions. Using travel, cultural arts, sports, and outdoor recreation, as well as social activities and hobbies, as part of a treatment regime, recreational therapists work for public, private, and commercial agencies. For example, commercial hospitals, private rehabilitation centers, nonprofit extended-care services, public recreation and park departments, colleges and universities, and many other different kinds of sponsors use a wide range of leisure expressions as a tool for curing, improving, or accommodating conditions.

Therapeutic recreation: The profession that provides recreation services as treatment for persons with illness or disabling conditions

For example, in hospice care, therapeutic recreation services assist the dying patient with an opportunity to increase sense of control, social interaction, social supports, task-oriented goals, and by providing an appropriate medium for the expression of feelings as well as creativity.

Figure 13.8. The "Pines of Sarasota" hosts a volunteer pet therapy program. Last year the dogs and their owners devoted 396 hours of service with visits to residents in the assisted living, skilled nursing, and memory care units. © Patricia D. Setser.

Box 13.6
The Study Says

Music Therapy in Palliative Care

Eighty-four patients of a hospice care unit were randomly assigned to one of two interventions: live music therapy or prerecorded mindfulness exercise. Results indicated that there were higher levels of heart rate in the music therapy group. Also, music therapy caused significantly stronger reductions of pain and other stress-related symptoms.

Source: Warth, Kessler, Hillecke, & Bardenheuer, 2016

Careers in the Leisure System

A career in the leisure services system can be gratifying and exciting. Just as the menu of leisure activity areas and leisure resource sponsors was numerous and varied in this chapter's discussion, so are the options for employment within it. Park, recreation, sport, and tourism professionals plan, organize, and direct activities at all levels and settings. Table 13.4 highlights some of the positions available in the most popular categories of settings. Notice that many of the settings and functions overlap, lending opportunity to be flexible.

Table 13.4
Selection of Employment Positions in the Leisure System

Outdoor Recreation and Resource Management	Park naturalist Outdoor education coordinator Outdoor programmer Outdoor resource manager Camp program leader Outdoor instructor Adventure leader Environmental education leader
Recreational Sport Management	Fitness instructor Amateur athletics director Industrial sports manager Collegiate sports leader Military/municipal recreational sports coordinator Resort visitor sport planner Sports leader in YMCAs/ Boys & Girls Clubs
Tourism Management	Meeting planning Special event planning Adventure travel companies Commercial recreation facilities Governmental and military tourism divisions Hotels and resorts Theme parks Conference bureaus and centers Visitor and convention bureaus
Public Recreation Management	Military recreation National parks and forests State parks and forests Municipal parks and recreation YMCA Scouting Boys & Girls Clubs
Therapeutic Recreation	Acute care facilities Adult day care facilities Assisted living facilities Developmental learning centers Public and private medical hospitals Mental health centers Public recreation and park departments Substance abuse centers Stress care units

Employment of recreation workers is projected to grow 10% from 2014 to 2024, faster than the average for all occupations. As more emphasis is placed on the importance of exercise, more recreation workers will be needed to work in local government parks and recreation departments, fitness centers, sports centers, and camps specializing in younger participants (*Occupational Outlook Handbook*, 2015).

So how do you get into one of these careers? The education, training, and experience required varies widely depending on the type and level of the position. Full-time career options for administrative positions or for large organizations typically require at least a 4-year bachelor's degree, preferably in a parks and recreation or leisure studies university program, although in some situations a liberal arts degree will suffice. Many positions in direct-service with customers and clients require only an associates' degree in parks and recreation or related fields, and masters and doctoral degree programs are also available for executive, professor, and research positions.

Box 13.7
In Profile

Professional Preparation History

One of the earliest leadership trainings specifically for leisure was an 1880s summer school conducted by Luther Gulick, then a professor of physical education for the School of Christian Workers (now Springfield College) in Massachusetts (Butler, 1965). In 1905, Guilick joined the faculty of New York University and offered the first university course on play, which included units on sports, games, theory of toys, and play and the exceptional child (Sessoms, 1993).

Later, the awareness of the need for special training for recreation leaders increased, resulting in the start of a 1-year graduate curriculum sponsored by the National Recreation Association. Known as the National Recreation School, its founding in 1926 confirmed the desirability of educating professionals in the functional use of leisure. Its curriculum included the construction and planning of play facilities and administering city and county recreation departments. It graduated over 295 students in its 9 years of operation.

Soon professional preparation programs in leisure began to appear within the curricula of forestry, landscape architecture, education, social work, and physical education at colleges and universities across North America. Among the first were those at the University of Minnesota (1937) and the University of North Carolina (1939). Quickly, other colleges and universities began to offer specialized and separate undergraduate degrees in leisure; by 1945, 37 were available, and by the 1960s, the number had nearly doubled (Kraus & Bates, 1975).

Today, accredited professional preparation programs in leisure (associates through doctoral) are provided in more than 75 colleges and universities (NRPA, 2016b). The predominant subjects of study include recreation management, programming and leadership, outdoor recreation and resource management, commercial and tourism services, therapeutic recreation, and recreational sport management.

Although a degree can be helpful, for many seasonal and part-time positions, such as camp counselors and activity specialists, on-the-job training, specialized training, or experience in a particular area, such as art, music, drama, or athletics is also necessary. Many full-time, part-time, and seasonal positions also prefer applicants with work experience, including volunteer positions and internships. Some leisure system jobs require certification, ranging from a lifesaving credential for water-related programs to national certification for therapeutic recreation positions.

What We Understand About Leisure Systems

Leisure is a significant institution in contemporary societies. It includes a wide range of leisure expressions and structures. Once chiefly the responsibility of thc family, leisure services have become the responsibility of a number of organizations, loosely formed into the leisure services system. From reading this chapter you should know the following:

1. Leisure is sponsored by numerous public, private, and commercial organizations.
   Name and describe a public, private, and commercial organization with which you have experience:

   ____

   ____

2. These sponsors include cities, hospitals, correctional institutions, the armed forces, universities, retail businesses, clubs, and thousands of others.
   Select one of the examples you cited above and describe its leisure services:

   ____

   ____

3. The leisure experiences provided by these sponsors primarily include outdoor recreation, cultural arts, travel, and sports.
   Give an example of an actual leisure service in each of these program areas:

   ____

   ____

4. Preparation for a career in leisure systems requires formal education and training, experience, and sometimes certifications.
   For a specific position that interests you in leisure services, what are the preparation requirements?

   ____

   ____

References

Bourdieu, P., & Passeron, J.-C. (1973). Cultural reproduction and social reproduction. In R. K. Brown (Ed.), *Knowledge, education, and cultural change* (pp. 71–112). London, UK: Tavistock.

Broadway League. (2016). Statistics in NYC. Retrieved from https://www.broadwayleague.com/research/statistics-broadway-nyc/

Brooks, D. (August 9, 2016). The great affluence fallacy. *The New York Times*. Retrieved from http://www.nytimes.com/2016/08/09/opinion/the-great-affluence-fallacy.html?_r=0

Butler, G. D. (1965). *Pioneers in public recreation*. Minneapolis, MN: Burgess.

Chubb, M., & Chubb, H. R. (1981). *One third of our time? An introduction to recreation behavior and resources*. New York, NY: John Wiley & Sons.

Cruise Forward. (2014). Impact. Retrieved from http://www.cruiseforward.org/impact/economic

Downey, D. B., & Powell, B. (1993). Do children in single-parent household fare better living with same-sex parents? *Journal of Marriage and Family, 55*(1), 553–715.

Dumais, S. A. (2002). Cultural capital, gender, and school success: The role of habitus. *Sociology of Education, 75*(1), 44–68.

Fantasy Sports Trade Association. (2016). Industry demographics. Retrieved from http://fsta.org/research/industry-demographics/

Freysinger, V. J., & Kelly, J. R. (2004). *21st Century leisure: Current issues* (2nd ed.). State College, PA: Venture.

Godbey, G. (2006). *Leisure and leisure services in the 21st century: Toward mid-century*. State College, PA: Venture.

Gordon, S. (December 29, 2014). Bookings for adventure trips to Afghanistan DOUBLE as curious travellers defy Foreign Office and pay £5,000 each to visit troubled country. *The Daily Mail*. Retrieved from http://www.dailymail.co.uk/travel/travel_news/article-2889853/Bookings-adventure-trips-Afghanistan-DOUBLE-curious-travellers-defy-Foreign-Office-advice-pay-5-000-visit-troubled-country.html

Gutcher, L. (5/27/2012). Ongoing conflict severely limits tourism in Afghanistan. *USA Today*. Retrieved from http://usatoday30.usatoday.com/news/world/afghanistan/story/2012-05-27/Afghanistan-tourism-limited-by-war/55237330/1

ICOM (International Council of Museums). (2014). Frequently asked questions. Retrieved from http://icom.museum/resources/frequently-asked-questions/

James, P., Hart, J. E., Banay, R. F., & Laden, F. (April 14, 2016). Exposure to greenness and mortality in a nationwide prospective cohort study of women. Environmental Health Perspectives. Retrieved from http://ehp.niehs.nih.gov/15-10363/

Katsillis, J., & Rubinson, R. (1990). Cultural capital, student achievement, and educational reproduction: The case of Greece. *American Sociological Review, 55*(2), 270–279.

Kraus, R., & Bates, B. (1975). *Recreation leadership and supervision: Guidelines for professional development.* Philadelphia, PA: W.B. Saunders.

Maclean, J. R., Peterson, J. A., & Martin, W. D. (1985). *Recreation and leisure: The changing scene.* New York, NY: John Wiley & Sons.

Mohr, J. W., & DiMaggio, P. (1995). The intergenerational transmission of cultural capital. *Research in Social Stratification and Mobility, 14*, 169–200.

National Recreation and Park Association (NRPA). (2016a) *NRPA field report: Park facilities.* Retrieved from http://www.nrpa.org/2016-Field-Report-Charts-Park-Facilities/

National Recreation and Park Association (NRPA). (2016b). COAPRT accredited programs. Retrieved from http://www.nrpa.org/Professional-Development/Accreditation/COAPRT/COAPRT-Accredited-Academic-Programs/

NPS. (2016). Visitation statistics. Retrieved from https://www.nps.gov/yell/planyourvisit/visitationstats.htm

Occupational Outlook Handbook. (2015). Recreation workers. Retrieved from http://www.bls.gov/ooh/personal-care-and-service/recreation-workers.htm

O'Flaherty, N. (October 26, 2015). New ships to increase tourist numbers. *Antarctic Report.* Retrieved from https://www.antarcticreport.com/articles/new-ships-to-increase-tourist-numbers

Putman, R. (January 1995). Bowling alone: America's declining social capital. *Journal of Democracy, 6*(1), 65–78.

Putnam, R. (2000). *Bowling alone: The collapse and revival of American community.* New York, NY: Simon and Schuster.

Russell, R. V., & Jamieson, L. M. (2008). *Leisure program planning and delivery.* Champaign, IL: Human Kinetics.

Sessoms, H. D. (October 1993). *Quo vadis physical education and recreation.* Paper presented at the Leisure Research Symposium, National Recreation and Park Association, San Jose, CA.

Stalker, G. J. (2011). Leisure diversity as an indicator of cultural capital. *Leisure Science, 33*(2), 81–102.

Stempel , C. (2005). Adult participation sports as cultural capital: A test of Bourdieu's theory of the field of sports. *International Review for the Sociology of Sport, 40*(4), 411–432.

Stengel, R. (July 22, 1996). Bowling together. *Time Magazine*, 35.

U.S. Census Bureau. (2012). Table 1249. Participation in selected sport activities: 2009. Statistical Abstracts of the United States: 2012. Retrieved from www.census.gov/prod/2011pubs/12statab/arts.pdf

Warth, M., Kessler, J., Hillecke, T. K., & Bardenheuer, H. J. (April 15, 2016) Trajectories of terminally ill patients' cardiovascular response to receptive music therapy in palliative care. *Journal of Pain and Symptom Management.* Retrieved from http://www.ncbi.nlm.nih.gov/pubmed/27090850

Wikipedia. (2016). ESPN. Retrieved from https://en.wikipedia.org/wiki/ESPN

Williams, T. (March 21, 2011). For law students with everything, dog therapy for stress. *The New York Times.* Retrieved from http://www.nytimes.com/2011/03/22/education/22dog.html?_r=0

Wingfield, N. (July 10, 2016). Forget beanbag chairs. Amazon is giving its workers treehouses. *The New York Times.* Retrieved from http://www.nytimes.com/2016/07/11/technology/forget-beanbag-chairs-amazon-is-giving-its-workers-treehouses.html?_r=0

World Data Base. (UNEP). (May 2, 2015). World database on protected areas. Retrieved from https://portals.iucn.org/library/sites/library/files/documents/2014-043.pdf

Index

O

P

V

W

Y

Z

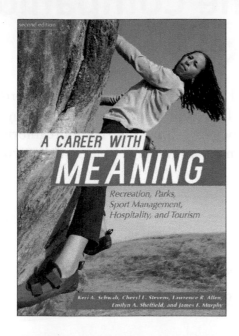

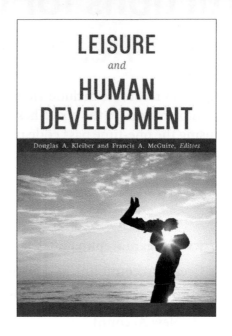

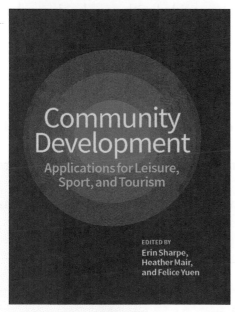

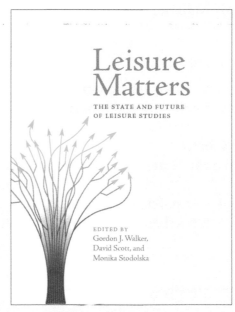

Instructions for Online Companion Resource Access

Online companion resources include videos, images, and other resources that the author provided as supplemental information for the text. These resources are found online and accessible only by creating an account using the one-time pass code provided at the bottom of this page. For more information about the use of or policies regarding the code for online companion resources, please visit www.sagamorepub.com

Steps to redeem access code if you DO NOT currently have a Sagamore account

1. Go to **http://www.sagamorepub.com**
2. Click on the **Create Account** link and fill out the requested information
3. Enter the code provided at the bottom of this page in the **online access code field.**
4. Click on **Create New Account.**
5. Click on **My Materials** tab to access all additional materials provided with your book purchase.

Steps to redeem code if you currently DO HAVE a Sagamore account

1. Go to **http://www.sagamorepub.com**
2. Click on the **Login** link and proceed to login
3. Click on the **Access Codes** tab for your account, enter the code provided at the bottom of this page and click **Submit**.
4. Click on the **My Materials** tab to access all additional materials provided with your book purchase.

If this book was purchased as a used book and the activation code is no longer valid, please call (800) 327-5557 to purchase a new activation code

Online Materials Access Code

BAT6-GAF9TFQVNJ29